# Monopolizing the Master

# Monopolizing the Master

HENRY JAMES AND THE POLITICS OF
MODERN LITERARY SCHOLARSHIP

Michael Anesko

STANFORD UNIVERSITY PRESS
STANFORD, CALIFORNIA

Stanford University Press
Stanford, California

This book has been published with the assistance of the College of the Liberal Arts and the Department of English of The Pennsylvania State University.

Printed in the United States of America on acid-free, archival-quality paper

Library of Congress Cataloging-in-Publication Data

Anesko, Michael, author.
  Monopolizing the Master : Henry James and the politics of modern literary scholarship / Michael Anesko.
     pages cm
  Includes bibliographical references and index.
  ISBN 978-0-8047-6932-7 (alk. cloth)
  1. James, Henry, 1843–1916. 2. Authors, American—Biography—History and criticism. 3. James, Henry, 1843–1916—Criticism and interpretation—History—20th century. 4. James, Henry, 1843–1916—Archives. 5. James, Henry, 1843–1916—Family. I. Title.
  PS2123.A66 2012
  813'.4—dc23

                            2011022751

Typeset by Bruce Lundquist in 9/15 Palatino

*This book is for*

        Warner Berthoff   Dan Aaron   Bernard Bailyn

                        *Teachers, Colleagues, Friends*

JUST AN EXCUSE TO USE JAMES TO DIG
AROUND FOR OLD GOSSIP ABOUT GAYS
NOTHING TO DO WITH LIT,

# Contents

# *Figures*

*Preface*

At least since Darwin's time, biologists have liked to remind us that the health of many ecosystems—indeed, the survival of many species—depends upon the otherwise unheralded work of parasites. The seemingly perverse symbiosis between such lowly creatures and the more conspicuous hosts who afford them life is a crucial element in nature's vast design. Much of the work of culture is done by similar organisms. The modern universe of literature would be unthinkable without the hungry tribe of critics, scholars, and biographers who feed on the lives and works of more celebrated others—the authors who inhabit and define the domain of public letters.

For reasons not hard to discern, the work of literary biographers, in particular, lends itself to this analogy. So many great writers have been shadowed by the men (of course they were men) who were in a privileged position to tell the life histories of their subjects: Doctor Johnson can hardly be imagined without his two-volume Boswell; Carlyle without his two-volume Froude; Dickens without his two-volume Forster. Lytton Strachey may have demolished the hagiographic archetype of such "life-and-letters" tomes when he published *Eminent Victorians* (1918); but modern literary biographers, if more critically disposed, have not escaped the veiled animus of parasitism that is concomitant with their work, which so often depends upon the discovery of materials—diaries, letters, drafts, and miscellaneous documents—rarely intended for others to see. The determined biographer, as James Joyce slyly anticipated, was ever more likely to become an author's "biografiend," an obsessive doppelgänger claiming exclusive priority to another's life history. *Monopolizing the Master* tells the story of not one but many such "biografiends"—all of whom have sought to shape our understanding of Henry James by cornering the market on that writer's cultural legacy.

Long before Pierre Bourdieu made the concept of "cultural capital" into a buzzword of contemporary literary criticism, another formidable thinker—the Canadian polymath, Northrop Frye—offered a salutary warning about the vagaries of defining it.[1] In the "Polemical Introduction" to *Anatomy of Criticism*

(1957), Frye took umbrage with the kind of "literary chit-chat which makes the reputations of poets boom and crash in an imaginary stock exchange." Wittily extending the metaphor, Frye commented, "That wealthy investor Mr. Eliot, after dumping Milton on the market, is now buying him again; Donne has probably reached his peak and will begin to taper off; Tennyson may be in for a slight flutter but the Shelley stocks are still bearish."[2] Since the time of his death, shares of Henry James have had their ups and downs, and his cultural valuation often has been linked to extraliterary factors and phenomena—particularly his citizenship and his supposed leisure-class allegiances. Although by now we have come to accept—even to presume—the Master's blue-chip status, the high reputation enjoyed by James's oeuvre (as Hilton Kramer has reminded us) "represents one of the most remarkable feats of literary exhumation in the history of twentieth-century literature."[3]

*Monopolizing the Master* chronicles the history of that recuperation, focusing especially on the strategies by which different critical cohorts have attempted to shape—ideally to control—the contours of James's posthumous reputation. Leon Edel's domination of modern James studies has long been obvious (and frequently complained of), but no one really has explained how he gained— and assiduously worked to maintain—his peculiar advantage: controlling others' access to the James archive. Still less appreciated is the extent to which Edel's career epitomizes a logic of restriction that already had been put in motion before James died in 1916. Even then, family scruples (inflected more than a little by homophobic paranoia) seemed determined to perpetuate a discreet hagiography of the author, and his collateral descendants worked deliberately to frustrate what they considered unwanted speculation or investigation. The appearance of Van Wyck Brooks's pseudo-psychological *The Pilgrimage of Henry James* (1925), which asserted that James's whole career was a testament to deracinated frustration and atrophy, galvanized his literary executors to thwart whomever they deemed "incompetent" from accessing sources that might disclose sensitive information about the James family.

James's contemporary acolytes (especially Percy Lubbock and Theodora Bosanquet) and the next generation of modernists who largely salvaged James's reputation (Eliot, Pound, and R. P. Blackmur) also, in their various ways, attempted to appropriate the Master's aura, wanting to transfer or borrow his cultural capital to shore up their own artistic agendas. While their motives and tactics differed widely, taken as a whole, they also worked to shape the contours of the "Henry James" with whom later readers and critics have had to reckon. Another key figure in this process was Harvard professor F. O. Matthiessen, whose "brief and busy excursion into James" (as Edel somewhat derisively described it) was largely responsible for the modern James revival. Edel was ready—at the time of Matthiessen's tragic suicide in 1950—to crown himself as sole successor, or at least majority shareholder, in what would rapidly become almost a new industry. Postwar enrollments at American universities expanded in tandem with a revolution in paperback publishing, and an unceasing stream of James reprints soon began to appear (in the vast majority of which Edel had not merely a scholarly but also a considerable financial stake). It is hardly a coincidence that the 1971 *New Yorker* profile of Edel ran under a satirically pecuniary banner—"Chairman of the Board." Edel's virtual monopoly of the field has of course been noted for some time, but only now can a detailed account of his campaign to ward off "trespassers," as he termed them, be given, since the vast archive of his own papers only recently has been open to public inspection and use. *Monopolizing the Master* fittingly concludes with that final chapter, for it was only when the last volume of Edel's biography was published that restrictions concerning the use and publication of the James papers were lifted.

Even though other scholars have touched upon certain aspects of this narrative,[4] a truly comprehensive account has had to wait. Michael Millgate concluded his important chronicle of James's "testamentary acts" by saying that "it seems impossible now to recover or even guess at" the reasons to account for the author's "final absolute dependence upon his own family" to lay the cornerstone of his posthumous reputation.[5] But new family materials since deposited at Harvard shed much light on those reasons; at the same time they expose many of the tensions and cross-pressures that would affect access to the archive for decades to come. Likewise, the more recent tactical forays made by researchers into Leon Edel's papers at McGill have glanced at topical issues—especially the details of his efforts to "police" the James archive at the expense of others—but have not sufficiently appreciated the extent to which such actions align themselves with the longer history of efforts to control the construction of "Henry James" as a subject for biographical or critical analysis.

Literary historians usually trace the beginning of the "James Revival" to the years immediately following the end of the Second World War, when

Matthiessen began to publish key source materials that previously had been locked away in the recesses of the Harvard library. In 1946, the same year that the James Revival formally was announced, already Lionel Trilling was forced to admit that "we are all a little tired of Henry James—or rather, we are tired of the Henry James we have been creating by all our talk about him."[6] That weariness has proved ephemeral, however. We have been talking about Henry James (more or less intelligently) ever since: creating—and re-creating—the forms of cultural capital he represents: possessing—or possessed by—the Master.

# Acknowledgments

In the years that it has taken to research and write this book, my debts to others have multiplied. I am grateful for the opportunity to thank

Bay James, the current executor of the family literary estate, for permission to quote from unpublished material in the James Family Archive at Harvard and from materials on deposit at the Center for Henry James Studies at Creighton University, Omaha, Nebraska

Deborah Edel, for permission to quote from the manuscript archive of her late uncle, Leon Edel

Professor Greg Zacharias and Katie Sommer, his assistant, for their unstinting willingness to field queries and forward documents from the invaluable archive of the Center for Henry James Studies

Professors Donatella Izzo and Carlo Martinez, who triumphed over the arcane impedimenta of Italian bureaucracy and helped me secure copies of the James family correspondence retained at the Museo Andersen in Rome

Dr. Richard Virr, for courtesies extended to me while working with the Leon Edel Papers at McGill University, Montreal

Professor Susan Gunter, for affording me access to portions of her biography of Alice Howe Gibbens James, when that work was still in manuscript

Leslie Morris, curator of manuscripts at the Houghton Library, who was willing to make generous concessions for the sake of scholarship

Susan Halpert, for kindness and courtesies extended to me in the Houghton Library Reading Room

Professor Robin Schulze, my department head, who has supported my research even as budgets for scholarship have continued to shrink

In much different form, parts of this book have appeared in a range of scholarly venues. For permission to include this material, I am grateful to

Susan Griffin, editor of *The Henry James Review*, for "O O O O that Ja-hame-sian Rag / It's so elegant / So intelligent: Tracing Appropriations of the Master's Aura in Modernist Critical Discourse," vol. 27 (2006): 264–74

Linda Smith Rhoads, editor of *The England Quarterly*, for "Monopolizing the Master: Henry James, 'Publishing Scoundrels,' and the Politics of Modern Literary Scholarship," vol. 82.2 (2009): 205–34

Ezra Greenspan and Jonathan Rose, editors of *Book History*, for "Collected Editions and the Consolidation of Cultural Authority: The Case of Henry James," vol. 12 (2009): 186–208

Cambridge University Press, for "Critical Response, 1916–1947," in *Henry James in Context*, ed. David McWhirter (New York: Cambridge University Press, 2010), 412–22

The following libraries and executors have given permission for material under their purview to appear here: Bancroft Library, University of California, Berkeley (Bruce Porter Papers); the Berenson Archive, The Harvard University Center for Italian Renaissance Studies, Villa I Tatti, Fiesole, courtesy of the President and Fellows of Harvard College; Boston Public Library, Boston, Massachusetts (portrait bust of Henry James by Derwent Wood); British Library, London (Macmillan Archive, Macmillan Letterbooks © The British Library Board, MS 55556); Brotherton Library, University of Leeds (Edmund Gosse Papers); Columbia University Library, New York (Paul Revere Reynolds Papers); Harvard University Archives and the Houghton Library, Cambridge, Massachusetts (James Family Collection, Houghton Library Librarian's files [James collection file, Librarian's Office Correspondence], Theodora Bosanquet Papers, New Directions Publishing Archive); Library of Congress, Washington, D.C. (portrait bust of Henry James by Hendrik C. Andersen); McLennan Library, McGill University, Montreal (Leon Edel Collection); Museo Andersen, Rome (Hendrik C. Andersen Papers); Manuscripts Division, Department of Rare Books and Special Collections, Princeton University Library, Princeton, New Jersey (Scribner Archive, R. P. Blackmur Papers, Anna Robeson Burr Papers); and the Watkins Loomis Agency, New York (Edith Wharton Collection, Beinecke Library, Yale University, New Haven, Connecticut).

*Michael Anesko    University Park, Pennsylvania*

# Monopolizing the Master

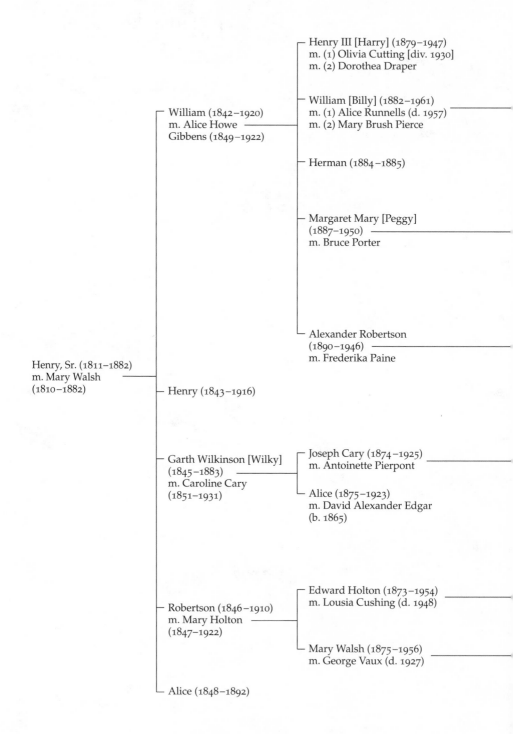

Henry, Sr. (1811–1882)
m. Mary Walsh
(1810–1882)

William (1842–1920)
m. Alice Howe
Gibbens (1849–1922)

Henry III [Harry] (1879–1947)
m. (1) Olivia Cutting [div. 1930]
m. (2) Dorothea Draper

William [Billy] (1882–1961)
m. (1) Alice Runnells (d. 1957)
m. (2) Mary Brush Pierce

Herman (1884–1885)

Margaret Mary [Peggy]
(1887–1950)
m. Bruce Porter

Alexander Robertson
(1890–1946)
m. Frederika Paine

Henry (1843–1916)

Garth Wilkinson [Wilky]
(1845–1883)
m. Caroline Cary
(1851–1931)

Joseph Cary (1874–1925)
m. Antoinette Pierpont

Alice (1875–1923)
m. David Alexander Edgar
(b. 1865)

Robertson (1846–1910)
m. Mary Holton
(1847–1922)

Edward Holton (1873–1954)
m. Lousia Cushing (d. 1948)

Mary Walsh (1875–1956)
m. George Vaux (d. 1927)

Alice (1848–1892)

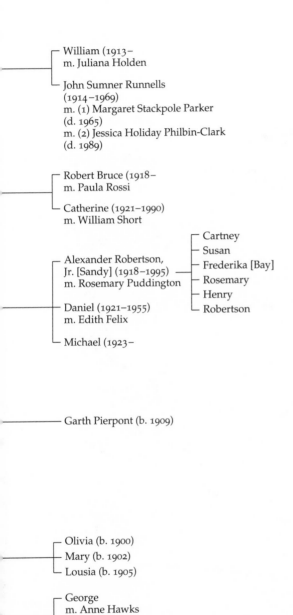

William (1913–
m. Juliana Holden

John Sumner Runnells
(1914–1969)
m. (1) Margaret Stackpole Parker
(d. 1965)
m. (2) Jessica Holiday Philbin-Clark
(d. 1989)

Robert Bruce (1918–
m. Paula Rossi

Catherine (1921–1990)
m. William Short

Alexander Robertson,
Jr. [Sandy] (1918–1995)
m. Rosemary Puddington

Cartney
Susan
Frederika [Bay]
Rosemary
Henry
Robertson

Daniel (1921–1955)
m. Edith Felix

Michael (1923–

Garth Pierpont (b. 1909)

Olivia (b. 1900)
Mary (b. 1902)
Lousia (b. 1905)

George
m. Anne Hawks

Henry James
m. Jean Macduff

James family tree

# 1

## Cornering the Market

### *Legacies of Mastery*

Before he left this world, Henry James took various steps to shape the contours of his posthumous reputation and direct the lines of critical inquiry that would affect it. That James entertained certain anxious intimations of immortality should not come as a surprise. Any reader of his work—especially those wonderfully wry stories about writers and artists—probably could anticipate the principal aims of his paradoxically posthumous authorial agenda. How many times in those taut works of fiction does the higher imperative of personal privacy trump public curiosity about the artist's life—often accompanied by the ritual destruction of the writer's manuscripts and letters? How often do we hear the lamentations of creative intellects who neither find genuinely satisfactory rapport with an audience nor receive insightful appreciation from the critical press? How many of James's artist figures ultimately succumb to the treacheries of the marketplace, whether as victims of misguided celebrity or knowingly complicitous devotees of a mercenary muse? Through all these permutations of an overarching theme—the relation of the artist to society, which James singled out as one of the "great primary motives" available to him[1]—a pervasive and telling irony adumbrates their autobiographical origins and implications, even when the author's notebooks betray more immediate moments of genesis or particular forms of instigation in the private chronicle of his own career. So many traps for the unwary, these stories often have snared readers into treating them as elaborate Jamesian exercises in self-pity, forms of retrospective consolation for the market's indifference to his work;[2] but their fuller resonance is best appreciated if instead we consider them as proleptic forms of constructed mastery, anticipations of the strategies that the author, his family, and his disciples would employ to consolidate and enhance the cultural capital of "Henry James."

James's yearning to frustrate future biographers is well known, especially since the most preeminent of them (Leon Edel) took pains to remind his readers at every turn how he had triumphed over his subject's nefarious intention to defy personal inquiry. Adamantly expressing the wish "to frustrate as utterly as possible the post-mortem exploiter," James also ruefully acknowledged that his desire was "but so imperfectly possible": death, when it came, would work to defeat his tactics of evasion, and postmortem exploiters inevitably would multiply. Jealous of all others, Edel became the postmortem exploiter par excellence, driven by an obsessive zeal that would have been the envy of any of the Master's fictional prototypes: those frequently foiled publishing parasites who seek to fatten their careers on the literary remains that less fastidious authors have left behind them. James certainly knew that the fabulous conventions he employed to safeguard his fictional authors from prying interlopers—the recriminating scruples that hamper Peter Baron in "Sir Dominick Ferrand" (1892) or the ghostly visitations that discourage George Withermore in "The Real Right Thing" (1899)—would hardly meet the necessities of his own case. "I have long thought of launching," he told his nephew Harry, "a curse not less explicit than Shakespeare's own on any such as try to move my bones." Provoked by this relative's query about the future disposition of his literary estate, James instantly made up his mind "to advert to the matter in my will—that is to declare my utter and absolute abhorrence of any attempted biography or the giving to the world by 'the family,' or by any person for whom my disapproval has any sanctity, of any part or parts of my private correspondence."[3] Such aggressive averments notwithstanding, James made no mention of these restrictions in the codicil that was appended to his will in late August 1915, just six months prior to his death. In fact, that document gives the merest nod to "manuscript or type-copied matter and letters," which were lumped with all his other copyrights and intellectual property in a bequest to his sister-in-law, Alice Howe Gibbens James.[4] It was she who moved his bones—or at least his ashes—from wartime London to Cambridge, Massachusetts, for burial in the family plot overlooking Soldiers Field. And it was she and her immediate descendants who gave to the world a substantial part of his private correspondence by allowing Percy Lubbock to publish a generous two-volume selection of *The Letters of Henry James* in 1920.

Though he never managed fully to effect an interdiction comparable to Shakespeare's, James already had taken precautions inspired by a like-minded scorn. Throughout his career, whenever "great changes & marked dates & new eras [&] closed chapters" were registered, the novelist unapologetically "committed to the flames a good many documents," wanting not merely to clean house but also to impede any prospect for subsequent inquiry.[5] Immortalized in the ritual burning of eponymous love letters in "The Aspern Papers" (1888), James's tactics of secrecy had become a confirmed law—a law, he told an old friend, "that I have made tolerably absolute these last years as I myself grow older and think more of my latter end: the law of not leaving personal and private documents at the mercy of any accidents, or even of my executors!"[6] Such confirmed habits of privacy only were exacerbated by symptoms of declining health. At particular moments of medical crisis, plumes of smoke would rise from his chimney or waft from the cottage corner of the garden at Lamb House, where the caretaker could keep a watchful eye on the Master's epistolary bonfires. The onset of deep depression in the summer of 1910 ("the blackness of darkness and the cruellest melancholia") provoked perhaps his most spectacular conflagration.[7] "Uncle Henry is burning his ships with a vengeance," his sister-in-law reported to Harry after she and her ailing husband arrived at Rye on their way to Bad Nauheim in Germany, where they hoped to find successful treatment for William's acute heart trouble. "Such a clearing of drawers and cupboards," with the servants "scudding & flying to do his bidding," she had never before witnessed.[8] Not surprisingly, then, later scholars and researchers have seldom been able to reconstruct fully reciprocal accounts of James's correspondence. Whereas those to whom he wrote safeguarded even his most trivial notes ("the mere twaddle of graciousness," as he freely confessed them), most of their letters to him never survived his periodic blazes. Even family letters sometimes found their way into the flames, resulting in lopsided lacunae amid the formidable accumulation of James papers at Harvard. As the author's nephew explained to Ralph Barton Perry (the first person granted access to the James archive), "As to the letters from my grandfather that were sent to Uncle Henry, I can only say that I don't think they were ever returned. His ways with papers were strange. My mother brought home what was found after his death but I know that some things will never be found again—probably don't exist."[9] Perry was just the first scholar who perhaps had reason to mutter a private execration in response to the Shakespearean curse that Henry James chose to hurl at posterity.

Wanting to forestall the more traditional modes of biographical inquiry, James insisted that his work, not his life, should be the proper focus of serious criticism. How little of *that* he had received in his lifetime was a perennial sore spot. His notebooks and correspondence bristle with contempt for the slovenly substitutes he found in the Anglo-American literary press—mostly a hodge-podge of puffing and publicity. A complaint he made to Robert Louis Stevenson in 1888 could have been lifted from almost any of his letters, early or late. "Criticism," he reported, "is of an abject density and puerility—it doesn't exist—it writes the intellect of our race too low."[10] Compared to the intelligent discussions of literary issues he heard during his brief stint in Paris (1875–76)—when he frequented the salons of Flaubert, Turgenev, the Goncourts, Daudet, and Zola—the chatter that filled the columns of newspapers and periodicals in London, New York, and Boston was worse than trifling. "There is almost no care for literary discussion here," he wrote from the British capital to his old American chum Thomas Sergeant Perry; "questions of form, of principle, the 'serious' idea of the novel appeals apparently to no one, & they don't understand you when you speak of them."[11] Even his deliberately provocative essay "The Art of Fiction" (1884) aroused not an echo: it simply fell into a void. On the one occasion when he chose to address the subject of "criticism" proper, James used the word ironically, since in contemporary practice it had become synonymous with the "platitude and irrelevance" of promotional journalism.[12] Sometime later, when the editor of the *Atlantic* rather tactlessly called James's attention to a vituperative review essay in the journal's pages that dismissed *The Wings of the Dove* for its "clouds of refined and enigmatical verbiage,"[13] a by now hard-shelled author simply shrugged. The article, James wrote back, "seems to me, certainly, as stupid as it is sprightly" (returning the favor); "but the stupid we have always with us," he continued, "& they are a very old story."[14] Certainly a very old story to him.

Critics have long recognized that the author intended his heroic labor in preparing the New York Edition of *The Novels and Tales of Henry James* (1907–9) as a kind of bulwark against such stupidity. The Prefaces he composed for that series, in particular, were "a sort of plea for Criticism, for Discrimination, for Appreciation on other than infantine lines—as against the so almost universal Anglo-Saxon absence of these things; which tends so, in our general trade, it seems to me, to break the heart."[15] All the same, it is worth remembering that those were *not* the words—decidedly—the author used when he first proposed doing the Prefaces for Scribner's as a special feature for the Edition. When James B. Pinker, his agent, was in early negotiations with the firm, the

Prefaces, he teasingly suggested, would be "of a rather intimate, personal character," hinting that for the first time in his life this notoriously reclusive author would share himself more freely with his public.[16] As plans for the Edition were firming up, James himself promised to write "a freely colloquial and even, perhaps, as I may say, confidential preface or introduction" for each of its volumes, underscoring the fact that "I have never committed myself in print in any way, even so much as by three lines to a newspaper, on the subject of anything I have written, and I feel as if I should come to this part of the business with a certain freshness of appetite and effect."[17] This was bait no publisher, ever eager for publicity, could resist—as James had testified in "John Delavoy" (1898), a tale in which a market-minded magazine editor rejects a serious critical essay about that author's work in favor of something more vividly biographical. Despite their final distinction as writerly texts (as Barthes might have said), the Prefaces were hawked on the basis of their readerly appeal and certainly envisioned as a major selling point for the whole venture.

When the time came to write them, however, the author felt compelled to subordinate popular expectation to a larger imperative for his own distinctive kind of critical formalism. Although many of the Prefaces give a brief nod to the particular circumstances of a given work's point of origin—the "germ" that had planted the seed in the author's imagination, the specific locale where he composed it—James announced from the first that, as he reread and revised his oeuvre, he found himself "in presence of some such recording scroll or engraved commemorative table—from which the 'private' character, moreover, quite insist[ed] on dropping out."[18] By the time he would write his final Preface, almost any vestige of "private" disclosure had been effaced altogether. As he continued to compose them, James would instead increasingly challenge his audience to appreciate the writerly demands, even more strenuous now by virtue of his textual revisions, that his fiction deliberately made. Acknowledging that the vast majority of what passes for "literature" makes no such demands, James anticipated Barthes's famous distinction without apology. "We may traverse acres of pretended exhibitory prose," he admitted, "from which the touch that directly evokes and finely presents, the touch that operates for closeness and for charm, for conviction and illusion, for communication, in a word, is unsurpassably absent. All of which but means of course that the reader is, in the common phrase, 'sold'—even when, poor passive spirit, systematically bewildered and bamboozled on the article of his dues, he may be but dimly aware of it." Preferring to engage the reader as an active spirit, James solicits his attention through forms "whose highest bid is addressed to the imagination, to the spiritual and the aesthetic vision, the mind led captive by a charm and a spell, an incalculable art. The essential property of such a form as that is to give out its finest and most numerous secrets, and to give them out most gratefully, under the closest pressure—which is of course the pressure of the attention articulately *sounded*."[19] James's aim, then, in this and every other Preface, is (as Paul Armstrong suggests) "to direct and even discipline the reader's attention without coercing or constraining it."[20] Precisely because each of the Prefaces was occasioned by a *re*reading of the work (or works) it addressed, their ultimate function is sublimely anachronistic: they bear as much relation to one another as to the various titles they rather arbitrarily precede. The author himself recognized that, taken together, the Prefaces constituted "a sort of comprehensive manual or *vade-mecum*" for the art of fiction and should, at some point, be collected as a freestanding volume.[21] Scribner's finally recognized the value of such a project in 1934, when R. P. Blackmur fulfilled James's ambition by publishing *The Art of the Novel*.

Those closest to James best understood his broader intentions for the Edition and responded generously in public venues to promulgate the significance of his achievement. Percy Lubbock, for example, extolled the Prefaces and declared that their appearance marked "an event, indeed the first event" in the history of the English novel. "The English novel," he maintained, "has hitherto been so boldly unconscious of itself that in any exact sense it cannot be said to have had a history at all." James's "summary achievement," then, was that "he has disengaged from a hundred misconceptions the question of form." "It is the form," Lubbock recognized, "and the form alone," that dictates the development of James's characters and directs their dialogue; and this "strict fusion of material with form" was James's necessary "point of departure."[22] Morton Fullerton collaborated with his lover Edith Wharton to arrive at a similar conclusion. The Prefaces, he forthrightly asserted, represented "the first serious attempt ever made in English to call upon [the] bewildered art [of fiction] to pause and give a conscious account of itself; to present its credentials and justify its existence."[23] To these already sympathetic readers, of course, James was preaching to the choir: their habits of devotion had long since been confirmed. But what of the uninitiated? The Edition's evidence of mastery was more than sufficient to win over even so skeptical a reader as William Crary Brownell (the Scribner editor who had been utterly exasperated by *The Sacred Fount*). Having received James's copy for the Prefaces to *Roderick Hudson* and *The Portrait of a Lady*, Brownell could not refrain from expressing his "absolute delight" with them, knowing that they would not only constitute "a real feature" of the Edition but would also "furnish something very nearly, if not quite, unique in literature itself"; he could not imagine "anything more enhancing" to the interest of James's readers or the "attractiveness of the volumes."[24] Even notices in the popular press recognized the Edition's importance, and they were surprisingly numerous: more than sixty appeared in newspapers and magazines all across the United States.[25]

Distinctive as the Prefaces were, just as important to the author, if not more so, were the painstaking revisions he made as he carefully sifted and selected his titles for inclusion in the series. Here was the opportunity, denied to Dencombe in "The Middle Years" (1893), for another go, the better chance. Although soon he would be chided for destructively tampering with the supposed freshness and clarity of his earlier style, James insisted on having the freedom "to revise everything carefully, and *to re-touch*, as to expression, turn of sentence, and the question of surface generally, wherever this may strike me as really required."[26] While James undoubtedly insisted upon a supremely aesthetic prerogative to justify his titivations, it is also worth noting that the wholesale revision of his works for the New York Edition also extended the author's legal rights in them. James could joke that while the laborious process of revision had added ten years to his age, it had also made his "poor old books . . . twenty or thirty years younger," but (knowingly or not) he was also affirming an important material fact.[27] By substantially rewriting his earliest novels and tales, James was in effect extending their terms of copyright, since many of these titles otherwise would soon have begun lapsing into the public domain.[28] Both artistically and commercially, James's New York Edition can almost be seen as the author's attempt to monopolize himself by patenting a style for futurity.

For a host of complex reasons, others in the literary field also had an interest in cornering the James market, however limited it may have been. From a certain angle of vision, James's *un*popularity by the end of the nineteenth century was calculated to make him all the more attractive to publishers, since having his name on one's list automatically would give it an indisputably aesthetic imprimatur, an added touch of exclusivity. Not all that coyly, even the titles James gave to his later short-story collections deliberately imply this; all of them—*The Soft Side* (1901), *The Better Sort* (1903), *The Finer Grain* (1910)—were meant to convey a palpable aura of *raffinement*, the enticement of unquestionable taste. ("'The Finer Grain,'" an obviously proud author puffed to his agent, "seems to me a thing to 'ask for'").[29] Even though James ruefully may have projected himself into the sorry character of Ralph Limbert in "The Next Time" (1895)—an author condemned to unsalability and a life beset my market-driven anxieties—in a peculiar way he also benefited from sharing Limbert's chronic incapacity for making sows' ears out of silk purses.[30] Commercial publishers in this period, who still wanted very much to think of themselves as genteel (even selfless) patrons of literary art, could sometimes demonstrate a rare indifference to the bottom line, if the author whose works they coveted possessed the appropriate hallmarks of writerly distinction. Henry James indubitably had them all. Why else would a turn-of-the-century New York real estate entrepreneur have built "The Henry James"—an uptown apartment house that would "specially appeal" (so its 1901 advertisements claimed) "to refined persons"?[31]

### THE HENRY JAMES,
### 501 WEST 113TH ST., COR. AMSTERDAM AV.

All outside light: 8 spacious rooms: bath, toilets, servants' stairs, most careful individual management; beautiful unobstructed views and healthful section; specially appeals to refined persons; liveried service; opposite St. John's Cathedral, Columbia University and many parks. Apply SUPERINTENDENT.

Such readers could only be such tenants: what a startling permutation of the author's cultural capital!

Not too surprisingly, the publisher who wanted James most was the one that had published him least: Charles Scribner's Sons. For years Scribner editors had watched from the sidelines as James serialized his stories and novels in their competitors' periodicals and published them under others' imprints. Early on the firm had snagged one of his titles for its magazine (the rather negligible fiction, *Confidence*, which appeared in *Scribner's Monthly* in 1879–80), but even then the book rights for this novel went to the Boston firm of Houghton, Osgood & Company, depriving Scribner's of the benefit of the kind of vertical market integration typically enjoyed by the *Atlantic* and *Harper's*. Since that time, only a handful of James's things—an occasional story or travel piece or critical sketch—had found their way into *Scribner's* pages, despite repeated invitations to the author for submissions. By the mid-1890s, a note almost of despair crept into these appeals. In 1896 senior editor Edward L. Burlingame wrote to James again, repeating "what I said in London last Spring, and in Paris two years ago, that I earnestly wish you would let me have more opportunities to see stories and papers from you." Not wanting in the least "to make *specific* requests" (commissioning articles from James as if he were merely any other journalist or literary hack), Burlingame still hoped that the author "would kindly consider my request as standing permanently," wondering too if James was crediting it "with the earnestness I really feel about it."[32] From these reiterated contacts with the author, and also from an editor's habit of keeping an ear open for literary gossip, Burlingame knew that James was increasingly dissatisfied with his existing publishing arrangements. Now was the time for Scribner's to make its move. And what better way to entice James to transfer allegiance and become a Scribner author than by offering to bring out a collected edition of his works?

Michael Millgate usefully has suggested that the building up of the Edition should be recognized as perhaps the most important "testamentary act" that James undertook in the last phase of his life, part of a pattern of "career closure" not unlike those of other writers "famous in their own time" who "have sought in old age to exert some degree of posthumous control over their personal and literary reputations."[33] Millgate fails sufficiently to appreciate, however, the extent to which the impulse to launch the New York Edition originated not with the author himself but rather with his not-quite-yet-publisher. James was hardly alone in seeing the impressive materiality of the collected edition, the author's magnum opus, as a mechanism for inviting (if not ensuring) future canonicity as well as the supreme opportunity to monopolize control over his posthumous reception. It is just as important to recognize, however, that through this particular form of cultural commodification, publishers also were asserting proprietary claim to the authors whose works they collectively issued, thereby trying to establish among the book-buying public an eponymous link between a particular house imprint and the writers grouped within its stable. Better than anything else, a collected edition of Henry James would consolidate and disseminate the perception of "Henry James" as a *Scribner* author.

It is not an accident that book historians have come to see the final decades of the nineteenth century as a kind of "golden age" for the production of collected editions of English and American authors. By the century's end, edition publishing was enjoying a kind of boom cycle, expanding the ranks of authors whose works received the benefit of uniform bindings and other marketing advantages. Unfortunately, no one has compiled anything like a complete census of these editions; but even a quick survey of trade periodicals from the time yields some impressive names and numbers. In 1903, for example, two of the leading American trade publishers, Scribner's and Houghton Mifflin, each were issuing the works of "standard" authors—from Emerson and Hawthorne to Dickens and Kipling—in collected sets that were available in a wide range of deluxe bindings, their cloth boards adorned with half-calf, half-morocco, or half-levant leather, suitably embossed with gilt, and targeted at minutely differentiated segments of the book-buying public.[34] Like other transformations in late nineteenth-century corporate capitalism, the phenomenon of edition publishing rightly should be seen as a reflection of the drive to rationalize and consolidate existing markets for symbolic forms of cultural capital. The practice went hand in hand with the other ways by which the major publishing houses of the time (trying to keep up with the trade's leading titans, Henry Oscar Houghton and Joseph Henry Harper) were vertically integrating their separate operations to make more efficient their control of intellectual property. While still concerned with the acquisition of publishable manuscripts (the editorial function would always be crucial in first assessing the potential cultural capital of a given work), these firms increasingly sought to profit from all the various stages by which the value latent in those manuscripts was transformed into marketable commodities: through serial publication in house-owned magazines, which also served as all-important vehicles for advertising and promotion; through in-house printing and binding, jobs that formerly had been contracted out to smaller regional presses and workshops; and now through direct marketing, since almost all collected editions were sold directly to consumers by subscription, circumventing retail booksellers altogether and thereby increasing the publisher's potential margin of return.[35]

Scribner's yearning to become James's American publisher and monopolize a claim to his oeuvre was hardly unrestrained. Certainly the firm knew that bringing out a collected edition of this by now notoriously recondite author would entail extraordinary risk. Like any other nervous gambler, the firm's senior editor was impelled by conflicting motives: Burlingame's hungry desire to corner the market in literary distinction could not altogether supersede the company's long-standing reputation for fiscal prudence, making his approach to the author both eager and cautious. From the very beginning, ambitions for the collected edition betray the latent contradictions between James's relatively inflated value as cultural capital and his correspondingly depressed value as a salable commodity. Because Burlingame knew that James was unhappy with his customary East Coast publishers—*What Maisie Knew* (1897) and *In the Cage* (1898) had been shopped around and finally placed with the upstart house of Herbert Stone in Chicago—the editor sensed in 1900 that "there might be an especially good chance at this moment of getting some collected form of James's books." At the same time, he had to question whether "the matter was worth following up at all" and was by no means sure that the company president, Charles Scribner, "would think it was." All the same, his instincts told him that this "was the 'psychological moment' for anybody who cared to have any chance at such a project," and he decided not to wait for his boss's approval before broaching the idea of a collected edition with James's agent. Conceding that such an edition "obviously [would have] so little commercial value," he nevertheless insisted that there were "many ways in which such a thing, if of reasonable proportions, could be a gratifying addition to a list like ours should it involve no sacrifice & not too much special work."[36] Though James demurred just then from accepting Burlingame's overture, it gave his agent the opening he needed later in 1900 to unload *The Sacred Fount* (which Scribner's published over their reader's considerable reservations[37]) and also kept alive the possibility of assembling a collected edition at a more opportune moment in the future.

When that moment arrived four years later, Scribner's unprofitable experience in marketing James's recent titles inspired renewed caution about the prospects for a collected edition. (Besides *The Sacred Fount* they had published *The Wings of the Dove* [1902] and *The Better Sort* [1903] with less than stellar results.) Still, Burlingame seemed convinced that readers of James were the real thing, and he urged Charles Scribner to relax the firm's pecuniary scruples with respect to a collected edition. Having been contacted again by Pinker about Scribner's interest in the project, Burlingame supposed that "if we want to meet the suggestion with cordiality, an early reply of some kind [would] be wise," but he conceded that he did not know "what effect our experiments in James since the idea was originally broached may have had upon it." But whatever the sales of those titles might have been, James's true audience, Burlingame felt, would respond less indifferently if his works had the added cachet of appearing in collective form. "To me [an edition] is still attractive," he affirmed, "not only for purely literary reasons but because it seems to me that James's audience, with all its limitation of number, is precisely the audience that buys a collected edition." Moreover, he insisted, such an audience "not only wants it when the cult is genuine, but even when it's only half so: there's a certain obligatory element."[38] Such market intangibles involved necessary risk, but in the end, to Scribner's, "Henry James" seemed a risk worth taking.

In retrospect, we can now see the whole complicated history of the New York Edition as a contest of competing intentions—Scribner's wanting to produce a series in line with the other "deluxe" editions they were selling, and James trying to reinvent the genre by making *his* edition distinct from others in what by then was an overly crowded literary marketplace.[39] His wholesale textual revisions, especially of earlier works; the magisterial, if somewhat forbidding, Prefaces;[40] the deliberately suggestive, rather than literally imagined, frontispieces; the thematic collocation of titles, rather than a strictly chronological sequence: in every respect James was deviating from consumer expectations and publishing tradition. No one knew this better than Scribner's, who then nervously attempted to convert each of these deflections into a marketing coup, as reflected in their advertising prospectus for the Edition. "To give the edition a literary unity such as, it is believed, no collected edition of any author's work heretofore issued has every enjoyed," Scribner's advertising claimed,

> Mr. James has devoted many months to the most careful and scrupulous revision of all the novels and tales, particularly the early ones. Those written many years ago, the first fruits of his genius, have thus been brought into alignment of style, color and general literary presentment with the work of his maturity—the work that has placed him in his present unrivalled position. . . . A still more important and equally novel feature is the set of Special Prefaces which Mr. James has prepared for the different volumes of the New York Edition. Nothing of the kind has ever been attempted. . . . The illustration of the edition has also been treated on a novel and, it is believed, particularly successful plan.[41]

Publishing hyperbole could not altogether conceal Scribner's anxiety about the very novelties they were obliged to tout. More circumspectly, Macmillan, the publisher who rather reluctantly agreed to distribute the New York Edition in England, omitted any reference to James's revisions in its prospectus, fearful that such information would discourage potential buyers.[42]

Emphasizing his selectivity was, at least for James, one of the selling points of the enterprise. As he told his agent during the planning stage, "It is best, I think, that it should be selective as well as collective; I want to quietly disown a few things by not thus supremely adopting them."[43] Disown them he did (only half of his short stories were included, and seven of his novels were chucked), and, once again, Scribner's was determined to convert that potential liability into a marketing advantage. "The edition will be complete in twenty-three volumes," their prospectus announced: "The entire set will include all of the author's fiction that he desires perpetuated in this definitive edition."[44] This smilingly glib commercial formula conceals an infinitely more complicated truth, for we also know that James would have preferred greater freedom to include "many things," as he told William Dean Howells, "that would have helped to make for rather a more vivid completeness."[45] Aesthetic discrimination played an important part in shaping the Edition, but blunter instruments of mere calculation also applied some determining strokes in forming its ultimate design.

Arithmetic, one gathers, was never James's strong suit. Even though Scribner's had insisted on a strict word limit (120,000) for the volumes of shorter tales and novellas to be included in the New York Edition, in preparing the various tables of contents for them James inflated that number to 150,000, a mistake that resulted in a wholesale reshuffling of constituent material down the line. Though we know that the author deliberately snubbed some of his works, especially early ones, as unworthy for inclusion,[46] the list of omissions grew not merely from judgments of taste but also from these errors of judgment. Martha Banta has called our attention to "The Excluded Seven"—the number, that is, of longer works absent from the Edition[47]—but to them we should at least add the titles of various shorter pieces that James originally envisioned as part of the series but then had to relinquish.[48] From correspondence in the Scribner Archive at Princeton, we learn that James's original tables of contents for the volumes of tales first included at least six stories that were later excised for want of space: "The Diary of a Man of Fifty" (1879), "A New England Winter" (1884), "The

Path of Duty" (1884), "The Solution" (1889), "Glasses" (1896), and "The Papers" (1903).[49] Even though some critics have drawn grossly inaccurate inferences from the "architecture" of the Edition (indeed, Leon Edel's whole academic career was launched by a paper that purported to discover it),[50] James and Scribner's both anticipated that its gradual success would allow for the later inclusion of many titles initially kept out. Their joint miscalculation of its prospects, which fixed the Edition's published dimensions, should not be misread as confirmation of James's imperial power in determining (à la Balzac) the ultimate shape of his literary legacy. Marketplace forces ultimately checked authorial intention.

Of course, James had more control over the texts he *was* able to include, and about his wholesale revision of them he was adamantly proud. When Charles Scribner himself expressed concern about the author's extensive reworking of his early fictions, James eagerly attempted to erase all doubt, affirming that he had conferred upon each of these titles a tremendous benefit—"and I mean of course benefit not only for myself, but for the public at large." "It is beyond any question," he continued, "that what I have just been very attentively doing for the 'Portrait' may must give it a new lease of such life as it may aspire to."[51] For James's publishers, however, such supposed rejuvenation was purchased at frightful expense. Setting type from the copy James had sent them—pasteups of pages from earlier editions, defaced by inky deletions and crisscrossed by wriggling interlineations scrawled up and down the margins—was a nightmare not just for the pressmen who had to untangle these serpentine scribbles but also for editors who worried that, through such wholesale overelaboration, the author was depriving his work of spontaneity and freshness.[52] The barrage of journalistic caricature that had shadowed James during and after his recent American lecture tour (1904–5), ridiculing his supposedly Byzantine sentences, could only have added to his publishers' anxiety about how well the much-revised texts would be received. Struggling to muffle their qualms about the invasive nature of James's emendations, which they feared would discourage sales, Scribner's preferred to address the issue in their prospectus with another liberal dose of rose coloring: "Purged thus of crudities while retaining their freshness these productions [of the earlier books] take their equal place in the harmony of the author's entire artistic output, and the whole edition thus constitutes an elaborate edifice whose design and execution are absolutely unique in their kind owing to their complete unity of effect."[53] Despite such sweeping claims, to some readers James's textual interventions violated a kind of literary ethics. "What an author has once deliberately given out to be published is not 'his own,'" the *New York Times* insisted. "His winged words have gone forth and found lodgment for themselves in other minds. Those who cherish them find incessant tinkering [with] them a 'perpetual impertinence' even on the part of the original writer, and are disposed indignantly to inquire, 'Who is he that he should tamper with a classic?'"[54] Well, he was Henry James (that's who), and Henry James tampered with abandon.

The Edition's failure to win popular approval, especially when James had invested so much time and energy in it, was, of course, a humiliating defeat. When he received his first almost imperceptible "returns" from the series, his letters groan with genuine despair. Returning his agent's accounting of meager royalties, James admitted that the document had "knocked me rather flat—a greater disappointment" than he was prepared for, "& after my long & devoted labour a great . . . & a bitter grief. I hadn't built *high* hopes," he insisted, "had done everything to keep them down; but feel as if comparatively I have been living in a fool's paradise. Is there *anything* for me at all?" he wondered.[55] When the remittance later came, James's check rewarded him with the princely sum of thirty-five dollars.[56] Somewhat larger amounts would follow, as more of the volumes eventually came into print, but the substantial returns he had hoped for never materialized. Overseeing the New York Edition turned out to be, as he had every reason to concede, "the most expensive job of my life."[57]

No less ironically, the expensiveness of the Edition also worked to restrict its circulation. In order to arrange for the Edition at all, Scribner's was obliged to market the series through their Subscription Department, committing the buyer to purchase twenty-four volumes at a minimum of two dollars apiece, and thereby removing individual volumes from competition with the sales of ordinary trade editions of James's scattered titles. Even the novelist's brother William (a full professor at Harvard) was grateful for the 25 percent courtesy discount that Scribner's afforded him ("thanks to the relationship") when he ordered two sets—as wedding presents![58] Because of their unusual size and cost, series like the New York Edition occupied an ambiguous place in the increasingly commodified world of consumer culture that American capitalism was creating in the modern era. Though these books were usually manufactured with the most up-to-date kinds of machine technology, their physical characteristics (and occasionally limited production numbers) seemed to defy the debasing tendencies of mechanical reproduction. Traces or evidence of manual labor often figured in their design (and were certainly promoted in their advertising). These pre-industrial vestiges might be incorporated bibliographically through the use of handmade paper or, possibly, hand-tooled bindings—or, at the very least, the hand numbering of a truly limited edition on the verso of the title page.

Ever mindful of the market, Scribner's followed all of these protocols in producing the New York Edition, wanting to invest "Henry James" with the necessary material features that would physically complement the aura of his symbolic capital. The firm used paper watermarked with an enlarged varia-tion of the art nouveau monogram (an *H* and *J* decoratively conjoined) that was stamped on the Edition's cover. Subscribers could purchase the trade issue in plum-colored cloth ($2 per volume / $48 the set) or half levant ($4 per vol-ume / $96 the set). And a genuinely limited issue of 156 hand-numbered copies, though struck from the same plates as the ordinary issue, was printed on Ruis-dael handmade paper ($8 per volume / $192 the set).[59] To well-heeled, if some-what pretentious, custodians of culture, the Edition was a testament to a kind of bookish exclusivity, and purchasers could be sure they were getting the real thing. "The aspect of these twenty-four volumes," said a writer for *The Bookman*,

> is such as to command the approval even of so exacting a connoisseur as Mr.
> James may be conceived as being: large, serious-looking volumes in their digni-
> fied binding of dull red, with their specially made, water-marked paper, their
> admirably novel and so distinguished illustrations consisting of photogravures
> made from photographs by Mr. Alvin Langdon Coburn. Everything is in keep-
> ing. Mr. James is no author for "pocket" editions.[60]

Perhaps not. But James's publishers (especially in England) soon realized that, in its expensive subscription format, the Edition would not find many buyers or readers. Macmillan, of course, could more easily reach that conclusion, because that firm had not invested serious capital in the Edition's production and man-ufacture: after their modest initial purchase of one hundred sets of sheets, they simply bought additional quantities from Scribner's as needed (and typically in very small lots).[61] Their role, essentially, was that of a binder and retailer, not re-ally a publisher. Because they were shielded from risk, why not, then, consider issuing the books in a cheaper format? Macmillan, in fact, proved amenable to the idea when James's agent first proposed it in 1915, although the less expensive series would not be published until several years after the Armistice. Scribner's, saddled with considerable overhead, could only pray that future sales of the New York Edition eventually would recoup the firm's up-front investment. Their supplications went largely unanswered by a market that remained churlish about acquiring the cultural capital that "Henry James" then could bestow.

## Sovereign Immunities

James's ambiguous national allegiance complicated his publishers' efforts to market the New York Edition. While Scribner's prospectus for the series touted the author as "the first of American novelists," his critical (often censorious) attitude toward his native land—expressed concurrently in the pages of *The American Scene* (1907), most chapters of which had been serialized in American magazines—encouraged many in the United States to dismiss him as an effete specimen of deracination, indifferent to the necessary claims of patriotism. Such views were frequently expressed in the newspaper accounts that chronicled James's recent American lecture tour and were echoed in no less a place than the executive mansion occupied by Theodore Roosevelt. "What a miserable little snob Henry James is," Theodore Rex complained. "His polished, pointless, uninteresting stories about the upper social classes of England make one blush to think that he was once an American."[62] Though James obviously prided himself on his deliberate cosmopolitanism, even members of his own family sometimes wondered about the cost entailed by cultivating it. William most famously addressed this when he described his younger brother (in a letter to their sister, Alice) as only superficially Anglicized, despite "all the accretions" from his years of living in London. "His anglicisms are but 'protective resemblances,'" William pithily observed. "[H]e's really, I won't say a yankee, but a native of the James family, and has no other country."[63] If citizenship in *that* country conveyed extraordinary privileges, it also imposed peculiar defensive obligations: and all the Jameses seem to have understood and accepted the need to shield the family and its sometimes vulnerable members from critical scrutiny.

In the autobiographical volumes he published near the end of his life, Henry James commemorated this sense of familial exceptionalism, tracing it back, quite naturally, to his father's rather fathomless financial independence and the freedom it granted them to migrate between Europe and the United

States. While the rest of antebellum American society conveniently could be pigeon-holed into three distinct categories—the Busy, the Tipsy, and Daniel Webster—the Jameses stood utterly apart; "our consciousness was positively disfurnished," the author admitted, "of the actualities of 'business' in a world of business. As to that we all formed together quite a monstrous exception; business in a world of business was the thing we most agreed . . . in knowing nothing about." The father's anomalous social status was a perpetual source of embarrassment, especially to young children wanting to befriend classmates at school and to enjoy the secure reputability that only "business"—a paternal calling in the law, medicine, or the church—seemed capable of providing. "'What shall we tell them you *are*?'" they would plead; and their bemused parent would unhelpfully answer, "'Say I'm a philosopher, say I'm a seeker for truth, say I'm a lover of my kind, say I'm an author of books if you like; or, best of all, just say I'm a Student.'"[64] When Henry James Senior called Emerson a man without a handle, he might just as well have been describing himself.

The patriarch's ambiguous legacy to his two elder sons elicited from both of them an aesthetics of defensive apology. After the father's death in 1882, William felt obliged to commemorate (and consecrate) his lifelong quest for religious truth by publishing *The Literary Remains of the Late Henry James* (1884), consisting of a long autobiographical fragment, thinly disguised by a pseudonym,[65] and two other compositions that had been left in manuscript. Undertaking the work was also something of a psychological recompense. As William confided to his brother, "I must now make amends for my rather hard non-receptivity of his doctrines as he urged them so absolutely during his life, by trying to get a little more public justice done them now." Having once drawn a telling cartoon depicting his father's obsession with theological abstractions—an India ink sketch of a man beating a very dead horse, jokingly intended as a frontispiece for one of Henry Senior's obscure self-published volumes[66]—William now needed to take a more sympathetic view of them. "As life closes," he wrote, "all a man has done seems like one cry or sentence. Father's cry was the single one that religion is real. The thing is so to 'voice' it that other ears shall hear,—no easy task, but a worthy one, which in some shape I shall attempt."[67] Obliged to admit that "few writers were in the end more prolix" than his father,[68] William successfully managed to recapitulate Henry Senior's principal doctrines in a masterful introduction to the *Literary Remains*. As R. W. B. Lewis tartly observes, "[T]he commentary offers the spectacle of the most lucid philosopher in American intellectual history expounding the salient ideas and the vision of our least communicative thinker."[69]

When Henry Junior received his copy of the memorial book, he had to admit that his brother's introduction was in some ways more illuminating than the father's dizzyingly esoteric prose, but he also appreciated the editorial discretion that William had employed in choosing "extracts from Father's writings" that were "selected so happily."[70] An even subtler discretion would reign when Henry assumed the mantle of family biographer twenty-five years later: he not only incorporated carefully chosen selections from the far-ranging archive of James correspondence into *Notes of a Son and Brother*; he also took considerable liberties with the texts of those letters, revising them to suit the needs of his imaginative reconstruction of the past. Anyone interested in objectively narrating the history of the family can hardly avoid wrestling with the Jameses' deep-seated impulse to control the representation of themselves to curious outsiders. Alfred Habegger has gone so far as to suggest that all reaches of the clan tacitly conspired to erect a defensive cordon either of silence (through the deliberate destruction of documentary evidence) or of selective revelation (through the misrepresentation of that evidence) when confronted with the need to address the public about itself.[71] While it is certainly understandable for scholars, especially, to be scandalized by such reticence and revisionary tendencies—as Habegger, Michael Millgate, and Carol Holly most conspicuously have been[72]—it is perhaps more useful to see this behavior as an extension of a kind of custodial instinct that was almost second nature to them. They also knew that the extraordinary freedom they indulged in verbal intercourse with one another (especially their exaggeratedly aggressive style and tone, so deeply inherited from Henry James Senior) might easily be misunderstood by others. As William once pregnantly observed about his father, "He is so little restrained by conventional considerations that if you or I or Mama were to die to night he would send off a contribution to the *Daily Advertiser* to morrow tearing us to pieces."[73] Such impulses necessitated close watchfulness, and the Jameses seldom let down their guard—even (or especially) with respect to one another.

No other event in the family's internal contest over its own documentary records is more revealing than the tremors that rippled through the ranks after Alice James's death (1892), when her survivors discovered that for years she had kept a private diary and that, even more alarmingly, she had bequeathed her manuscript to someone outside the kinship circle: Katharine Peabody Loring, who had been Alice's loyal companion and caretaker for almost two decades. Since 1884 the two women had resided in England, wandering to various watering holes and seaside resorts, where Alice unsuccessfully sought treatment for the neurasthenia that condemned her to invalidism; then they had settled in London, taking rooms not far from brother Henry in Kensington. In the final months of her confinement, terminally ill with breast cancer, Alice had begun dictating her journal entries to Katharine, who now added the responsibilities of an amanuensis to the list of her other household duties. Unbeknown to the family, when Katharine Loring returned to America with Alice's ashes in March 1892, she also brought with her two manuscript scribblers—much like her brother's notebooks, some 450 pages in all—containing the text of her companion's diary. Appreciating Alice's so tragically limited literary ambitions and opportunities, she prepared a (reasonably accurate) typescript of the journal and then arranged for four copies to be privately published by a printer in Cambridge, intending one for each of Alice's three surviving brothers and one, of course, for herself. William and Henry each received his copy in short order; the copy intended for Robertson James was withheld after Katharine Loring received a sharp remonstrance from Henry about what she had done. Hoping all the while that the brothers would consent to the diary's formal publication, Loring instead had to stomach their disapproval. She was not able to honor Alice James's wish to have the diary published for another forty years.

For his part, William James immediately recognized the vitality of the diarist's style, which nevertheless could only leave "the impression of personal power venting itself on no opportunity." Alice's straitened circumstances had prevented that, but now, perhaps, she might find her chance. Such "really *deep* humor!" he found in her pages: surely one day the volume ought to be published, he insisted to Henry; it could only become another "leaf in the family laurel crown." His brother, however, shared no such enthusiasm; he was mortified "by the sight of so many private names & allusions in print" and stricken with fear lest the diary circulate more widely. Even though he was quick to appreciate his sister's literary achievement—the sharpness of her social observations and her frequently caustic satire—"the printedness-*en-toutes-lettres* of so many names, personalities, hearsay, (usually, on Alice's part, through *me!*)" made Henry "intensely nervous & almost sick with terror about possible publicity, possible accidents, reverberations &c," the effect of which was to poison his *"enjoyment* of the wonderful character of the thing," even though it did not dim his perception of it. If only *he* had had the chance to edit the manuscript: *then* they could have freely given it to the world and "carefully burn[ed] with fire our own 4 copies." James had said as much, apparently, in his stern rejoinder to Katharine Loring ("a letter which . . . she may not have liked," he admitted); and he saw no reason why the diary's unfortunate private publication could not be kept "an absolute & utter secret"—even from their brother Bob. "It has only—the secret—to *be* really kept," Henry underscored, and the others eventually acceded to his almost hysterical reasoning.[74]

Henry James *did* burn his copy of Alice's diary, and he enjoined the others to do the same. He was especially fearful that, should a copy make its way to the ever unreliable Robertson, his chatterbox wife and daughter would pass it around among their neighbors in Concord, Massachusetts, "with the fearful American newspaper lying in wait for every whisper, every echo."[75] But the three remaining printed volumes escaped the flames. William James preserved his (locking it away to prevent casual inspection by visitors to 95 Irving Street); Katharine Loring certainly cherished her copy; and, deferring to Henry's strenuous appeal, she withheld Robertson's copy, which remained in her possession until she presented it to Harry James in 1923, after he had made public his intention of giving William James's professional library to Harvard. Having by then inherited his parents' copy, Harry, in turn, gave this duplicate to his sister, Peggy, who was very much in league with him as a cautious guardian of family confidences. Mindful of Uncle Henry's adamant injunction, neither of them had any interest in circulating the diary more openly. Neither, apparently, did they have much interest in giving Katharine Loring the time of day: she later remarked that Robertson's descendants were the only members of the James family who had ever shown any concern for her welfare or desire to know more about her relationship with Alice. (Neither brother had even so much as thanked her, it seems, for having been given his precious printed copy of the diary.)[76] When, years later, Robertson's daughter, Mary Walsh Vaux, inquired about her long-dead aunt (of whom she would have had the dimmest memory, having been only nine years of age when Alice left to take up residence in England), Katharine Loring generously responded by sending the original pair of manuscript scribblers to her Bryn Mawr home.

Armed with these and other family documents, Mary Vaux hoped now to redress a host of long-simmering family grievances. William and Henry had become world-renowned figures—didn't the recent publication of volumes of their letters (in 1920) confirm it?—and their combined reputations had overshadowed those of all the other members of their illustrious American family. Even though Robertson James seems to have had less in common with his elder brothers than with Pap Finn (sharing the latter's wily ability to secure others' trust and money, resources he would then use to get hopelessly drunk),[77] his daughter nevertheless felt that both he and Wilky—not to mention Alice—deserved better. Mary Vaux entrusted all the family manuscripts in her possession to Anna Robeson Burr, a distinguished biographer and essayist (whose husband, like Mary's, was a successful attorney in Philadelphia), wanting her to produce some kind of memorial volume—*A Gathering of the Family* she called it—that would allow the otherwise invisible Jameses at least to gain some measure of sympathetic understanding and stature. In 1934 Burr edited and published *Alice James: Her Brothers—Her Journal*, bringing Alice's diary to public awareness for the first time.[78] In her lengthy introduction to this volume (a biographical essay devoted to Alice's more- and less-famous brothers), she also reprinted selections from letters that clearly were intended to correct misconceptions that had accrued because of the very selective nature of the family documents that the Jameses had allowed to be published up till then. Because so few of the exchanges among the siblings and their parents had been brought to light, critics and biographers often drew mistaken inferences from the silence occasioned by their apparent absence. It was all too easy to assume, as had one recent biographical study, that "Wilky and Bob never counted for much" in the lives of their more celebrated brothers, since almost none of their correspondence was known (or available) to outsiders.[79] This volume was intended to correct such unfortunate imbalances.

Having access to so many previously unpublished primary sources, Burr also recognized the extent to which Henry James had tailored them—self-aggrandizingly—when he wrote *Notes of a Son and Brother*. The familiar image that James had projected of himself—as the "innocent, very powerless-feeling brother"—did not square with the aggressive egotism Burr found in suppressed passages of the family archive. "It must not be forgotten," she insisted, "that his main weakness—or was it perhaps strength?—lay in his dread of responsibility and in that egotism, twinborn with shyness, which caused him to protect and shelter his own self-respect."[80] If first she had been infected by Mary Vaux's resentment of Henry's willful monopoly of family history, Burr was also influenced by the allegations about the author's unfortunate deracination that Van Wyck Brooks had sensationalized in *The Pilgrimage of Henry James* (1925). Since Burr was mindful of the younger brothers' service and severe wounding in the Civil War, their sad vulnerability to the economic upheavals of agricultural and industrial business cycles, the contrast between their losing struggles with implacable American realities and the expatriate's more comfortable life abroad was too painful to go unremarked. Burr echoed Brooks in concluding that, because he was "too ceremonious and reserved for America," Henry James

> drifted at length into the quiet harbor of his spiritual home—to that Victorian England, where one was admired without interference, never bothered, never asked to think about anything but oneself and one's art, and where "the passions of luxurious aristocrats," as he told Edith Wharton, surrounded him with a profusion of literary material. It was fortunate he did not live to see the Europe he delighted in as bare as a rifled cupboard and as emptied of kings and pageantry as the United States itself.[81]

Whatever their failings, the younger brothers at least had felt the clutch of patriotism. Besides, Henry's disloyalty extended even to his own family. The editor clearly knew that it was Henry who had urged the destruction of his sister's journal: the first line of acknowledgment Burr wrote expressed her gratitude to "Miss Katharine Loring, first and foremost, by whose piety the Journal was originally preserved."[82] By then Miss Loring's eyesight was too poor to allow her to study Burr's work unaided, but hearing its pages read aloud to her, she dictated a note on the spot to tell the editor that she had "enjoyed every word of your family history and find it interesting and brilliant."[83] Mary Vaux's gadabout brother, Edward Holton ("Ned") James, likewise voiced his approval of the volume. "I cannot find a fault in it," he blithely reported, feeling too that "a big success for it" was "assured."[84]

Whatever satisfaction Robertson's descendants and Katharine Loring may have received from seeing Alice James's diary at last in print, their happiness was hardly shared by other members of the James family. For years Harry confidently had assumed that, at her death, Katharine Loring intended her printed copy of the diary—and the original manuscript—to be returned to him for safekeeping; indeed, she had promised him as much in a letter. Instead, now the diary was in print, advertised in all the major papers, even noticed—twice—in the pages of the *New York Times*. (One can only imagine his reaction upon reading there that his Uncle Bob's symptoms of mental anguish made him out to have been "all the brothers Karamazoff wrapped up in one package"!)[85] "The whole thing would make me weep," he told his sister, Peggy, "if anything of that kind were worth weeping about." Seeing the diary in circulation was bad enough, but even worse, in Harry's view, was the puerile biographical essay that Burr had written to exaggerate the supposed virtues of the younger brothers—a performance "so thin, clumsy and unintelligent as to be pathetic."[86] Receiving her copy from Mary Vaux, Peggy was even more incensed. Publishing the diary, she bitterly wrote by way of acknowledging the gift, was "a betrayal of trust of the older generation and as such shameful"—"to say nothing of its bad taste," she added.[87] Peggy also lashed out at Katharine Loring for having given Alice's diary to Mary Vaux in the first place: why couldn't she have respected Uncle Henry's judgment? What he had published in *Notes of a Son and Brother* was more than adequate, she felt, as a family chronicle. "Why parade the failures, neurasthenias, and depressions of its younger members, as does Mrs. Burr?" she hissed. "I consider it a disloyalty to them, and that instead of an enhancement of the family, the book is an exposure, in the worst possible taste." To see all this in print simply made her "shrink and shudder."[88]

The other Jameses found whatever consolation they might in the scolding the editor received from some of her reviewers. While most of the notices simply reveled in the wealth of new documentary evidence her book had made available, a few took exception to the slant of Burr's biographical chronicle. To Ralph Barton Perry, Harry had ridiculed her sloppy methods and misinformed interpretations. "She is careless, lazy," he spluttered, "both sentimental and spiteful, innocent of any real understanding of the history of the time she is dealing with, superficial minded, inept." Her prejudices were only too conspicuous. Burr seemed "to harbor a real dislike of my Uncle Henry," he complained, and could "hardly refer to him without scratching him."[89] Consequently, Harry could only chuckle with "malicious glee" when he saw these judgments repeated in the *Times Literary Supplement*.[90] "The editing of this beautiful little book has not been given all the care that it deserved," the *Times* reviewer shrewdly suggested. "One scents misreadings in some places, and in others more annotation is required." Turning the tables on Burr, the reviewer openly wondered what "language . . . Alice would have launched upon her head" had *she* had the opportunity to read the book's introduction (and its condescending treatment of brother Henry)? "To speak plainly," he confidently asserted, "Miss Burr would have been scorched."[91] That the anonymous reviewer was none other than Percy Lubbock could only add clout to this counterfactual criticism. Had Harry James known who had written the piece, his gleeful chuckle would have resonated with added scorn.

We should also remember that, two decades before, Harry had voiced very similar criticisms of his uncle's handling of the family documents that Henry James had chosen to incorporate into the pages of *Notes of a Son and Brother*. In fact, he and Uncle Henry had almost come to an open rift over the disposition of these materials. Much of that misunderstanding can be attributed to Henry James's evolving (and expanding!) conception of the so-called Family Book that in 1911 he had promised William's widow he would write as a memorial to his older brother. Having returned to the United States with heart-stricken William and the ever-devoted Alice in August 1910, Henry stood at his brother's bedside when the elder James died, barely a week after they had reentered the country and removed to the family's rural outpost at Chocorua, New Hampshire. Shortly after they had taken his brother's body back to Cambridge for cremation and burial, Henry vowed to Alice that he would remain with her for a year, placating her ardent desire for his presence in the event that William's spirit should try to speak to them from the other side. Exactly how many séances Alice convened at 95 Irving Street is not a matter of record, but none of them resulted in any addition to William James's verbal legacy. That gnawing silence probably encouraged Alice to suggest that Henry compile a family memoir so that William's voice might yet be heard; perhaps it also contributed to his eagerness in taking up the idea? At any rate, he later told Alice that "it was in talk with you in that terrible winter of 1910–11 that the impulse to the whole attempt" came to him, an impulse that would result in two fat volumes of autobiographical recollections and a fragment of a third.[92]

The fraternal impulse to commemorate William—and the opportunity, during the otherwise dreary months spent in America, to rummage through the vast collection of letters and other family documents filed away at 95 Irving Street— led the younger brother to conceive of a book that would allow William to speak for himself by incorporating significant portions of his youthful correspondence into its pages. Letters from the other Jameses—especially their long-dead mother and father, and sister Alice—could also tenderly invoke sacred memories of their early days in New York, their seasons of European sojourn and summers in Newport. Knowing that some formal compilation of William's correspondence would someday be expected, his widow and Harry already had begun to sort through the mass of documents in their possession, having many of them type-copied for easier consultation but also destroying many letters that were deemed too private for others ever to see.[93] Even when Henry was traveling away from Cambridge that winter, packets of the type-copied correspondence chased him through the mail, dutifully sent by his nephew as they were compiled and sorted; and the overstuffed envelopes continued to arrive after James returned to England later in the summer. Henry clearly was delighted that Alice and Harry were so forthcoming. A voluminous letter sent that November expressed "the interest & pleasure" he took in Harry's generous response to his "asking for more—from your Dad; & in my understanding that you have still something more to send me." Harry, just as clearly, was trying discreetly to coach his uncle on the best use of these materials. "I am absolutely at one with you," James affirmed,

> as to your idea of the atmosphere & setting that should flow round & encircle all these things—and that should (& shall) be filled with all the evocations that I can summon up of the old figures & feelings & times, all the personal & social & subjective (& *objective*) furniture of our family annals. Seen this way & in the light of my own "genius," the whole subject-matter opens out to me most appealingly & beguilingly, & if you will but trust me so to *keep* seeing it & doing it, I think something altogether beautiful & interesting & remarkable & rare will be the issue—for I now have got thoroughly into the vein & the current; so much so that I hope really to go very straight & uninterruptedly & quite swiftly.[94]

Not too surprisingly, James's progress on the "Family Book" was slow, broken, and crooked; before very long, he began to deviate quite markedly from the common assumptions with which he and those back in Cambridge had started.

Once he remounted the stream of time, James found that the work's first intention to enshrine William was superseded by another aim altogether: instead of composing a narrative about his older brother, Henry began to reconstruct a sensitive chronicle of his own youthful development and coming to artistic consciousness. Within a year, the writer realized (as he told his agent) "that I seem to have sufficient material, quite, for *two* books, two distinct ones, taking the place of the one multifarious and comprehensive one that I originally saw." The solution, he felt, was "to detach and disengage" from the family memoir a separate volume that would "stand upon its feet" as the 'Earlier letters of W. J., edited by H. J.'" "My only way not to be too copious and too complicated," he continued, would be "to take these, to produce and present, to comment and accompany, or in other words duly and vividly *biographise* them, by them-selves."[95] Since, almost from the moment of his father's death, Harry himself had begun work on his own edition of William James's letters, he and his more famous uncle now, unwittingly, were poised to wrestle for control of them.

Given the disappointing commercial failure of the New York Edition, Henry James was also eager to generate income, and he certainly knew that William's death inevitably had created a ready market for documents pertaining to his life. Earlier that year, in fact, J. M. Dent, an enterprising British publisher, had suggested that James write a biography of his elder brother, a book that could only catch fire with the public. "I think we could arrange satisfactory terms for this," his agent was told, though, of course, "with Henry James the terms would not be the first consideration." All the same, the proposal was a sign of security: "if I am," Dent wrote, "as I think I am, the first in the field with this sugges-tion, that will profess our desire for the book."[96] This overture did not result in a contract, but it surely could have prompted James to reconsider his handling of the "Family Book" and its constituent materials. The incentives for treating William's letters independently began to multiply after Pinker began hawking the idea to other publishers. Not long after William's death, the family had been pressured by Ida Tarbell to serialize some of his correspondence in the pages of her *American Magazine*, but Alice and Henry both felt that a more dignified out-let should be found. Now, with Pinker circulating word that Henry James was at work on his brother's letters, better options started to materialize. Charles Scribner himself promptly invited the novelist to prepare two installments of his brother's letters for serialization in *Scribner's Magazine*, and he promised to pay generously for them. So eager was Scribner to scoop this material, his firm began to advertise the forthcoming "Letters of William James" as a bribe for purchasers to renew their subscriptions.

Because of William's high visibility in England, Pinker was also able to negotiate an extremely lucrative contract with Macmillan for a selection of the philosopher's letters[97]—a turn of events that allowed a rather invidious Henry James to reject another piddling offer that had come to him from William Meredith (on behalf of Constable & Co.) for the same book rights. Thinking of that stingy prospect, James confided to his agent, "I had all the while at the back of my head the perfect remembrance of W.M.'s connection with quite the least remunerative episode of my literary career (which is saying much)—his having given me a dozen years ago that small scrap of a sum for 'The Wings of the Dove.' . . . So I shall answer his letter today or tomorrow in the manner that will serve him right; and I beg you to go on with Macmillan."[98] Similarly advantageous terms with Scribner's prompted James to dismiss the notion of giving anything to Ida Tarbell's *American Magazine*; that poor rag, "with its short newspaper-form snippets," "couldn't either *touch* it—or pay for it," he brayed.[99] Besides, who could match the five hundred pounds that Charles Scribner had agreed to advance him as a condition for securing the serial installments of William's letters?[100] All in all, James's disposition of his brother's literary remains promised to be one of the most profitable book-making arrangements to which he had ever signed his name.

Quite unknowingly, James's boastful letter to his sister-in-law tipped off the Cambridge contingent to what could only strike them as his overreaching designs. When the November issue of *Scribner's Magazine* arrived at 95 Irving Street, soon promising a two-part serial "composed of letters of William James edited by his brother," alarms clearly sounded.[101] Alice confessed to her son that it was "a great shock" to see the advertisement, though she urged him not to overreact. "*But*, dear Harry," she implored, "let us be very gentle with poor, sick Uncle Henry" (who was then suffering terribly from an attack of shingles).[102] Earlier that September, as soon as Harry had learned of his uncle's plans, he had cabled "STOP" to enjoin any contract with Scribner's for William's letters. Believing that his uncle had, at most, been culling a few quotations from all the documents that Harry had sent him—to flesh out what he all along had supposed to be a volume of early family reminiscences—it now came as both a shock and a surprise to discover a much different enterprise afoot. Averse to confronting his uncle directly, Harry instead wrote to Pinker, hoping that the agent's typical diplomacy would find a way to resolve the inevitable contest for control. Trained in the law, Harry knew how to present a clear line of reasoning. "Of course my father's letters cannot be published even by my uncle without the consent of his representatives," he began. The evasiveness of his uncle's replies to his queries about the use of his father's letters—and now the recent advertisement from *Scribner's*—made his appeal for specifics more urgent. It was absolutely out of the question, Harry emphasized, "for any considerable number of my father's early letters to be published" until certain questions as to the treatment of the rest of his correspondence (which he and his mother had been collecting for eighteen months) had been settled. If Uncle Henry had already signed a contract for such material, it would have to be broken—an event that would deeply "embarrass him and me," Harry admitted. He also knew the marginal diameter of the ice on which he was treading. "Frankly," he wrote, "it would upset [Uncle Henry] very much to know of my writing to you about this. If you don't want to answer without his knowledge and consent, please simply tell me so and throw this away without referring to it." But Harry did not want to think of that alternative as viable. "I'm really enquiring about what is not wholly my uncle's affair but partly mine," he insisted; "and I've also got the feeling that it would be well for you to know . . . that I take more than a passive interest in my father's literary remains."[103]

Harry's confusion and resentment were amplified because he thought he had made abundantly clear to his uncle his own "more than passive interest" in William's epistolarium. Dutifully following established family practice, he had already collected some of his father's literary remains and published them as a freestanding volume (*Memories and Studies* [1911])—a clear assertion of executorial authority as well as an expression of filiopiety.[104] More recently he had enlisted Uncle Henry to help in the process of soliciting letters from Britons with whom William had corresponded. James obliged by having special insertions made in the "Literary Gossip" columns of the *Spectator* and the *Athenaeum* ("much the best & most conspicuous place," he advised), formally asking that copies of such letters be sent to Harry in Cambridge.[105] "Casual or brief letters may have an interest or importance not apparent to the person preserving them," these notices pointedly remarked, adding that "news of the whereabouts of any of [William] James's letters" would be "gratefully received."[106] Now it seemed as if Uncle Henry was trying to usurp his nephew's legal priority in the rights to his father's letters and, not incidentally, to profit handsomely from

them. Such premature publication could only jeopardize Harry's more comprehensive intentions for the controlled dissemination of William's correspondence and possibly lessen the appeal that any later publication would have.

The nephew's sharp rejoinder to his uncle prompted a long and tortured exchange of letters between them about the use (and misuse) of family documents—
only fragments of which have been disclosed in published accounts—and which
typically have been understood as Henry James's long-winded apologia for having tinkered with the texts of his brother's correspondence in *Notes of a Son and
Brother*.[107] Since Henry James destroyed almost all of his nephew's missives, it is
understandable that later researchers have been obliged to draw inferences from
only one side of this exchange; but one of the few letters from Harry that did
not perish in the flames offers keener insight into the larger question of editorial control that supersedes the more technical issue of revision itself. Harry's
first letter of objection (which no longer survives) prompted James to compose
a twenty-eight-page explanation of the manner by which the intended "Family
Book" had now grown disproportionately into an account of his own personal
development, for which he even envisioned a very revealing title—*Earliest Memories: Egotistic*. From the uncle's response, we can assume that Harry had also laid
out an elaborate rationale for his own editorial project. "I enter intensely into
your letter's so interesting pages on all that matter," James affirmed, intimating
that "the degree and manner of my manipulation of the whole material in which
your Dad's letters are employed and embedded will conjure away sufficiently
any danger of a suggested connection or continuity with, or implied reference to,
the fact of your reserved array of his correspondence proper."

Such vague assurances did not altogether satisfy Harry, who was especially
concerned that, should his father's correspondence appear in *Scribner's*, his own
vested interest in its copyright would be compromised. His confusion about his
uncle's intentions, he wrote,

> was based, as you say, partly on your "clinching" a bargain with Scribners for
> an use of the title "Early Letters of W.J. with Notes etc."; and partly also on your
> saying in your letter of Aug. 26 to Mama that the "Early Letters,"—for which
> you described yourself as "in conspicuous treaty with Scribner," and "for"
> which, you said, "with notes I can do everything I want"—would be the *first*
> publication; and partly on your referring to the Family Book as "broken down"

and more or less unuseable. All this led me on to think that if ~~negotiations~~ terms were ~~on~~ being arranged with Scribner, Pinker would be more or less conducting ~~them~~ negotiations; and in searching for explanations of what, I can't help admitting to you, seemed to me a most strange inversion of the natural order of publication, I thought it possible that he might have reported to you an immediate eagerness on Scribner's part for "Early Letters of W.J." by which you might have been influenced to formulate the plan you seemed to be announcing.

Harry's compunction to suppress the pecuniary inflections of his answer powerfully suggests that the driving force of his concern was hardly a prissy fear of textual adulteration—rather, of surrendering his rights to whatever portions of William's correspondence that his relative intended to publish. To make sure that his uncle understood this point, Harry wrote explicitly that "Scribner must have no right to restrict the re-printing (through another publisher) of such letters, and I trust you will not find it irksome to inform us adequately before the time of printing, just what letters you are planning to use."[108]

With the manuscript of *A Small Boy and Others* now almost ready to go off to Scribner's, James pleaded for renewed patience from his nephew, because work on the second installment of the "Family Book," *Notes of a Son and Brother*, was still at an early stage. "I wish I could persuade you to a little greater confidence," James implored (on 25 November 1912),

> in my proceeding with the utmost consideration for—well, whatever you want most to be considered; and I shall feel this confidence most, and most happily and operatively profit by it, if you won't ask me too much in advance, or at any rate now for some time to come, to formulate to you the *detail* of my use, of my conversion into part of the substance of my book, of your Dad's Letters; which will have to wait so, as to the quantity and variety etc. in which they figure, on their relation, from point to point, to the whole, and to the rest of my ingredients.

He then dismissed the thought of serializing any of the letters in *Scribner's* and brushed off their announcement as "a mere publisher's piece of precipitation and 'enterprise.'" To placate his nephew further, James was likewise willing to surrender the "pecuniary bribe" the magazine had offered for two installments of the correspondence. What better sign of good faith could he want?

To forestall any future misunderstandings and resentments, all through 1913 James dispatched almost monthly letters to Harry (or Alice), allowing each to peek over his shoulder as composition of *Notes of a Son and Brother* proceeded. "The Book will have to be a longer one than 'A Small Boy,'" he rightly surmised, "but even with this there must be limits involving suppressions and omissions." Letters from Henry Senior and William were too precious to exclude, but by giving latitude to them, he had "little room for any one else's," notably those from sister Alice.[109] As he went forward, James tried to be as explicit as possible about which of William's letters were likely to be featured; he was almost sure that those written from Europe in 1868–69, when his brother was studying in Germany, would be the last he would incorporate. "The air I can breathe round *them* will, I think, be missed if they are published without it," James felt; "but with the cessation of my nearness, as it were, that is with the opening of '69, that nearness begins to cease, and I leave everything thereafter for [your] Collection. Let so much serve, for the moment, as a sort of rough prefiguring statement. What seems to be indicated is that I can embody (for space-reasons) a good bit less of everything than I had dreamed."[110] Harry and his sister, Peggy, traveled to Rye that summer, bringing with them an even more voluminous transcription of William's later letters. Tantalizing as they were—"treasures of vividness, pages & pages so characteristic that the difficulty among them will be as to what to publish & what to leave"—James was obliged to leave them all; his manuscript already was so overstuffed that "large, very large, *chunks*" would have to come out.[111] Even letters from Ralph Waldo Emerson fell under the knife: how else could James include those from Henry Senior to *him*? (Besides, he said, those written by his father were "much the better of the lot!")[112]

Despite all these precautions—and forms of family flattery—Harry recoiled when he learned that *Scribner's* planned to publish portions of his father's letters that were culled from *Notes of a Son and Brother*. His uncle quickly reversed his earlier decision *not* to serialize this material after Charles Scribner strenuously renewed his demand for it. "Why is it," Scribner inquired of James's agent, "that you give us no information concerning the two articles to be made from the selected Letters of Mr. William James?" Having been kept in the dark about James's changing plans for *Notes of a Son and Brother*, Scribner now feared "that the Letters themselves (which were expected to make the bulk of the volume)" would "not appear in it at all." He could not hide his doubt and disappointment from Pinker. "We started with the idea of a volume of William James's Letters," he almost audibly moaned, "and we shall have two volumes on Mr. Henry James's early life."[113] As soon as Pinker communicated Scribner's obvious desire for the William James correspondence to his client, James began to "shake the Letters . . . as free as possible from the (I hope) very interesting comment hanging round them in my Book" and then cobbled them together for separate publication.[114] In the meantime, however, Harry inadvertently was able to see firsthand what his uncle was doing with (or to) William's correspondence. Having decided against using any letters that his brother had written during a scientific expedition to the Amazon (1865–66) with Louis Agassiz, James had returned that batch of typescripts to his nephew, but not before he had marked them up editorially and massively overscored them with his own preferred expressions. Seeing the extent to which his uncle had tampered with the texts of his father's letters, Harry was appalled; he could find no justification whatsoever for such meddling; and he was inclined to prohibit *Scribner's* from publishing these or any revised texts.

With such blatant evidence in front of him—and who knew what he *hadn't* seen?—Harry's response was immediate, angry, and loud. Unfortunately, this scorching rebuke has not survived, but his uncle's pained answer to it—once again filling twenty-eight sides of stationery!—has. James's letter is, as Tamara Follini has wisely pointed out, "less a record, as some critics have seen it, of unquestioned confidence and belief in his method than an anguished epistle of self-justification in which certainty coexists with doubt and defiance consorts with humble self-reproach."[115] On the one hand, James insisted that the claims of artistic license necessarily trumped the drudgery of mere facts; on the other hand, he came very close to admitting that he was ashamed of having indulged that license too freely. James even went so far as to suggest that, unlike the silent séances at 95 Irving Street, as he was writing, William's spirit had hovered at his elbow, imploring him not to "'give me away, to hand me over, in my raggedness & my poor accidents, quite unhelped & unfriended.'" Nevertheless, the writer also had to admit that "strange withal is the 'irony of fate' that has made the very intensity of my tenderness on your Dad's behalf a stumbling-block & an offense—for the sad thing is I think you're right in being offended." To that, Harry could only slash a vivid exclamation point (!) in the margin.

As a last resort, James suggested—in a lengthy postscript—that Harry himself supply the much anticipated William James letters to *Scribner's*. He would withdraw his own submission in favor of whatever Harry might want to publish first. "[T]hese being utterly *textuels* & the exact originals, the thing would be an extremely good & quickening preliminary to the [collected] Correspondence," James urged, "& wouldn't at all 'interfere' with my Volume—on the contrary." What could be easier, Uncle Henry thought? "They would *need* no introduction nor commentary whatever," he rather disingenuously suggested, "& might perfectly be printed in their order of date simply—& so present & explain themselves—with the excellent effect of announcing the further body of Letters." His last appeal—almost brazen—was to modesty. "Your name," he told Harry, "even would scarcely be necessary—if you shouldn't wish to put it forward." Again, resistingly, his nephew noted in the margin, "Of course this is not feasible."[116] Determined to prevent his father's altered texts from circulating in *Scribner's*, Harry confronted Charles Scribner with his objections, and the publisher was obliged to concoct a diplomatic means for James to withdraw the article he had just submitted. Telling the author that, after all, the failure to print something already advertised "would cause us no serious embarrassment," Scribner opened the door for a graceful exit. "The whole possibility of the two articles has miscarried," James gratefully replied. But he also added a further—and telling—rationale. "I found myself in possession of much less of a free hand than I had presumed," he confided, "and this made much difference." With a typical rhetorical about-face, James then recast the whole abortive exercise as the happiest accident of fate. "I am glad to have buried the question," he affirmed, "and not less glad, as well, not to have deflowered a little the contents of my Book by the offer of any imperfectly-served foretaste."[117] His silent violation of others' texts, deflowering their contents, for now remained concealed, sovereignly immune from critical scrutiny.

## *Notes of a Son and Nephew*

Henry James had much to say on the subject of revision. In his Preface to *The Golden Bowl* (volume 23 of the New York Edition), the Master gave a rationale for—and formal imprimatur to—his reappropriation of work already in print and framed a generous license for the massive undertaking he was just then completing. Sifting through his various volumes of fiction, deciding which titles should be retained—and, accordingly, revised—James at first mistakenly confused, he admits, revision with rewriting. But as he began to reread his work, the author found himself empowered to make a vital distinction between the two operations, enabling him to valorize revision as "the act of seeing it again," a process by which a given intention, latent in an earlier form of expression, might "flower before me as into the only terms that honourably expressed it." "What re-writing might be was to remain—it has remained for me to this hour—a mystery," he claimed.[118] It seems safe to say that nephew Harry solved that mystery for his uncle in no uncertain terms. In that now-missing letter of indictment, Harry made it quite clear what rewriting was and accused James of having perpetrated the ignoble act upon the family documents that had been shared so magnanimously with him. (In his letter Harry included a deplorably long tabulation of all the textual peccadilloes his uncle had committed, line by line, chapter and verse.) As we have seen, James's long-winded response to his nephew's charges wavered between haughty condescension (justifying the "exquisite inevitability" of his manipulation of others' texts, his refusal to settle for "any mere merciless transcript") and groveling abjection ("Never again shall I stray from my proper work"). Harry's criticism came too late to have much of an impact on the project at hand—the manuscript of *Notes of a Son and Brother* was already on its way to the printers—but the high-pitched exchange between the two Henrys certainly illustrates how competitive the custodial instincts within the family could become.

When we recall that the "Family Book" was first envisioned primarily as a vehicle for William James's correspondence, how much that conception changed over time is confirmed by the fact that, in the end, Henry James included only sixteen excerpts from letters by his older brother—some 8,700 words out of the almost 140,000 that *Notes of a Son and Brother* comprises. (Then again, not all those 8,700 words even *were* William's, since James freely modified the fraternal texts to suit his own autobiographical needs.)[119] To read James's family memoir in light of the intense squabbling occasioned by its composition can only call renewed attention to these emendations, which were themselves calculated to smooth over past rifts and aggressions within the family ranks and to allow the public to see its members most favorably and advantageously. As James fondled the leaves of William's early letters (the same leaves he would silently alter), he confided to the reader that "these familiar pages of youth testify most of all . . . to the forces of amenity and spontaneity, the happy working of all relations, in our family life."[120] In order for these texts to evoke such domestic bonhomie, however, James first had to revise their language—softening their tone in some places and suppressing whole passages in others.

The most economical way to illuminate the extent and effect of James's emendations is to superimpose the wording of his memoir upon that of a letter he pretends to be quoting. A single example will serve. In this instance, William, who had just come up to Cambridge to study medicine at Harvard, is writing to the rest of the family still at Newport; a brief visit from Henry has just concluded, while Wilky remains with him for some days more; the date is 10 November 1861:

The radiance of ~~Harry's~~ [^]H.'s[^] visit has not faded yet & [^] and[^] I come upon gleams of it 3 [^]three[^] or 4 [^]four[^] times a day in my farings to and fro, but it has never a bit diminished the lustre of far[^]‾[^]off shining Newport[^]'[^] all silver and blue ~~&~~ [^]' and of[^] this heavenly group below

Sketch of the James family, by William James. From *Correspondence of William James.*

{[^]‾[^]all being more or less failures, especially the two outside ones}. The more so as the above[^]‾[^]mentioned ~~Harry~~ [^]H.[^] could in no wise satisfy my ~~cravings to know~~ [^]craving for knowledge[^] of ~~the~~ family and friends ~~as~~ [^]‾[^] he ~~did not~~ [^]didn't[^] seem to have been on speaking terms with ~~any of them~~ [^]anyone[^] for some time past[^]'[^] and could tell me nothing of what they did, said, or thought[^]'[^] about any given subject. Never ~~was~~ [^]did[^] I see a so[^]‾[^] much uninterested creature in the affairs of those about him. He is a good soul[^]'[^] though[^]'[^] in his way[^]'[^] too, ~~much more so~~ [^]'[^] and less fatal[^]'[^] than the light fantastic ₍^₎and ever-sociable₍^₎ Wilky₍^₎ʸ₍^₎ who has ~~been doing nothing~~ ₍^₎ wrought little₍^₎ but disaster ~~since he has been here,~~ ₍^₎during his stay with me;₍^₎ breaking down my good resolutions about ~~eating keeping~~ ₍^₎food, keeping₍^₎ me from ~~any~~ ₍^₎all₍^₎ intellectual exercise, ~~ruining~~ ₍^₎working havoc on₍^₎ my best hat ₍^₎by₍^₎ wearing it while dressing, while in his nightgown, ~~wishing to wash~~ ₍^₎while washing₍^₎ his face ~~with it on, insisting on sleeping in my bed inflicting on me thereby the pains of crucifixion and hardly to be prevented from taking the said hat~~₍^₎, and all but going₍^₎ to bed with ~~him. The odious creature~~₍^₎it.₍^₎ [121]

Here, James clearly has refrained from representing his older brother in all his "raggedness" and instead has corrected his "poor accidents" of grammar and his occasional slips of the pen. One might even concede that such cosmetic changes are merely incidental and perhaps even helpful. Of greater significance (and curiosity) is the revision of William's treatment of Wilky, who, in the original, suffers more damningly from invidious comparison with Henry James himself. Even if one assumes that William's aggressive humor was playful and meant expressly to entertain the letter's recipients, his phrasing stings much more sharply than the milder wording his brother has substituted for it. If, to William, Wilky was an "odious creature" who could only "do nothing but disaster" and was intent on "ruining" his best hat, in the revised text the younger brother is simply "ever-sociable," one who can't help "working havoc" on William's prized millinery. Even more revealingly, if sharing a bed with Wilky condemned William to the "pains of crucifixion," no one reading *Notes of a Son and Brother* (no one, that is, outside the family) was going to know.

No one, that is, until 1920, when Harry chose to include this letter—unemended, and in its entirety—in his own two-volume edition of *The Letters of William James*. Besides this one, Harry chose only two others that his uncle had (mis)printed in *Notes of a Son and Brother*, but he took every step to ensure that readers of his authoritative edition would give priority to his account of the James family over the more imaginative reconstruction of their history that his relative earlier had disseminated. Perhaps now that his uncle had died, Harry was able to criticize his relative's work more openly? With respectful discretion, Harry acknowledged that a "good deal of biographical information about William James, his brother Henry, and their father has already been given to the public," but he felt obliged to observe that, "unfortunately it is scattered, and much of it is cast in a form which calls for interpretation or amendment." Harry then pointed his criticism more directly at his uncle's methods, noting that "he wrote without much attention to particular facts or the sequence of events, and his two volumes were incomplete and occasionally inaccurate with respect to such details." In his own succinct "Introduction" to the *Letters*, Harry meticulously corrected numerous errors of fact in his uncle's autobiographical volumes. Just as forthrightly, Harry explained his editorial criteria and procedure without apology. "Verbal changes have not been made," he averred, "except where it was clear that there had been a slip of the pen, and clear what had been intended. It is obvious that rhetorical laxities are to be expected in letters written as these were. No editor who has attempted to 'improve away' such defects has ever deserved to be thanked."[122] The recently deceased Henry James may not be mentioned by name, but he is certainly the kind of "improving" editor that Harry had in mind as a fitting candidate for scorn. If Uncle Henry had dismissed a commitment to textual accuracy as a kind of "pedantic conformity,"[123] his nephew embraced the principle gladly—and almost, one might say, reflexively.[124]

Such differences, important as they are, concern matters of detail, not disposition; and it should be emphasized that, in his own way, Harry carried forward entrenched Jamesian habits whenever he had to deal with the family annals. He would not have disagreed with his uncle's affirmation that a "man has certainly a right to determine, in so far as he can, what the world shall know of him and what it shall not; the world's natural curiosity to the contrary notwithstanding."[125] For his own edition of his father's letters, Harry compulsively excluded any documents that might have provoked controversy, and, in those that did appear, he pruned out potentially offensive phrases or allusions. Harry also made very discreet use of other family materials—especially Alice's still-secret diary, from which he occasionally drew information or extracted quotations but without revealing the source.[126] In many respects, William James's letters were edited with an even tighter measure of control than that exerted over Percy Lubbock's edition of *The Letters of Henry James*, which appeared in the same year. Soon after, in 1923, when Harry decided to present Harvard with his father's professional library—numerous works of psychology and philosophy that William had carefully annotated—he stipulated that access to those books be granted only to persons who were, "in the opinion of the University authorities, qualified to consider and respect the marginalia" and that, for the next twenty-seven years, none of his father's commentary be published without the joint consent of himself and the chairman of the Philosophy Department.[127] As we shall see, Harry would devise even more rigorous restrictions when he donated the vast archive of James Family manuscripts to Harvard almost two decades later.

Harry and his uncle, then, shared more than a name—though that in itself, psychologically, might have primed them for conflict. As soon as his own eponymous father was in the grave, Henry James discarded the much-despised generational suffix. "Please," he insisted to his publishers, "in any more announcements or advertising, (of things of mine), direct the dropping of the *Jr.*"[128] Much later in life, he urged his nephew Billy not to repeat the family mistake of saddling *his* children with the names of their forebears. Now the family patriarch (after William's death), James felt obliged to admit that it was "happy and delightful that your father's first grandson should be a William again—but I can't but feel sorry that you are embarking afresh on the unfortunate mere *Junior*. I have a right to speak of that appendage—I carried it about for forty years—and both you and Harry ought to know much of it; poor dear Harry in particular, who isn't even a *real* one!"[129] No one had to remind poor dear Harry of *that*: it was hardly an accident that, when he published *The Letters of William James*, the title page of that volume declared that its contents had been "EDITED BY HIS SON / HENRY JAMES." Even though his uncle had been dead for four years, poor dear Harry wasn't going to let that other "Henry James," even posthumously, receive credit for *his* more scrupulous handling of his father's correspondence.

By the time they had their standoff over William's literary remains, uncle and nephew had developed a relationship that was close, but wary. Living on opposite sides of the Atlantic, they had never shared much time together; their occasions for meeting—from Harry's boyhood on—typically were separated by long stretches of time; and even then such encounters were brief. When, at his mother's insistence, Harry made his first independent trip abroad to visit his uncle at Lamb House, the nineteen-year-old (about to enter his senior year at Harvard College) kept a pocket diary to record his impressions. These were not always happy. Several days after his arrival, Harry confided, "I doubt myself how much Uncle H. cares for me. He takes no interest at all in my plans projects or ambitions, and at any rate does not w[ish] to show any curiosity about my taste or peculiarities. And as his only way of condemning seems to be by faint praise, I don't feel much reassured by his commendations."[130] Already intent upon pursuing an advanced degree at Harvard Law School, perhaps it was inevitable that Harry would feel somewhat distant from his uncle? In rather uncanny fashion, he was on his way to becoming the Henry James that his uncle might have been, had he remained in the United States and stuck to the career path he had initially chosen.

Henry James later distinguished his decision to forsake a law career as the "turning point" of his life. Harking back to the winter of 1862–63, "I must there, in the cold shade of queer little old Dane Hall, have stood at the parting of my ways," James recalled, and "recognised the false steps, even though few enough, already taken, and consciously committed myself to my particular divergence." In this unpublished fragment (which dates from 1910, almost a decade after his nephew matriculated at Harvard Law), James denies that any particular dishonor attached itself to his decision: if he was "withdrawing . . . prematurely," it was "under no precipitation" that he could "not now comfortably enough refer to."[131] In *Notes of a Son and Brother*, however, James's memory of this event is blackened by a sense of shame and humiliation, his withdrawal having been precipitated by a disastrous performance in moot court, an event in which his voice "quavered away into mere collapse and cessation"; his exposure, that grim day, was no better than that of "some actor stricken and stammering" upon the stage, an appalling spectacle that could only be suspended by the merciful drop of the curtain.[132] The "particular divergence" that James had chosen, freighted with such ambivalent (if not contradictory) psychological associations, could only have been magnified by his nephew's pronounced success upon the same stage from which he had fled.

These same intense feelings of otherness, of oppositional forms of selfhood—all the result of early vocational choice (or avoidance)—are at the very center of "The Jolly Corner" (1908), a tale James composed shortly before he turned to the "Family Book." The outlines of this story are so familiar that rehearsing them will be unnecessary. To almost everyone who has written about the tale, middle-aged Spencer Brydon, a newly repatriated aesthete, has seemed an obvious stand-in for James, who himself recently had returned to the United States to rediscover his native land and gather the impressions that he would shape into *The American Scene* (1907) and most of the very late short stories collected in *The Finer Grain* (1910). Not long after reentering the New York house in which he was born ("his house on the jolly corner"), Brydon is haunted by the specter of the man he thinks he would have become, had he spent his adult life in America, instead of following the "perverse young course" that took him to Europe, where, for thirty years, he has led "a selfish frivolous scandalous life."[133] These voluntary self-reproaches seem unavoidable to him, now that he is forced to measure himself by the only standard that New York allows—a scale of strictly pecuniary values—especially since his return has provoked the "lively stir" of an unsuspected capacity in him "for business and . . . construction" (699). In the money-hungry air of the city, he is more at home than he ever would have imagined: and therein lies his dilemma.

The owner of two increasingly valuable parcels of Manhattan real estate (his hallowed birthplace and another, less consecrated row house), Brydon is now renovating the latter building, eager to profit from New York's incomparably lucrative version of the unearned increment: air rights. Adding story upon story to what had once been a more modest and humanly scaled structure, Brydon will soon be the owner of a modern up-scale apartment house (not unlike the entrepreneur who, just a few years before, had raised the exclusive "Henry James" on the corner of Amsterdam Avenue and 113th Street). He throws himself into the enterprise with such resolution, and displays such managerial prowess, that even Alice Staverton, his old New York companion, can't help remarking upon these surprising talents.

> She had come with him one day to see how his "apartment-house" was rising; he had helped her over gaps and explained to her plans, and while they were there had happened to have, before her, a brief but lively discussion with the man in charge, the representative of the building firm that had undertaken his work. He had found himself quite "standing up" to this personage over a failure on the latter's part to observe some detail of one of their noted conditions, and had so lucidly argued his case that, besides ever so prettily flushing, at the time, for sympathy in his triumph, she had afterwards said to him (though to a slightly greater effect of irony) that he had clearly for too many years neglected a real gift. If he had but stayed at home he would have anticipated the inventor of the sky-scraper. (700–701)

Lucidly arguing cases was a skill that James conspicuously lacked when he attended law school (the "fierce light" of a moot court had thrown that liability into embarrassing relief), and he had always been content, from the time that his father died, to let surrogates manage the family's rental properties in Syracuse.[134] Harry, on the other hand, actively excelled where his uncle could not. The young man's diligence at Harvard, besides earning him a degree, not only landed him a job with a prestigious Boston law firm (where, in short order, he would be made partner);[135] it had also emboldened him to step in personally to reconfigure the family's real estate portfolio in western New York. Just months before he wrote "The Jolly Corner," having just received a much-larger-than-expected check from America, Uncle Henry felt obliged to express his admiration for his nephew's obvious gifts (and his gratitude for the enhanced pecuniary returns made possible because of them). "Very interesting & valuable to me is your statement of the new Syracuse arrangement," he commended Harry, "—your admirable action over which . . . had already filled me with wonder, admiration & gratitude. It's a brave & masterly act," he gushed, "& I feel as if it had placed my declining years *à l'abri* of destitution—so that you may know the brute of an uncle at least feels that you have done *that* for him. With what wisdom, judgment and firmness you must have proceeded!"[136] Without much effort, the unexpatriated Henry James (Harvard 1899, LL.B. 1904)—namesake, if not alter ego—could have stepped across the threshold and taken up residence in the family house his uncle imaginatively would place on the jolly corner.

For all the autobiographical readings of this story (which cheerfully affirm, at one extreme, Brydon's reconciliation with America, or lament, at the other, his refusal to accept a closeted queer identity),[137] none has yet examined "The Jolly Corner" within the broader, but no less curious, context of Jamesian family dynamics. To locate it there can help us understand the tale's *unheimlich* psychological projection of an alternative (and threatening) namesake as the epitome of the Jamesian uncanny, undeniably central to its particular textual locus but reaching out, as it were, beyond the frame of the story in which it originated to foreshadow the struggle for control that erupted when Henry James attempted to reclaim—to renovate (i.e., revise)—the family's literary patrimony. Like the suddenly remasculated Brydon in the tale, Harry was not afraid of "standing up" to his transgressing uncle (who had not lived up to their mutually agreed "conditions"); and he had his own "Alice"—his mother, Alice Howe Gibbens James—to provide whatever "sympathy" his "triumph" might have elicited. The dizzying dualisms of this story make it difficult unambiguously to ascribe motives when, correspondingly, there are two Henrys also for whom to account. But when we recognize that Brydon's ultimate goal is to rewrite his life—to disrupt its linear history and reconstruct it within a different grammatical dimension, the realm of *what might have been*, the realm of the past conditional—we can see a rhetorical anticipation of Henry James's idealized autobiographical project. "The Jolly Corner" is the "Family Book" writ small—or large, as one chooses.

How strangely these two narratives interpellate goes far beyond the biographical evidence already adduced. Several critics have pointed out that James's most frequently employed rhetorical device in "The Jolly Corner" is the quotation mark itself. Pairs of them—"scare quotes," in common parlance—surround many of Brydon's usages, giving such expressions a double meaning: a fitting narrative technique in a story about alterity and doubleness.[138] How strange, then, that persistent *mis*quotation in *Notes of a Son and Brother* should have opened the severe rift between William's son and brother, those two other Henrys. Harry clearly felt that his uncle's revision of his father's English had made William's words signify in other, unwanted (and unwarranted) senses. Such meddling was a form of trespass—even, perhaps, a form of violence, perpetrated against a helpless victim. As we read "The Jolly Corner," scare quotes gradually begin to become legible as they surround the word *Jolly*: inexorably, we sense that the house on the "jolly" corner is divested of its sentimental associations and will become instead a gothic setting for predation and attack.

Once Alice Staverton's conditional words—"if [you] had but stayed at home"—fix themselves in Brydon's consciousness, he responds to them by imagining that, somewhere within the recesses of the deserted birthplace on the jolly corner, his alter ego, the might-have-been self, lurks. With his newly discovered business acumen working as a catalyst for curiosity, Brydon yearns to track him down, to confront him. "He knew what he meant and what he wanted; it was as clear as the figure on a cheque presented in demand for cash. His *alter ego* 'walked'—that was the note of his image of him, while his image of his motive for his own odd pastime was the desire to waylay him and meet him" (711). Brydon's ghostly embodiment of the alter ego, his prosopopoeic investiture as a felt but shadowy presence, again uncannily anticipates James's defense of his textual misappropriations—his claim that William's abiding spirit had been there in the room with him (speaking, if not "walking"), abetting him in the very act of altering his texts, making them conform to "what he meant and what he wanted." "I found myself again in such close relation with your Father," James pleaded to Harry,

> such a revival of relation as I hadn't known since his death, & which was a passion of tenderness for doing the best thing by him that the material allowed, & which I seemed to feel him in the room & at my elbow asking me for as I worked and as he listened. . . . These were small things, the very smallest, they appeared to me all along to be, tiny amend[me]nts in order of words, degrees of emphasis &c, to the end that he shld. be more easily & engagingly readable & thereby more tasted & liked—from the moment there was no excess of these *soins* & no violence done to his real identity.[139]

What Brydon, of course, fears at the end of the tale is that some kind of terrible, disfiguring violence has been done to *his* "real" identity. Imagining that, when he corners his alter ego, the phantom will present to him the smug visage of the millionaire he might have been, Brydon is hardly prepared for what he finds. When at last, at midnight, he confronts the awful specter and forces him to reveal his face, Brydon recoils in horror, "for the bared identity was too hideous as *his*. . . . The face, *that* face, Spencer Brydon's? . . . Such an identity fitted his at *no* point, made its alternative monstrous" (725). Turning the tables, it was Harry who would express his horror at the disfigurement suffered at his uncle's hand—a breach not merely of text but of trust—that indeed seemed monstrous.

At the very time that James was choosing which much-modified documents he would stitch together with the personal narrative that would become *Notes of a Son and Brother*, his nephew was making a different, but no less significant, choice. Forsaking New England and chucking his career in the law, Harry moved to New York in 1912 to become the high-ranking business manager of the Rockefeller Institute for Medical Research, the first of its kind in the United States. Harry James would never again live in Cambridge. When the news reached him in Sussex, Uncle Henry sounded (just as Spencer Brydon might have) a note of vicarious triumph. "[W]hat a noble & interesting & glorious cause to be associated with," he exclaimed, "—*that* whole range of things, with its inspiring perspectives & possibilities, its chance to *make* new great activities

& conquer new great worlds." Better still was what the return to New York more broadly signified. Abandoning the puritanical byways of Boston for *the* American metropolis was more than a happy twist of fate: the move would restore the Jameses to the native ground on which their earliest namesake had secured his prodigious fortune. The elder Henry James could barely express the "pleasure somehow taken in the fact that we are brought back as a family, in your person & by your reversion, to a 'stake' in our old original New York. I am independently glad, really—as merely for the poetic justice of it." *This* family version of "The Jolly Corner" was going to be *jolly* indeed: no need for scare quotes here. "I seem to myself really now to have taken it in as if I had had a mystic prevision that these things were going somehow to work round to us," James proudly wrote.[140] Indeed, he had had that "mystic prevision"—and given it symbolic form—in his most uncanny short story.

How fitting, then, to know that the last quarrel Harry had to pick with his uncle was precisely over the writer's use of the word *jolly* in the draft version of *Notes of a Son and Brother.* The word itself does not appear even once in the published text of the book, perhaps because Harry had raised such strong objections to it. In some ultimately rejected portion of his manuscript, James seems to have adopted the word to refer to the idiosyncratic patois in which he and William and their close boyhood friends often would converse. Responding to his nephew's criticism, James defended his usage for their "talking in 'jolly.'" "My recollection of the time," he averred, "is that we never talked in anything *else*; we had known in our time abroad nothing *but* jolly—we should have had nothing at all if we hadn't had it; & I remember no moment & no influence for our foreswearing it."[141] In context, it seems clear that James had forced that usage upon William, changing his adjectives into nouns and thereby distorting his brother's meaning. "Uncle H. seems here to be using the word *jolly* in the sense of 'joshing,'" Harry scribbled in the margin of this letter. "That was not Dad's meaning—nor yet the natural interpretation of his altered text."[142] A youthful Henry James may have cornered the market on "jolly," but his watchful nephew would not permit him to enjoy a jolly corner on the rest of the family's literary inheritance.

## 2

### *Remains of the Day*

James invited the family's ire not merely because he had mishandled William's letters: Alice and Harry also feared that Uncle Henry had, in fact, mislaid or inadvertently destroyed them. Trying to meet both his publishers' deadlines and his relatives' expectations, James kept asking for more of William's letters to be sent to him in England, even as the "Family Book" was distending itself out of all proportion as a vehicle for those documents. Since Harry, too, was under new pressure (occasioned by his momentous move to New York), he did not always have the time—or the foresight—to have type-copies made and instead began dispatching packets of the original manuscripts to England. When the family biographer decided against using any of William's so-called Brazilian letters (those he had written from the Amazon basin in 1865–66), what he returned were not the autograph letters themselves but instead his much-made-over transcriptions, which had been dictated to his amanuensis, Theodora Bosanquet, at her faithful Remington. Alarmed by their absence, Harry pressed for the return of the originals, but James had to confess that he wasn't sure where to find them. "I have the superstition of keeping papers overmuch & overlong," he whined to Harry, "& giving them the benefit of every doubt, & no remembrance whatever of anything done with *these*." They might have been taken up to London, he suggested (without much conviction): "dimly I seem to recall a large japanned box of them last winter, but I am vague & things had much slipped from me there."[1] Unless the originals were restored to his possession, how could Harry ever hope to include any of this material in his own edition of his father's correspondence? It would be impossible to reconstruct their contents, especially now that his uncle had so utterly defaced William's texts with revisions and suppressions. What possible excuse could there be for such carelessness? It must have seemed as if the grim prophecy of "The Death of the Lion" (1895) was going to be borne out by the very man who wrote that story (another minor masterpiece detailing the conflict between life and art). As

Neil Paraday's philistine admirers smother the newly discovered author with unwanted social attention, lionizing him and handing him round at his patroness's country house, the priceless manuscript on which he is working slips through their heedless fingers, lost in the promiscuous comings and goings of other weekend guests. His manuscript gone, the author has no more reason to live, and he quickly surrenders to a suddenly recurrent illness. Saddened as he is by the "death of the lion," the narrator of the tale is even more deeply affected by the irretrievable loss of his manuscript. "It's impossible," he muses, "and at any rate intolerable, to suppose it can have been wantonly destroyed. Perhaps some hazard of a blind hand, some brutal ignorance has lighted kitchen-fires with it. Every stupid and hideous accident haunts my meditations."[2] One can only imagine that similar thoughts ran through Harry's mind when he discovered that some of his father's letters had gone missing.

As James himself was nearing death, after suffering in early December 1915 the first of what would be a series of debilitating strokes, his nearest relative braved the submarine-infested waters of the Atlantic to come to his bedside. Alice Howe Gibbens James had promised this five years before, when her husband lay dying, and she was not a woman to go back on her word. At earlier moments of medical crisis—notably the nervous breakdown that crippled James in 1910—nephew Harry had been the principal nursing emissary,[3] and he knew all too well what a strain his mother would face. For almost a year, in fact, the James children had discouraged their mother from going to be with their uncle, whose persistent attacks of angina already had become worrisome, awakening Alice's deeply ingrained sense of duty. "Nobody who has been alone in England with Uncle H. during an illness can understand," Harry had warned earlier that year, "with what suffocating and nerve-exhausting weight he throws himself on one under the circumstances. If Mama were to go over he'd lie down completely, and use every art and artifice to keep her from coming home. Not that he'd urge her frankly to stay—But he'd put it up to her to have pity on him at a rate that would send her home more morbid and worried than she is now."[4] Deferring her departure as long as she did, however, weighed heavily upon Alice's conscience and made her ministrations, once she did arrive in London, that much more obsessive.

Alice's first concern was to restrict the number of visitors who were admitted to see her ailing brother-in-law. As soon as the news of his condition had circu-

lated among the throng of his London acquaintance (efficient little Bosanquet got
the word out fast), anxious friends began streaming to James's flat at 21 Carlyle
Mansions; but Alice actively discouraged them, preferring to keep close vigil herself. As one friend could see, "[H]aving nothing to report but this slow, terrible
decay," the family took "refuge in silence, determined to shut themselves in with
the sad spectacle, & shut the rest of the world out." Knowing that James "would
hate to be seen in his present condition," the one thing Alice could do was "to
interpose a screen & shield between him & the world."[5] Before long, even James's
trusted amanuensis was told to stay away: the clattering of her typewriter (James
had not lost the urge to dictate) was too upsetting to Alice's nerves. Until James's
relative arrived in London, the care of him and his household had largely been
in Bosanquet's hands. (It was during this brief interval, free from family surveil-
lance, that she typed out most of James's rambling Napoleonic utterances—and
kept one copy for herself.) The value of Bosanquet's solicitude was not lost upon
Alice, who immediately described her to Harry as "a wonder of judgment and
capacity."[6] Increasingly, however, she felt the secretary's presence to be an intru-
sion—especially since she seemed always to be sending letters and cables to
Paris, apprising an all-too-nosy Edith Wharton of every up and down in James's
medical condition. Soon, Alice closed the door of James's sickroom to anyone but
his doctor, his devoted servants, and herself.

Anxious both for Uncle Henry and for their mother's well-being, Peggy at
first and then Harry crossed the ocean to attend to James's inevitable down-
lying. Alice understandably was grateful for their presence. Now they could
take turns at James's bedside and relieve one another during the dreary winter
weeks that preceded his death on 28 February 1916. Even as the family circle
closed around the dying writer, his relatives knew that they could not dis-
pense altogether with the services of his amanuensis: her knowledge of his
affairs was too intimate and long-standing. Despite their jealous apprehensions—the secretary, to her chagrin, had glimpsed a letter of Peggy's ("left very
much exposed") in which she read that she had given the family the impression of having behaved too much above her menial station—they summoned
Bosanquet to Carlyle Mansions to discuss the status of James's uncompleted
manuscripts and to inventory his other papers. Arriving there on the last day
of January 1916, Bosanquet immediately was struck by nephew Harry's formidable appearance. "[N]early white-haired, but still black-moustached," she

noted. "He has a tremendous chin—the most obstinate-looking jaw." Still, he was at least civil (unlike Mrs. James) and asked her "to go through his uncle's typescripts—the unfinished novels, etc.—and make lists of them for himself and Pinker."[7] Once again, a death within this family of writers would occasion conflict as to the proper disposition of the decedent's literary remains.

Not to be confused with the money-grubbing heirs of Mrs. Stormer in "Greville Fane" (1892), who have sponged off the proceeds of their mother's fame for years and then publish "every scrap of scribbled paper that could be extracted from her table-drawers,"[8] the James family hardly made a rush to cash in on the variety of manuscript materials that Uncle Henry left behind. Understandably, his literary agent and publishers were more keenly aware of the un-

Henry James III. Harvard University Archives, call #HUP James, Henry III (1).

usual marketing advantage that the death of the author would create (if only for a time)—the solemn publicity attending his last rites, the train of commemorative tributes appearing in major newspapers and journals, all the peculiar ways by which grief can be superseded by curiosity—but neither was the family stupidly indifferent to the circumstances of James's posthumous literary situation. Not long after she arrived in London to nurse her brother-in-law through his final illness, Alice took up the question forthrightly. "I shall do my best to find out his wishes about his literary remains," she told her son Harry. "Ten days hence we can talk," James had murmured to her in the aftermath of the stroke he had suffered, "and I shall have much to tell you."[9] With several projects still in manuscript (two unfinished novels, *The Ivory Tower* and *The Sense of the Past*, and a small portion of a third autobiographical volume, *The Middle Years*), James already had confided his plans for them to his amanuensis and to Pinker: indebted to Charles Scribner for a staggeringly large advance on future royalties made in 1912, the author felt it only proper to cede the rights to his last works to his generous American publisher. Bosanquet quickly informed Alice of her employer's express wishes, but no action was taken then.[10] As James's literary executrix, Alice would superintend the final disposition of these properties; and she preferred to proceed only after consulting with other advisers.

Just two days after the novelist's body was cremated, Alice invited Pinker to come to James's flat in Carlyle Mansions to take stock of the manuscripts she had found there.[11] Before that meeting could take place, Alice also discussed the matter with Edmund Gosse (1849–1928), James's close friend and preeminent Edwardian man of letters, who prudently advised her not to make any rash decisions. Always in correspondence with Harry about legal and professional matters, Alice reported that Gosse insisted "on no account" should she "yield to so uncalled-for a sentiment as the *giving* of all three fragments" to Scribner's.[12] If the family took a more deliberate stance, Gosse was sure that the publisher would relent any claims for the return of the advance and might even be persuaded to pay more for the serial use of the remaining texts in their widely circulated magazine. The ultimate fate of James's manuscripts—and vast corpus of letters—would hinge upon a complex custodial struggle that had been set in motion even before he took his last breath.

What neither Gosse nor Alice James could have known was that the money James had received from Scribner's back in 1912 came not from the publishing firm but rather from his lordly (and conniving) friend Edith Wharton. More-over, this was only one of several stratagems she had devised to help relieve the novelist's perpetual money worries in his declining years—and the only one to succeed. Unbeknown to James, the munificent sum—eight thousand dollars—Scribner advanced for "another novel to balance the *Golden Bowl*" had in fact been funneled through the publisher by Wharton,[13] from whose incom-parably more bloated royalty account it was siphoned. James understandably rubbed his eyes in disbelief when the offer first came—such generous terms from a publisher were unprecedented in his experience—but he never got wise to Wharton's ruse.[14] Market-savvy Pinker probably saw through Scribner's un-precedented generosity, but he happily kept the secret from his client. Not long before this, Wharton had conspired with Gosse, William Dean Howells, and other prominent academicians to secure James the Nobel Prize for Literature in 1911; to their regret, the "mysterious Swedish committee" in Stockholm gave the award to Maurice Maeterlinck instead.[15] Even more disappointing to Whar-ton was the botched plan she initiated to raise a lavish purse from American donors on the occasion of James's seventieth birthday in 1913, an effort bitterly abandoned when James denounced the scheme after having been tipped off about it by his relatives in the United States. Knowing that James's friends in Britain and on the Continent were financing a subscription to honor him with the gift of a golden bowl and a portrait commissioned by John Singer Sar-gent, Wharton felt that his American acquaintance should act in concert and, if anything, respond even more generously. Circulating an appeal for "a sum of money (not less than $5,000)" to a restricted number of James's well-heeled "friends and admirers," Wharton tried to act in secret, but her impetuously devised scheme was disclosed to the author's family in New York and Boston, and one of the nephews wrote to Uncle Henry at once. "I took care to inform him so *gently*," Billy explained to one disappointed contributor, and "had he been ready for one moment to accept of the gathered gift he could have done so." On the contrary, an obviously incensed Henry James cabled back immedi-ately: "Immense thanks for warning. Taking instant prohibitive action. Please express to individuals approached my horror. Money absolutely returned."[16] Already suspicious of Edith Wharton's morals (her 1912 novel *The Reef*, rife with sexual betrayal, had scandalized Alice),[17] the Jameses became even more wary of her motives and her meddling. "Who was it who said that the trouble with women is that they haven't the instincts of a gentleman?" Harry snidely inquired. "Mrs. W. seems to me quite feminine."[18]

Harry's gruff assessment notwithstanding, Wharton's instincts were generous, but controlling. All these various attempts to relieve James's late financial anxieties can be viewed as a pecuniary extension of her wish to assume a kind of managerial responsibility for the author's immediate and, ultimately, for his posthumous, career. As James's health deteriorated, Theodora Bosanquet dutifully kept Wharton posted—at least until the secretary was banished so unceremoniously from Carlyle Mansions. "Whatever Mr. James's relatives may think," Wharton wrote to console her, "all his friends owe you a deep debt of gratitude for the promptness with which you kept them informed of his condition in those first harassing weeks, & for your perfect understanding of what they felt & of all they longed to be told."[19] Bosanquet sent almost daily reports to Paris—not only to honor Wharton's long-standing friendship with James but also to position her more favorably as a candidate to become his literary executor. Both she and Pinker agreed that James "ought to be got to leave his literary baggage in the hands of Mrs. Wharton rather than run any risk of its falling into Harry James'."[20] Only someone wholly sympathetic to James's art, in their view, was to be entrusted with such an important task.

Wharton may not have coveted that role for herself, but she certainly cherished it for Percy Lubbock—surely the most intelligent and capable of all the Master's devoted acolytes—and she quickly started maneuvering to bring about this desired outcome. Given her rather testy relations with the Jameses in the recent past, any assertion of influence on Wharton's part would have to be discreet, if not altogether clandestine. Although Alice may not have been aware of it (and almost certainly would not have approved), Bosanquet was not the only person in close communication with Wharton during the period of James's sad decline. Not only had nephew Harry written to Wharton; he had come in person to see her in Paris (probably to lend some kind of support for her wartime philanthropy). Here was a chance, perhaps, for the "Angel of Devastation," as James facetiously called her, to repair any bad feelings still lingering from the birthday fiasco, and she was not above using words of consolation and flattery to win the nephew's trust. "What you tell me of your uncle's state only adds to the sadness of the situation," she commiserated, "but I am glad that, at least when you wrote, he was having an interval of relative restfulness.

I can only hope the great rest may be less far off than it now appears." Wharton also wanted Harry to know that the manuscript of his uncle's contribution to *The Book of the Homeless*—a charity effort she had organized on behalf of Belgians displaced by the horrors of World War I—had fetched a very high price at auction. A generous bidder had paid five hundred dollars for "The Long Wards" in New York. "I wish he could have known of this great help given to my refugees," she added. A week later, when James at last had died, Harry telegraphed Wharton himself. "I am glad it is over," she responded simply, "as you all must be."[21]

Through the period of James's last illness, none of the Master's disciples showed his loving attention more thoroughly than Percy Lubbock. Almost as soon as she had arrived in London, Alice wrote to Peggy to tell her of Lubbock's admirable behavior. "Percy Lubbock asked to speak with me," she noted. "He has been devoted. Not Hugh Walpole."[22] When the end came, it was Lubbock who wrote the stirring eulogy for the *Times*. Alice dutifully clipped the columns from many papers and sent them to America, where James's recent adoption of British citizenship was still so wrongly comprehended. In his tribute, Lubbock had been careful to emphasize that "through all his long residence in Europe, his relations with America were closer and more constant than may perhaps have been generally understood; and the whole American question, in whatever aspect, was one in which he was always eager to keep himself instructed."[23] Lubbock displayed similarly sympathetic intelligence in a longer essay he wrote soon after for the *Quarterly Review*, the invitation for which came when he happened to be at Carlyle Mansions in the company of the editor's wife, Fanny Prothero, another of James's devoted friends. "Percy Lubbock was here Sunday," Alice told her son Billy, "curiously inarticulate—but so fine. Mrs. Prothero had asked him to write a long article for the National Quarterly in July which he has agreed to do."[24] Once again, James's disciple insisted that the more closely the writer "was held by the claims and interests he found on this side of the Atlantic, the more intensely he became an American." One only had properly to weigh *The American Scene*—and the loving recollection of his early years poured into *A Small Boy and Others* and *Notes of a Son and Brother*—to appreciate the true measure of his national affection.[25] These public testaments, so much valued by the grieving family, helped persuade them of Lubbock's fitness to attend to their relative's posthumous literary affairs.

At the time of the author's death, however, the best choice for that job was far from clear, and all the Jameses instinctively felt that it should be reserved for someone within the family circle. Not long after Alice arrived on the scene, she interrogated Bosanquet as to whether James "had left the arrangement of his letters to Harry." Knowing how much consumed with work he already was, Alice openly fretted that "he was so frightfully busy—he hadn't even time to arrange his Father's letters yet," though William had been dead five years, "so certainly he [couldn't] do his uncle's."[26] James's will would name Alice as his literary executrix, but she understood her role principally as one of delegating particular responsibilities to the those best suited to complete the tasks at hand. With her long experience as James's secretary, Bosanquet was the obvious person to inventory his manuscripts and prepare multiple type-copies of surviving drafts. When they were in presentable shape, surely Pinker would know how best to dispose of them. Dealing with the question of James's correspondence was a much more complicated affair. Everyone knew that some kind of memorial volume was called for and would be expected, but to whom should that work be entrusted?

Wanting to respect a long-established family precedent, Alice turned first to her children, hoping that they would want to retain oversight of the project under the watchful eye of common kinship. While Harry and Peggy understood their almost obligatory role, they also appreciated its magnitude—Harry, especially, who already was impatient to complete the much-deferred edition of his father's letters. Since the family by now was consulting frequently with James B. Pinker about other literary matters, they also turned to him for advice about this most vexing dilemma. As we know, at first Pinker had hoped that Edith Wharton would be involved, but he quickly must have sensed the family's disapproval of that option (Alice and Harry, in particular, were adamantly opposed to it). The agent's next suggestion was George Prothero, of the *Quarterly Review*; if Wharton's were dubious, *his* editorial credentials—and moral respectability—were beyond reproach. Harry quickened to the possibility, acknowledging that "in some respects he would certainly be an admirable solution" to the problem of who should edit the correspondence. "Three or four other suggestions have also been made," Harry added, "and I don't think that we shall try to come to any decision on that point for a while yet."[27] The names of some other British men of letters had also been tossed around—Edmund

Gosse? Desmond MacCarthy?—but for now the family suspended judgment and seemed willing to let the work progress in the hands of Peggy and
Mrs. James (who would always be within earshot, to be sure, of ever-mindful
Harry). In the meantime, the two women began to solicit, collect, and transcribe
documents from many of James's English friends and correspondents.

Not surprisingly, the question of who should edit James's letters was also
much discussed outside the family circle. Suspicious of the Jameses' provincial limitations, close London friends of the writer feared from the outset that
the enterprise would be botched by his relatives' flat-footed underappreciation
of his most distinctive qualities: his devastating sharpness of wit, his extravagant inventions of intimacy, his Rabelaisian powers of innuendo. Gosse and
Wharton were convinced that Percy Lubbock was the ideal candidate, and they
privately conspired to do whatever was necessary to make his sterling qualifications irresistibly apparent to the Jameses. Bosanquet, too, was a quiet partner
in this strategy, for Lubbock had long valued her willingness to share with
him her privileged knowledge of the goings-on within the relatively closed
quarters of Carlyle Mansions. A week before Easter, Lubbock came to Bosanquet's modest rooms to sip tea and share gossip. "He wanted really to discuss
the question of what's to be done about the editing of the private letters," she
confided to her diary, "and joined with me in a regret that Mrs. Wharton hadn't
been left in charge. He feels that it's awfully difficult to offer advice to people
like the Jameses, and yet that they do need some very badly!" The best way
to give them advice was to channel such wisdom through the small handful
of people in London whom Peggy and Alice still seemed to trust—Lucy Clifford, Fanny Prothero, and, somewhat more distantly, Edmund Gosse. Behind
the scenes, then, Bosanquet began making rounds to enlist their discreet advo-
cacy on behalf of Lubbock. Telling Fanny "how iniquitous it would be if Harry
James edited" his uncle's letters "and how fitting it was that Percy Lubbock
should," Bosanquet happily recorded that her interlocutor "entirely agreed,
and so did her husband."[28] She also pressed Lubbock's as yet unarticulated
claim upon Pinker, with whom he was as yet unfamiliar. "I don't know if you
have any idea of what is to be done about Mr. James's letters—who is to edit
them and write about him?" she asked the agent. "I've heard nothing from
Mrs. James herself, but I know the letters are being more or less collected."
Since "Mrs. Wharton isn't in question (as I'm afraid she certainly won't be),"

Bosanquet was sure that Lubbock "would really do the thing as well as anyone could. He has plenty of discriminating taste and nobody could bring a greater measure of sympathy, affection and admiration to the task."[29] At Bosanquet's request, Pinker agreed to meet with Lubbock and talk things over. Slowly, but surely, a formidable alliance was taking shape.

Lubbock himself was eager (even desperate) to be given the work, but he also knew that his desire had to be concealed from the very people for whose consent he yearned. No stranger to the closet, Lubbock was perhaps ideally suited to play the subtle game that lay ahead, because superabundant discretion was the one criterion above all others that the Jameses most prized. Aware that "his name had been suggested to Mrs. James," he also doubted whether "they will be able to gather themselves up to do very much until they hear from Harry, and all depends on his giving them some positive directions — any word of his will be law, of course." Lubbock could hardly have suspected the full history or significance of the family's jealous executorial prerogatives, but already he apprehended their looming presence. Simply in talking to the Master's relatives, "one seems," he confessed to Bosanquet, "to move in such a cloud of fine discretions and hesitations and precautions that it is difficult altogether to know where one is."[30] As the weeks of spring went by, revealing little but dawdling and clumsy incompetence on the family's part, Lubbock's frustration boiled over. "Of course it is perfectly sickening that the Jameses elect to treat as a family matter what is not really much more of a family matter than the plays of Shakespeare," he fumed. Their refusal to let an outsider handle the letters was just another example of what the Master famously had called "the high brutality of good intentions," but Lubbock rightly sensed that if anyone confronted the relatives directly, or put their backs to the wall, it would "be the devil, & useless besides." Still, the family's stupid squeamishness in approaching the job at hand was unforgivable. Having given Peggy and Alice her own precious bundle of letters, Lucy Clifford was disconcerted to learn that they were "a little taken aback at discovering how many began 'My dear dearest Lucy, never have I loved you as I do at this moment'" — or with other, similarly extravagant, salutations. The implication was plain enough: if the collected correspondence was left to the family, such letters as these either would be ignored altogether or bowdlerized according to some ridiculously provincial standard of gentility. Howard Sturgis (who knew the family better than most) feared that, once his niece and sister-in-law discovered the kind of life James really had lived, they would "loyally destroy every scrap of his writing!" (Hadn't James himself foretold such a possibility in "The Author of Beltraffio" [1884] and "The Abasement of the Northmores" [1900]?) "*Imagine* that *literature* should positively be at the *mercy* of a pair of *women!*" Lubbock (somewhat misogynistically) wailed: "It *is* sickening."[31]

While Peggy and Alice dutifully had begun the task of soliciting letters, they clearly were inclined to privilege the Master's American acquaintance at the expense of the infinitely more cosmopolitan reach of his friendships. To many who received their appeal (even more so to those who *didn't*), the very language they ingenuously employed struck an ominous note. "We are collecting Uncle Henry's letters," Peggy wrote,

> because my brother and I hope to make a selection of them later for publica-
> tion. I hope you approve of this, and think as we do, that they will be all that is
> wanted in the way of a Biography and also that it is wise to have the family do
> it, as we have such wealth of material in the shape of letters to the family, that go
> back as far as his first European times.[32]

When Edmund Gosse showed Peggy and Alice a box containing the more than four hundred letters addressed to him, they displayed almost no interest in them (so he told Edith Wharton) but "harped" instead "(as they did when I saw them at Chelsea)" on James's "American history." Gosse inferred that the family were "desirous to ignore his European existence, and it was plain that they thought his English citizenship a blot on his career." To him it seemed painfully clear that "Henry's non-American friends are to be excluded as rigidly as possible from all participation in his posthumous glory"—an unforgivable blunder. To make matters worse, Gosse was convinced that the family's attitude was too desultory, that they were heedless of proceeding in a timely fashion. Alice James had told him that she and Harry "were so fully occupied with the life and correspondence of William James that it would be several years before they were likely to do anything with the letters of Henry."[33] By maintaining such tight control over James's literary remains, James's relatives would smother his posthumous reputation with delay and distort his true artistic legacy. This Gosse and Wharton were determined to prevent.

From war-torn France, the Angel of Devastation continued her private campaign on Lubbock's behalf, exchanging letters with the extraordinary inner circle of (mostly homosexual) confidantes who had become a kind of exclusive entourage, snared by the force of her personality and, to a certain extent, by the lavishness of her generosity. James, of course, had been the other vital figure holding this group together. But its existence also owed much to Arthur Christopher Benson, the Eton headmaster (and son of the Archbishop of Canterbury) who first introduced Lubbock to James, who renewed Howard Sturgis's acquaintance with him, and then, somewhat later (having been named reader in English literature at Magdalene College, Cambridge), who brought Gaillard Lapsley (like Sturgis, an Anglicized American) into relation with all the others.[34] From each of them Wharton sought close advice: how best might she persuade the Jameses to abandon their misguided plan and allow Lubbock instead to take charge? Her first impulse was to refuse to cooperate with them—declining to send them her letters—and to see that all the others in her circle do likewise. "*Of course* I will back you up!" Lapsley shouted back. "It's only a question of *how*." He was at a disadvantage (the family hadn't even bothered to ask him for his letters); and even though he knew Harry from their time together as

Percy Lubbock, Howard Sturgis, and Arthur Christopher Benson, at Magdalene College, Cambridge (1906). From David Newsome, *On the Edge of Paradise: A. C. Benson, the Diarist* (Chicago: University of Chicago Press, 1980).

undergraduates at Harvard, he doubted that the starchy nephew would yield to outside pressure. "Can't you see the dear, grim, Boston scruple at work?" Lapsley mused: "Jealously screening the 'family' & their privacies just as dear Henry screened his father's wooden leg." Dropping into the macaronic French to which the group often resorted when they wanted to cloak their sharpest insults, Lapsley could only think that dull-witted Irving Street, so ill equipped to do the job successfully, would make a *gâchis* (i.e., a mess) of the material.[35]

Once she had drafted a guarded response to Peggy, Wharton circulated it confidentially to see what suggestions her coadjutors might have. Howard Sturgis best appreciated the delicacy of the affair, recognizing immediately that "the matter is one requiring immense caution & diplomacy." "Any appearance of *dictating* to the family would at once stiffen their determination," he perceived, wryly adding that long-under-siege Verdun would prove "pregnable compared to the J. family." Sturgis's fears were well placed. He was sure that if the family "got hold of an idea that you & I, Gosse, Lapsley, Fullerton etc. were in a *conspiracy* to foist our candidate upon them, it would be fatal." "Of course it is very unfortunate," he added, "that such wealth of literary richness should be left entirely in the hands of *un*literary people. . . . They look on the matter entirely from the point of view of the necessity for suppressing the 'undesirable,' & presenting to the world a portrait of what they would like a highly respectable member of a highly respectable family to appear."[36] Undiscouraged, Wharton tinkered with her wording and stepped down a bit from her pedestal of condescension, but she still made a very strong case for Lubbock's candidacy: not only—as she finally wrote Peggy—because of his "extraordinary literary sense and his experience in biographical work, but because he had an almost magical insight into your uncle's point of view."[37] Although this message was addressed to Peggy (with whom she was still on reasonably good terms), Wharton knew that the family would do nothing without consulting "the great & grim brother"—and that was "the real stumbling block." Harry, she feared, simply loathed her ("I don't know why, but I fancy simply for the cosmopolitan & bejewelled immorality of which he regards me as a brilliant & baleful example"), and for her hand to be visible in any scheme of persuasion might well condemn their hopes altogether.[38]

Peggy, at least, was politely grateful for Wharton's interest. "Everyone has approached us in the same way about Mr Lubbock's doing the letters," she replied, "and we are ourselves impressed by his apparent understanding of and sympathy with, my uncle so that now what you say of him on every score, may tip the balance, and make my brother, as it would me, decide on the entrusting of the large and delightful work, to him. I hope it will."[39] Despite Wharton's apprehensions (obviously profound), Harry finally did accept the logic and fitness of her suggestion—perhaps because her candidate had also been pressed upon him by Gosse. Before the end of July, he made a formal offer to Lubbock, who could scarcely imagine what kind of high-pressure diplomacy had been enacted behind the scenes on his behalf. "I have had a really *nice letter* from Harry James," he bubbled over to Lapsley,

> —making me the Great Offer. I dimly see, & easily imagine, with Mrs Clifford telephoning to me finger on lip & writing to me with her handkerchief stuffed into her mouth—with Gosse summoning me to high fateful interviews—what webs of history have been spun during the last weeks—a maze of scruple & debate & desperate resolves, such as the mere newspaper-reading public have had no suspicion of. But the upshot is that I am plainly asked to do the thing, & am to dine at Carlyle Mansions tomorrow to discuss the detail of it. For the moment the cream of the whole thing is this—which I just can't keep to myself, though I suppose I must keep it from all but you—Gosse has been asked (by Carlyle Mansions) to *watch* the proceedings so as to shield me from a certain influence. He told me this, pleasantly twinkling, and if you will believe me I simply gaped & asked *what* influence! I did really—& he had to tell me, still twinkling—the influence of the rue de Varenne! The last fine flower of farce—who could have *invented* such a touch? I can't help it—at present it is *this* that infuses the scene—& can you wonder? But the gratitude, underneath, for such an opportunity, is deep & wide, naturally.[40]

No wonder Gosse would "twinkle," enjoined by the family to keep a watchful eye on Lubbock and to prevent Wharton's meddling fingers from interfering with the editor's work! How little did they suspect that it was Wharton who had approached him in the first place about landing the job for Lubbock! This was a situation almost worthy of the Master himself, just the kind of donnée upon which he might have dilated in the pages of his notebooks. On the other side of the channel, Wharton was ecstatic. Writing to her co-conspirator Gosse, she could not resist a festive metaphor: "I have had to restrain for a long time my effervescent joy at your good news," she bubbled, "but luckily it is a vintage that keeps!"[41]

The question of editorship settled in Lubbock's favor, there were still many other details that had to be ironed out. What would be the best method for the letters to be collected and transcribed? How should Lubbock be compensated? What sort of deadline should be imposed for completion of the work? Still reveling in the delicious irony of the situation, Lubbock confided to Lapsley that "the Jameses have been ALL kindness. . . . They give me the freest possible hand, & the most generous help. Peggy will go through the family letters, & undertakes to collect (not *select*) the various series of letters to friends in America. The 'arrangements' (which is our delicate & only term of allusion to the indecent subject of my remuneration) are placed in the hands of Pinker— much the best plan."[42] In close consultation with Pinker, Harry hammered out the terms of Lubbock's contract, offering him a flat fee of six hundred pounds for all editorial work, together with a travel allowance to subsidize a trip to America that they assumed he would make at some point along the way. One hundred pounds was to be paid up front, the balance upon completion of the work, everyone agreeing that the editor would finish the job by 1918.[43] Lubbock's time-consuming work with the Red Cross through the duration of World War I impeded such timely progress, but as soon as the Armistice was signed, he was able to reorder his priorities. Days after the cessation of hostilities, Lubbock gleefully wrote, "The wild thought of a return to literature, early in next year, is almost too much for me altogether—I move in dreams—I seem to wake to peace & victory every morning for the first time—most incredible of all is that it is not yet a week old."[44] The Allied victory—for which the dying Master so desperately yearned—liberated Lubbock to honor James's steadfast commitment to a "decent and dauntless people" by continuing his editorial labors.[45] When that task at last was done, *The Letters of Henry James*, in two volumes, appeared in April 1920.

## From Keyboard to Ouija Board

Getting to that point involved many tactical difficulties, not least of which were assembling and accurately transcribing the letters themselves. As Lubbock told Wharton, Peggy had agreed "to harvest the family letters, and certain other notable batches" of correspondence in America, prepare typescript copies of them, and then send her work to England.[46] Meanwhile, Lubbock would issue his own appeal for documents, which would then also need to be type-copied by a reliable hand. Though James's amanuensis might have seemed the logical person to do this clerical work—certainly *she* thought as much—the Jameses were not eager to extend Theodora Bosanquet's involvement with family affairs, and Lubbock eventually agreed that it would "be better to get someone else."[47] Harry concurred that the family was under "no obligation to engage Miss Bosanquet for this"; indeed, he suggested, it might be "easier and pleasanter to get some one more skillful who would not be tempted to assume an intimacy with matters with which she really has only a limited acquaintance."[48] Until other arrangements could be made, Bosanquet continued to work on documents as they came in; but it seems likely that her service was terminated before very long. When Pinker volunteered space and clerical support for the project at his place of business in Arundel Street, Harry expressed his satisfaction and confirmed that Lubbock would "be very glad to avail himself of your offer of a room in your office for a typist to do copying in, and I shall be very glad if that arrangement goes into effect."[49] Lubbock certainly knew that "little B." was going to be disappointed (Wharton had told him that such a decision would "kill" the devoted helper), and he had to find a way of letting her down gently.[50]

Lubbock's task was made even more disagreeable because earlier he had relied so much on Bosanquet's confidences and treated her almost as an equal partner in the heroic mission to rescue the recently deceased Master from his misguided and ill-informed relatives. Besides, it had been Bosanquet who first brought him to Pinker's attention: surely a pivotal step in the successful prosecution of the plan to secure him the editorship. Lubbock's attentions certainly flattered Bosanquet's sense of her own social and literary prospects, and she seems not to have suspected that the suave Etonian might be patronizingly disposed. When he invited her to dine with him at the Hyde Park Hotel grill room, Bosanquet was almost giddy. "Met P. Lubbock at . . . 8.15 and we had an excellent dinner, with champagne!" she scribbled. In the shaded candlelight they discussed plans for the editing of James's letters. "Mrs. James, apparently, definitely said to him that it would be better to have the letters copied by a stranger than by me!" she noted, incredulously. This irritating revelation—together with the champagne—encouraged a resentful tongue. Afterward she feared that she had been "very indiscreet and let myself go far too much," a thought that kept her up all night.[51] Taking account of the Jameses' obvious dissatisfaction with their uncle's former secretary, Lubbock eventually felt obliged to distance himself from her. Already he had wondered whether "little B." would "be equal to very much of a day's work" (Bosanquet's stenography had always been something of a fallback, for she also cherished the hope of pursuing an independent literary career);[52] now, with the family squarely opposed to her continued involvement, Lubbock had to sunder their connection. In early November 1916, the two met again, Bosanquet noting that they "spent the evening going through the letters I've been copying, and making out obscure words etc." Lubbock "was very charming—just as much so as always," but Bosanquet, rather dejectedly, left his quarters "feeling rather dismally conscious that after all there *won't* be much work on these letters for me to do." Somewhat disingenuously, Lubbock suggested that his wartime work was too distracting and that there was no longer a need to retain her service. Little B. understood, but she had to confess—at least to her diary—that it was "rather disappointing after the high hopes he held out earlier."[53]

Despite her diminutive stature, feisty Little B. was not about, in the face of this setback, to relinquish her own claims as a guardian of the Master's posthumous reputation. She had been too much near the center of things not to cherish such hopes. If the family had treated her indifferently, no less a person than Edith Wharton had written to console her after James's death. "You will be feeling a great void now," she tenderly affirmed, "but you will have happy & dear memories of the long years of your collaboration with one of the wisest & noblest men that ever lived. We who knew him well know how great he would have been if he had never written a line."[54] Bosanquet's greatest credential was just that intimacy of understanding. Not much satisfied with Lubbock's *Quarterly Review* essay (which she thought "very sympathetic and understanding but a little indefinite and disconnected"),[55] already she had been trying "to lick an article on H.J. into shape," and she was not afraid to solicit advice about it from Lubbock himself and others among James's almost exclusively male cadre of disciples.[56] Howard Sturgis offered her some useful suggestions—he dissented from her first physical description of James ("he was short, square, fat if you will," Sturgis admitted, "but there was nothing unwieldy or ungainly about him")[57]—and she quickly emended her manuscript and sent it to Pinker, who for some years had been acting as her literary agent, too. Pinker had no problem landing the piece with an American magazine (the *Bookman*), but Bosanquet could only express regret that there seemed to be "no room in an English periodical of good reputation for a first-hand study of the method of a great artist."[58] It was not long, however, before Pinker surmounted this obstacle; Bosanquet's article first appeared in the June 1917 number of the prestigious *Fortnightly Review* and was quickly reprinted in the American *Bookman* and the British literary digest *Living Age*.

Bosanquet's tribute was both modestly autobiographical and immodestly hagiographic. After recounting her first impressions of the Master and their characteristic mode of dictation-to-the-typewriter, she then addressed the more seriously literary question of the scale of revision that James insisted upon for the New York Edition. Acknowledging that many readers had objected to the Master's later style, Bosanquet offered a heroic defense of his unappreciated labor. "His struggle was always to stretch his power of expression to the compass of the things he saw and felt," she affirmed; "and it seemed to him, when he re-read his forgotten stories, that he had missed in writing them countless precious opportunities for rendering vision and feeling which the process of revision allowed him at last to retrieve." Fortunately for his art (she fervently, if mistakenly, believed), James never had to compromise his aesthetic ideals and could hold himself aloof from the petty necessity of chasing a philistine public. "The whole course of his life showed him to be without the least taint of the sordid passion," she claimed, and this "economic independence of his work enabled him to fashion it in the mould he desired, irrespective of the demands of the market."[59] She would develop and expand upon these fundamental convictions in all of her subsequent writing on James.

"Isn't little Bosanquet an amazement?" That was Edith Wharton's surprised reaction when she read the July *Fortnightly*. "Her article wrung my heart," Wharton confessed; "it brought *him* back so intensely."[60] Bosanquet's skill as a writer and critic was not lost on others. For her next public utterance about the Master, Bosanquet would appear among the distinguished company—most notably T. S. Eliot and Ezra Pound—whose opinions were promulgated in the August 1918 "Henry James" number of the *Little Review*. Once again her subject was "The Revised Version," and once again she cogently assembled a series of texts for comparison, always at pains to demonstrate that the "loose vague phrases" of James's early compositions inexorably were transformed in the New York Edition to reveal "close-locked intensities of meaning." Here, too, Bosanquet commemorates the lonely heroism of James's supposed indifference to marketplace pressures—an aesthetic credo that by now had reached biblical proportions. "Not to revise," she urged, "would have been to confess to a loss of faith in himself and it was unlikely that the writer who fasted for forty years in the wilderness of British and American misconceptions without yielding any scrap of intellectual honesty to editorial or publishing tempters should have lost faith in himself."[61] Bosanquet's indirect identification with the Master

"Little B."—Theodora Bosanquet, secretary to the Master from 1907 until the time of his death and vigilant guardian of his literary remains and posthumous reputation. By permission of the Houghton Library, Harvard University (MS Eng 1213.8 b. 1).

increased in direct proportion to the extent that she was being marginalized by those who laid straighter claim to James.

Having spent many days and hours assembling James's stray unfinished manuscripts, Bosanquet was particularly concerned with the ultimate fate of those compositions. What she witnessed (and overheard) at Carlyle Mansions was not especially encouraging, since the Jameses seemed curiously indifferent to the literary value of those splendid fragments. As she was working on them, Bosanquet confided to Pinker, "I have reason to believe that it is entirely owing to your suggestion that copies are being made at all, which is a fact no one who cares for the preservation of his writings can be too grateful to you for." Whereas Bosanquet felt that *The Middle Years* "would have been the most wonderful book of Victorian portraits ever published," Alice James told Pinker that, in her opinion, it wasn't even worth publishing! (After seeing it in print, Harry was inclined to agree.)[62] Hoping to snag a publisher's interest before curiosity about the Master might wane, Pinker sent Bosanquet's typescripts of the three unfinished works (*The Middle Years*, *The Ivory Tower*, and *The Sense of the Past*) to Scribner's, further suggesting that, together with James's detached notes on these projects, an introduction by his former secretary might be of especial interest. "Mr. James," he nudged, "never took the public into his confidence in the popular sense and revealed his methods, and it is only the few who came into intimate contact with him during the progress of his work who are aware of them."[63] Since he was also trying to place the article that Bosanquet had written about the Master, this suggestion must have seemed both right and logical. Contracts for these volumes were not drawn up until the following spring, however; and when the family got wind of the details, their displeasure was immediate. Alice told Pinker that publishing these titles with "notes by Miss Bosanquet, perhaps touching upon Mr. James' methods of work would be a mistake." "Why should Scribners suggest so clumsy an expedient?" she wondered. "It would have been most unwelcome to H.J.," she magisterially asserted, instead insisting that any editorial work be done by Percy Lubbock. In her view, he would "not over-load the book with elaborate or needless comment."[64] Once again, poor Little B. was sidelined by others jealous to control James's posthumous legacy.

These disappointments did not deter Bosanquet from composing an even ampler testament of devotion, her invaluable essay, *Henry James at Work*, first published by Leonard and Virginia Woolf's Hogarth Press in 1924. In this piece she gathered together the principal insights of her previous publications (including some from her very generous assessment of Lubbock's edition of James's letters) to produce a condensed but vivid and appealing monument to the Master. It is not surprising that she should have chosen to conclude the work with a (slightly revised) passage from her 1920 essay on *The Letters of Henry James*: no one then or since has framed a more eloquent defense of James's deliberately indeterminate nationality, a cosmopolitanism that he always subordinated to the higher claims of moral earnestness. "The cardinal fact," Bosanquet stipulated,

> is that everywhere he looked Henry James saw fineness apparently sacrificed to grossness, beauty to avarice, truth to a bold front. He realized how constantly the tenderness of growing life is at the mercy of personal tyranny and he hated the tyranny of persons over each other. His novels are a repeated exposure of this wickedness, a reiterated and passionate plea for the fullest freedom of development, unimperilled by reckless and barbarous stupidity.[65]

It was only fitting that, having commended the work of James's other most industrious disciple, Bosanquet should have received some kind words in return from Percy Lubbock, who affirmed in print that "the blessing of Henry James" was "surely upon her pages." "Fortunate that Henry James employed a secretary," Lubbock declared, "and fortunate that Miss Bosanquet observed and understood so shrewdly. Her account of what she saw is a contribution of value to the criticism of Henry James's art."[66] To Bosanquet herself, Lubbock added a more personal touch, telling her that he had "seen & read & admired" her "deeply interesting pamphlet": "it *is* good—through & through," he underscored, "so clear & so quick & so right, so sharp to the eye."[67]

Beyond her intimate acquaintance with James's working life, Bosanquet also possessed uniquely privileged knowledge about his subconscious fantasies. Having been present to take down his inspired (but weirdly delusional) Napoleonic dictations, James's amanuensis retained her own copy of those strange documents after disclosing their existence, first to Lubbock and Wharton, and then to Alice James, who arrived at Carlyle Mansions a few days after they were typed out.[68] (She confided to Wharton that "the fragments he dictates do, in the queerest way, hang together—they seem to form part of a book he is writing in his mind about Bonaparte. He leaves huge gaps undictated, but everything somehow fits into the scheme.")[69] Though the family and Lubbock must have pledged to keep these papers secret, rumors about them began to surface, enticing one of James's earliest biographers, Pelham Edgar (1871–1948), to inquire further. In 1925, Ferris Greenslet, an acquisitions editor at Houghton Mifflin Company in Boston, wrote to Harry, informing him that a book proposal had arrived that alluded to "an unpublished fragment by your uncle, Henry James, entitled 'The Autobiograph[ic] Relation of Episodes in the Great Napoleon's Life,' said to be of extraordinary interest, both in relation to Henry James and to Napoleon." Enticed by the prospect of a previously unknown James manuscript, Greenslet hoped that Houghton Mifflin might issue the piece in an expensive limited edition. "If the thing is as interesting as it is said to be," he pregnantly added, "it certainly ought not to be permanently withheld from publication." Harry, not surprisingly, scoffed at that notion and denied, furthermore, that such a document was "among the papers which were in my Uncle's own possession at his death." Tipping his hand more freely, Greenslet then told Harry that "a Miss Bosanquet was said to know all about the manuscript in question"—perhaps that detail would "help you to find out more about it?"[70] Harry immediately wrote to Eric Pinker (who had succeeded his father as the James estate's literary agent), asking him to verify these reports. When Bosanquet confirmed the existence of the dictation (and sent along a copy of it), Harry enjoined the agent to maintain continued silence about it. In his opinion, the fragments conveyed "so slight an indication of whatever may have been my Uncle's intention, that I fully agree with what I infer were my Mother's and Mr. Lubbock's opinions— that there's no use saying or doing anything about it."[71] Nevertheless, in his 1927 biography, Edgar disclosed that Bosanquet had allowed him to read her copy of the dictation, and he declared that "the fragment is of unique interest, revealing as it does the strange and powerful workings of his dormant brain." If published, Edgar added, it would "rank among the curiosities of literature."[72] The full text of the dictation would not be published for another forty years, but listeners of the BBC could have heard Theodora Bosanquet read portions of it over the airwaves on the evening of 14 June 1956, when she participated in a group interview of the select few still living who had known Henry James. With such documents still in her possession, the former secretary's credentials as a uniquely privileged Jamesian confidante were impeccable.[73]

Bosanquet's abiding interest in the Master's legacy would continue. In 1932 she told a Jamesian neophyte named Leon Edel that she was assembling an omnibus volume of the author's short stories and preparing an introduction for the volume based mainly on the Prefaces to the New York Edition "and partly, for some of the later, post-preface ones," on her "own memories of their respective origins."[74] That book never materialized, but even later, after the horrors of the Second World War were behind the British nation, Bosanquet planned to recover her copyright in the now-long-out-of-print Hogarth Press pamphlet and to supplement it with a longer memoir and critical study of James's oeuvre. In 1948, the newly important publisher Rupert Hart-Davis pressed her about this. With something of a James Revival already under way (Hart-Davis was one of the first to sense the commercial potential latent in it), the publisher hoped to capitalize on Bosanquet's unique relation to the Master. "What has happened to *the* book on James for which we are all waiting," he asked: "—I mean, of course, *your* book?"[75] Perhaps because she knew by then that Edel was expecting soon to undertake a full-fledged biography of James, she never followed through on her own intentions. It was she, in fact, who had brought Edel to Hart-Davis's attention, affording the still-unknown Jamesian an enviable foothold in one of the more exclusive echelons of British publishing.[76]

Even though Bosanquet never realized her larger Jamesian ambitions, that omission is almost overshadowed by her apparent belief that she herself was the living medium through whom the deceased Master might yet speak (or write). Her peculiar convictions about parapsychology and the power of automatic writing led Bosanquet to continue (so she believed) as James's amanuensis even after his death. Having access to the Bosanquet files in the papers of the Society for Psychical Research, Pamela Thurschwell has provided transcriptions of these odd communications, through which the former secretary found a way to re-create—and significantly intensify—the intimacy of her relationship with Henry James, rehabilitating the privileged status that his relatives (and even Lubbock) had begrudged and progressively stripped from her. Ostensibly reunited with the Master's consciousness, Bosanquet heard James's voice expressing "a desire to return to relations that existed in a distant past between me and the lady who kindly acted as my secretary." This phantasmagoric James wanted only to encourage Little B.: "In the past she acted to a great extent as a mouthpiece for me, recorder perhaps might define the relationship still better now, although we have not entered into what might be described as fluent cooperation her efforts suggest the past relationship. A lending of the mind to follow mine, or should I say a willing perception of my work and intention."[77] Bosanquet's remarkable indulgence of such transgressive fantasy led her to imagine the Master's posthumous reaction to her close-knit little study of his working life. "Henry James is here now," she transcribed,

> just to wave you his friendly blessing. Yes, he knew you would recognize the words that he used to use so often in his letters to his friends but he means it with a very different kind of love and greeting now for he loves you now and he did not in the least then, for he thought that you were a very uninteresting young woman who had a marvellous gift for transcribing his words correctly, but he . . . finds now that all the time you were observing his style and taking mental notes and that afterwards you wrote a little book about him which he has never had the courage to look at, but he thinks he will have to now if you don't mind.

Hoping that this disembodied spirit was aware that Edith Wharton had "liked" *Henry James at Work*, Bosanquet's James then affirms,

> Yes he knows that and he thin[k]s that in that case it must have been a good little book but he must read it for himself and he asks you to leave a copy unopened on the table by the window tonight when the sitting is going on for he will be in the room most of the time and he can read through the covers of any book in the world quite easily but he can't make out what is locked away in a cupboard as this book is.

Bosanquet's uncanny identification with the Master resonates on many levels, articulating, as Thurschwell notes, "an erotics of exchange, not simply of money, information or sex, but rather of recognition."[78] Snubbed by James's family but still devoted to his memory, Bosanquet cultivated a fealty so intense that only the transports of an unseen world could reciprocate her undying esteem.

Bosanquet's peculiar experimentation with the uncanny might also remind us (yet again) of "The Real Right Thing," the tale in which the ghostly presence of a deceased author seems first to encourage—but then to frustrate—biographical investigation of his life and work. To recruit the services of the young

writer Withermore, Ashton Doyne's widow flatters both his talent and his privileged intimacy with her deceased husband. "'You're the one he liked most,'"
she tells him: "'oh, *much*!'—and it had been quite enough to turn Withermore's
head." Agreeing to write the author's life, Withermore is given access to "diaries, letters, memoranda, notes, documents of many sorts," and he soon begins
to feel, as he bends over his papers, that "the light breath of his dead host was
as distinctly in his hair as his own elbows were on the table before him." Increasingly, however, Withermore entertains doubts about the rightness of his
work: "'We lay him bare,'" he tells Mrs. Doyne; "'We serve him up. What is it
called? We give him to the world.'" When the widow rejoins, simply, "'And
why shouldn't we?'" Withermore summons his strength to answer:

> "Because we don't know. There are natures, there are lives, that shrink. He
> mayn't wish it," said Withermore. "We never asked him."
> "How *could* we?"
> He was silent a little. "Well, we ask him now. That's, after all, what our start
> has, so far, represented. We've put it to him."
> "Then—if he has been with us—we've had his answer."
> Withermore spoke now as if he knew what to believe. "He hasn't been
> 'with' us—he has been against us."

Withermore now recognizes that the artist's ghost just wants "to be let alone,"
and he abandons his assignment.[79] Bosanquet's fitful and fantastic intimacy with
James's spirit betrayed similar self-questioning. Even as she was summoning the
Master's otherworldly approval for her well-intentioned pamphlet, Bosanquet
couldn't help recording, "Here my mind flashed to what M.R. told me about
Elizabeth Robins having said it was a book that would make H.J. turn in his
grave."[80] One can only wonder if such second thoughts discouraged her (like
Withermore before her) from continuing her critical work on James.

Not long before these ghostly encounters with the Master, Bosanquet had
received a different kind of communication from a much more worldly source.
It came from Paris in the form of a letter from someone very much like young
Withermore—a biographer/critic beginning his pursuit of a very elusive author: Henry James. Bosanquet was one of the first people Leon Edel contacted
when he began to assemble the chronicle of James's "dramatic years," the proj-

ect that would become the larger half of the doctoral thesis he submitted in 1931 to complete his program of study at the Sorbonne. It was she who led him to Bernard Shaw and Harley Granville-Barker and all the other Londoners whom he would interview (and whose letters he would copy); without her generous interest in his career, Edel would neither have been able to compose *Henry James, les années dramatiques* nor to become the Master's authorized biographer. As their friendship matured, and her confidence in his ability deepened, Bosanquet made typescripts of her diaries, which she presented to him—a remarkable gift for any biographer—and assisted him in various other ways. Along with Edith Wharton, she endorsed Edel's (successful) application for a Guggenheim Fellowship in 1937, enabling him to work for the first time with the archive of James Family Papers that Harry had deposited in the basement of Widener Library at Harvard. There he found the "Napoleonic fragment," the existence of which Bosanquet earlier had confirmed for him. That, too, was a special confidence. "People bother me from time to time to know about the 'Napoleonic fragment' so unfortunately emphasized in Pelham Edgar's atrocious book," she complained to him. "The last was a jaunty young New York journalist intent on disinterring any corpse."[81] Edel himself was (as yet) such a journalist, but for him, at least, Bosanquet would make exceptions.[82]

As Edel began to make more serious inroads on Jamesian territory, Bosanquet generously deferred to his claims and even seems to have taken an almost maternal interest in the biographical enterprise he had staked out for himself. When the first volume of his life of James appeared in 1953, Bosanquet was ready to hymn its praises in *Time and Tide*. In keeping with the family's view, Percy Lubbock had insisted in 1920 that the two volumes of James's letters then published, together with the autobiographical volumes already in print, would properly serve any and all interest in the Master's life. "Dr. Edel," Bosanquet rejoined, "politely and firmly disagrees." Anyone hoping to surmount the obstacles in writing such a life would require "a sympathetic imagination, linked with an inexhaustible appetite for every scrap of relevant material and a sound critical judgment."[83] In her view, Edel possessed them all. Entitling her review "The Son and the Brother," Bosanquet knowingly closed the circle that surrounded her own earliest memories of the Master (who had dictated *Notes of a Son and Brother* to her) and effectively ceded the defense of his honor to a successor she deemed worthy.

## The Queer Case of Percy Lubbock

The other champion in the arena, Percy Lubbock, by then had pretty much hung up his shield. But in the first decade after James's death, no other figure worked more tirelessly to consolidate the Master's cultural capital. Having at last gained the family's blessing, Lubbock edited James's unfinished manuscripts for the press; he compiled the two-volume edition of James's letters that would serve for more than fifty years as the principal source of the author's published correspondence; and he oversaw the publication of Macmillan's thirty-five-volume edition of *The Novels and Stories of Henry James* (1921–23), which brought back into print almost all of James's fiction. Lubbock also enshrined the Master in *The Craft of Fiction* (1921), his own high modernist critical treatise, which redacted—and made elegantly persuasive—the compositional principles James had (more discursively) articulated in the Prefaces to the New York Edition. This gospel of Anglo-American formalism was enthusiastically received when it first appeared and would enjoy numerous reprintings for decades to come. Whatever vicissitudes James's posthumous reputation had witnessed, Lubbock confidently could assert (in a preface he added to the 1954 reissue of his book) that there was "no need in these days to point to the only begetter of all our studies in this manner of approach to the novelist at work. . . . [T]here he stands, foursquare to all our theories of the novelist's art; and they may blow where they list, but it is still with the burly figure of Henry James that they have first to reckon."[84] The Master's steadfast monopoly of the field owed much, indeed, to Percy Lubbock.

In order to accomplish all this, Lubbock first had to consolidate his own status as James's most fervent and favored disciple, the surrogate in whom his watchful relatives could place their abiding trust. With considerable help from Edith Wharton and the others of her so-called inner circle, Lubbock eventually won the confidence of the ever-suspicious Jameses, who otherwise might have remained unaware of his peculiar qualifications. Habitually shy and self-effacing, Lubbock never would have been one to broadcast his own credentials. The Jameses would have had little reason to know, for example, that for years he had been writing intelligent and adulatory notices of their uncle's work or that he had already demonstrated his professional competence as a literary biographer.[85] It would have been up to his many confidential allies (Gosse, Sturgis, Pinker, the Protheros, Jessie Allen, Lucy Clifford, not least Little B.) to

parade Lubbock's merits for the family's consideration, a campaign they willingly prosecuted with discretion—and success.

Once he had received the family's approval, Lubbock moved deliberately
to build a fitting monument to the artist whose towering achievement seemed
still too-much undervalued and unappreciated. With Peggy and Alice compil-
ing transcripts of letters in America, Lubbock worked through a list of James's
favored British correspondents, asking that they lend any documents in their
possession for transcription and possible inclusion in the forthcoming volumes.
To prevent unintended omissions, in January 1917 the editor placed a formal
notice in the *Times*, soliciting responses from anyone who might have James
letters at hand.[86] As documents came in, clerical help in Pinker's London office
made surprisingly good typescript copies, which Lubbock then checked for
accuracy against the originals. (A great many of James's later letters, of course,
had themselves been dictated to his typist, making the task of retranscription
much easier.) Still, progress was slow and much interrupted. In the midst of
war, Lubbock was preoccupied with his work for the Red Cross—sometimes
crossing the channel to assist Edith Wharton, who coordinated various chari-
table activities from her Paris quarters at 53 Rue de Varenne—and he could not
address himself to the equally challenging tasks of editorship until hostilities
ended. As he told Pinker in July 1917, "[T]he final selection, & the introduction
& notes which must go with it—all this absolutely depends on the War, like all
else."[87] When the Armistice at last was signed, Lubbock returned to the James
project with pent-up gusto. "*How* interesting it is going to be to gather it all in
& *see*," he marveled in anticipation, "—& to try to exhibit it as it should be exhibited—to put one's best critical care into the doing of it—to be relieved of the
fear, at any rate, that the thing will be *badly* muffed" (by the family, he meant)
"through want of perception."[88] Having to defer such pleasure seems only to
have magnified the work's intrinsic importance to Lubbock, whose already considerable veneration for James was becoming almost a sacred rage. While Howard Sturgis wanted to remember the Master principally as the kindest of human
fellows, he sensed in Lubbock a deep-seated need to extol and appropriate a
much different Henry James. Percy "is so penetrated with his *greatness*," Sturgis
shrewdly glimpsed, "that he is even *glad* that he died before he began in any
way to decline; he seems to think of him so exclusively as the Genius, the reputation, the possession of the ages."[89] To be charged with the consecration of *that*

could only have been a thrilling prospect, and Lubbock took up the cause with single-minded fervor.

Knowing full well the almost morbid scruples of the Jameses, Lubbock understood in advance that the faculty he would need most to exercise in preparing his edition of the Master's letters would be discretion. Every batch of typescripts sent from America already had been marked up by various family censors, with sections of many letters bracketed and flagged with a marginal inscription to "Omit." Of course, many of these exclusions would have been understandable and probably necessary for any editor to make. It would have been imperative, for example, to elide James's occasional derogations of people still living: no one wanted to invite prosecution for libel.[90] The Master was a delightfully incorrigible gossip, "unprintable," as Lubbock said, "when he was at his best," because of the extraordinary freedom of his private confidences.[91] Many other recipients (including Edith Wharton), jealous of words they felt had been meant only for *them*, also sent the editor letters with such strictly personal passages clearly marked for omission.[92] But the family's editorial rigor extended far beyond the obvious question of legal decorum. James's incessant—and often grossly detailed—discussions of his personal health were obvious candidates for elision, as were his frequent—too frequent—complaints about impending destitution. Money matters and the specifics of the writer's professional life were also deemed off limits, tinged, presumably, with a vulgarity that could not be reconciled with the enduring image of the Master— aloof from marketplace necessities—that this edition was intended to enshrine.

Perhaps even more unsettling to the family was their uncle's habit of beginning and ending letters "to anyone for whom he cared, by enveloping the person addressed in some kind of affectionate hug."[93] These almost physical epistolary gestures were especially pronounced in James's late letters to younger men, and Harry, in particular, was afraid that their amative intensity might be misconstrued. What Leon Edel would later term the "relaxed homoeroticism" of these documents was an element that neither the family nor Lubbock wished to advertise, and most traces of it were carefully pruned away by James's vigilant disciple.[94] Edmund Gosse, for reasons (as Whitman might have said), also had recommended such excisions, and Harry was only too glad to concur with his cautious judgment. "I agree more and more with your suggestion that terms of endearment had better be omitted in a fair number of letters," he told Gosse, and Lubbock trimmed accordingly.[95] The extravagances that remained when Lubbock's volumes appeared were more than enough to invite speculation—even the ever-modest Howells was struck by them[96]—but, by and large, this edition of James's letters played an important role in the broader biographical conspiracy to evade questions about the Master's sexuality and to restrain the legitimate circulation of his cultural capital within acceptable social bounds.

Before Lubbock's volumes went to press, the Jameses insisted on having an opportunity to review them, unwilling to relinquish ultimate editorial control to someone outside the family. All along they had assumed that Lubbock would travel to the United States (financial provision for such a trip had been written into in his contract), so he could place his finished manuscript in the family's hands (or, just as likely, at their feet); but when it seemed as if James's relatives were going to be sidestepped, Harry immediately intervened to halt the publication process. "Considering the family's pretty intimate and substantial interest in this book and the fact that it was originally assumed that Lubbock would come to the States before finishing it," Harry confessed to Pinker that he was "somewhat surprised" to learn that the book was ready to go to press: the editor had neither said a word about his progress nor given them a chance to see it. "My mother and I ought to know what the book is going to be before it is published," the nephew insisted, "—not because I fear anything in particular or expect to have to make any suggestions or objections, but simply because it is obviously appropriate and necessary to take that course."[97] Since Harry was still in Paris, working for the postwar US Reparations Committee, he suggested that Lubbock bring the manuscript to him there, as the editor was about to depart from London for a sojourn in Italy and was planning to spend a few days en route with Mrs. Wharton at 53 Rue de Varenne. Pinker hastily arranged for a duplicate of at least some of the manuscript to be typed up, for which Harry expressed much satisfaction. "It will be possible for me to go over part of it at least while Lubbock is here," he added, affording him the desired opportunity to restore a certain measure of family control over the edition.[98]

Constraints of time, however, meant that Pinker could provide Harry only with copies of Lubbock's main introduction and the sundry editorial headnotes he had written, which, taken in sequence, composed an extremely concise biographical portrait of Henry James. The vast bulk of the manuscript—the edited letters themselves—would not be subject to closer family scrutiny until several months later, when the book was already in proof. Meanwhile, in Paris, Harry found himself at a curious crossroads. From the very beginning, the family had been deeply suspicious of Edith Wharton's possible influence: that was the principal reason for having Gosse serve as Lubbock's editorial mentor and consultant—to keep the distrusted divorcée out of range (and in the dark). Now, rather unhappily, Harry was obliged to meet Lubbock under Wharton's very roof and to try to legitimate the family's controlling priorities in precisely the quarter where those narrow imperatives were least likely to garner much respect. Somewhat nervously, Harry wrote to his mother that "dealing with Lubbock against a Wharton & Geoffrey-Scott back-ground is not just what I should have asked of Fate"—the Anglo-Florentine Geoffrey Scott, another member of Wharton's inner circle, was the man who had invited Lubbock to come with him to Italy.[99] Knowingly or not, Harry was surrounded by a ring of conspirators, all of whom found the mental (and moral) horizons of Cambridge, Massachusetts—as Uncle Henry did—embarrassingly provincial.

The contradictions of the moment become even more queer when we realize that the English art historian Geoffrey Scott—whose homosexuality was openly acknowledged—was now a kind of soi-disant brother-in-law to Harry, since both of them recently had married women with kinship ties to the family of William Bayard Cutting, a fabulously wealthy New York lawyer and financier. Harry had waited until age thirty-eight to marry Olivia Cutting (1892–1949) in June 1917, she being the youngest of the four Cutting children. Their engagement had been very brief—less than two months—and their happiness, as a couple, probably briefer: "Olivia James revealing herself after a certain painful time to be" (in R. W. B. Lewis's words) "by every inclination a full-fledged lesbian."[100] Less than a year into the marriage, Harry marched off to the war, refusing the officer's rank that easily would have come with his advanced age and professional experience; instead, eager to see battle, he enlisted as a private in the United States Army. When peace came, he deliberately prolonged his exile from New York through civilian service in postwar Europe. Meanwhile, Olivia (described by one biographer as "a reticent . . . woman, somewhat manly in appearance") abandoned the couple's Manhattan apartment and went back to live with her mother at the family's fabulous estate—Westbrook—on Long Island.[101] In 1930, after years of separation from his wife, Harry "stage-managed a divorce proceeding with himself as a defendant," even arranging for one of his sisters-in-law to testify "as to his cruelty and misbehavior."[102] In one of his meanest tales about marital betrayal, "A London Life" (1888), Uncle Henry almost had arrived at such a tortuous plot; but the depressing dénouement (ruthlessly up to date) of Harry's failed marriage was even more false than anything James could have imagined.

Reversing genders—and sexual orientations—in 1918 Geoffrey Scott became the husband of Sybil Cutting, the wealthy widow of the youngest Cutting heir, Bayard Junior, who had died in 1910 of chronic tuberculosis. That earlier marriage, too, had been considered ill advised; but, when Sybil bore the Cuttings a grandchild, she guaranteed her in-laws' generous, if grudging, support. (Aware of his wife's anxiety about her future, Bayard had reassured Sybil, telling her that "Papa and Mama would never let my widow be in difficulty. They are *really* rich you know.")[103] At the time of her first husband's death, Sybil received an immediate bequest of twenty-five thousand dollars, with another three hundred thousand dollars to be held in trust for her lifetime, after which the principal would revert to her daughter.[104] This fortune enabled Sybil to purchase the Villa Medici in the hills of Fiesole above Florence, where she became a close neighbor—and, soon, adulterous lover—of Bernard Berenson. At nearby Villa I Tatti, undergoing restoration and expansion to accommodate Berenson's vast art collection and library, Geoffrey Scott had been installed first as landscape architect (with his companion and business partner Cecil Pinsent) and then as librarian and personal secretary to the great historian of Renaissance art.

Sybil's affair with the notoriously philandering Berenson lasted about three years (longer than some of his), and, as with all the others, their dalliance was an open secret among the Anglo-Florentine community. In time, however, Sybil began to turn her attentions to the much younger Geoffrey Scott, whom she had commissioned to redesign the extensive gardens at her own palatial residence. Sybil's imperial promiscuity now invited the open displeasure of Berenson's wife, Mary: she could hardly believe that "both [her] men should have been snatched away" by a "chatterbox" like her regrettable neighbor. (In her autobiography, even Sybil admitted that "silence," to her, was an "unnatural" state.)[105] Without success, Mary Berenson tried to get Scott to break off the liaison, warning him that Sybil was "a case of arrested development," a hypochondriacal vampire.[106] The Berensons' mutual friend Edith Wharton took a similarly jaded view of such an unashamedly opportunistic affair, sure that Scott, rather pathetically, was seeking financial independence by affecting heterosexual inclinations for an heiress only too eager to use her wealth as a cynical aphrodisiac. "Poor Geoffrey," she quipped; "it will be bed and board, with a vengeance, and bored in bed."[107] Scott himself surely knew this—he admitted to Mary Berenson that he would never find in Sybil the "mate" of his "deeper nature"—but to their marriage she would bring "many gifts as the mistress of a hospitable house" and secure for him all the "good traditions of English civilized life."[108] Neither was Sybil completely blind to the implications of this undisguised marriage of convenience. To Berenson she confessed that, until very recently, both Geoffrey and Cecil "had always been 'the boys,' companions and friends but with no other thought ever coming in at all, and no chance of any other relationship ever springing to life." "I want to be needed so much," she pleaded to her former lover: "—*so* much, and somehow I feel with Geoffrey that he *does* need me that I shall be able to give him *what he needs*, that *all* one's tenderness & care as well as one's sympathy and interest and companionship will be *wanted*." Afraid that such a confession might invite Berenson's derision, she commanded, "Don't smile—or at any rate don't laugh. You know I *was* lonely, you know what a dear Geoffrey is. Surely it is natural enough?"[109] With such mixed motives—on both sides—that this marriage should flounder hardly provokes much surprise. Strangely enough, though, after *their* unhappy time as man and wife, Scott would arrange for his divorce through a legal charade almost as depressing as Harry James's. In 1925, having lived away from Florence for years, he and another woman (a "flaxen haired" prostitute) falsely registered at a London hotel as "Mr. and Mrs. Geoffrey Scott," thereby giving Sybil material grounds to initiate proceedings against him.[110]

   All of this might be dismissed as mere collateral gossip were it not for the fact that Sybil's next husband would be Percy Lubbock, whom she married as soon as a London court certified her divorce from Scott. Fully to appreciate the complex psychosexual agendas and anxieties that were in play as Lubbock completed his work on *The Letters of Henry James*, we need to flesh out what Harry rather cryptically referred to as the "Wharton & Geoffrey-Scott back-ground" in which, to his obvious dismay, he found the editor enmeshed. Wharton had long been viewed by the Jameses as a dangerous sybarite, whose personal influence—like that of her books—could only be corrupting. The sexual preferences of many of her closest friends were ambiguous at best; some, like those of Howard Sturgis (who never went anywhere without a pair of knitting needles[111]) and his male companion, William Haynes Smith (familiarly known as "The Babe"), were unambiguous altogether. Harry's personal discovery of his wife's lesbianism must have given him qualms about his own powers of psychological discernment—or at least an uncomfortable awareness of the confusing folds in which sexual identity might be muffled or submerged. Not long before his ill-starred nuptials, Harry had told his sister, Peggy (who was also soon to wed Bruce Porter [1865–1953]—a man old enough, it might be noted, to have been her uncle), "I begin to suspect that marriage for you & me, who've taken to it after the first blush of you[th]—is going to reduce a number of hitherto pleasantly demonstrative relationships to their solid dimensions."[112] Just of what those "pleasantly demonstrative relationships" might have consisted is unclear, but we do know that during her years at Bryn Mawr (1908–10), Peggy had formed an intensely homosocial attachment to the poet Marianne Moore.[113] For both James children, the belated acceptance of heteronormative roles and conventions would seem to have implied a welcome end to a protracted period of (quite possibly confused) identity formation. This cluster of circumstances could only have reinforced the family's guarded sensitivity to ambiguities of sexual orientation and their fear that disturbing innuendo might besmirch Uncle Henry's posthumous reputation, unless the writer's letters, soon to be made public, were edited with unstinting discretion. Confronting Lubbock about such matters—just then and there—was a task Harry scarcely could have relished.

Sybil Cutting was hardly the only thing that Percy Lubbock and Geoffrey Scott had (or would have) in common. The two were near contemporaries (Lubbock was born in 1879; Scott, in 1884) and had emerged from similarly privileged backgrounds. Lubbock attended Eton and Cambridge; Scott was first enrolled at Rugby and then Oxford; both distinguished themselves academically as undergraduates. The young men also were deeply affected by the intensely homosocial worlds of the British public school and university, having to wrestle there with their own same-sex attractions during the very period when homosexuality was being criminalized in Britain (and elsewhere). Neither man was in line, genealogically, to inherit his father's wealth or social position; but neither did their formal schooling, exquisite as it surely was, equip them to pursue especially lucrative careers. For most of their adult lives, both men were frankly dependent upon the patronage of wealthy elders of both sexes; and their professional work, however accomplished, was nevertheless occasional, dilettantish, and largely unremunerative.[114] Ultimately, both yearned for the kind of social respectability and economic security that only marriage to a much wealthier woman seemed likely to provide.

For decades after leaving Eton, Lubbock remained the occasional companion of his former tutor, the prolific poet, essayist, and man of letters Arthur Christopher Benson. It was Benson, in fact, who in 1897 had first introduced his shy young pupil to Henry James, bringing the Master to the young man's lodgings. Lubbock's much-later evocation of the moment is characteristic, teasing the reader by asking,

> Who was it? He hadn't the sparkling forwardness of the other [Edmund Gosse, to whom Benson had introduced Lubbock some time before], and somehow between his hesitation and his massiveness the introduction was bungled; I didn't catch the name. He was sturdy and large-headed, with a close dark beard. He did his best, I am sure, to see an interest in the wretched little room and its inconspicuous owner; but it was a laborious proceeding, and I felt myself that there was none in either. We toiled at a few trivialities, where we could find them, but the chill and the gloom and the squalor were too much for us all; even my resourceful tutor was at a loss. I still had no idea who the stranger might be when he was released; with all courtesy but no particularity he said good-bye and was borne away. A chapter that was to develop so memorably never opened so lamely; for this was my first sight of Henry James.[115]

Between Benson, on the one hand, and that other gregarious gay Etonian, Howard Sturgis, on the other, Lubbock was always guaranteed comfortable quarters, male companionship, and frequent access to James, for whom Sturgis's country house at Windsor (Queen's Acre, or Qu'acre ["Quaker"], as the regulars called it) was a familiar retreat.[116] Lubbock's devotion to James and his work—regarded by most observers as a kind of idol worship—was soon complete. As early as 1904, the Master confided to Sturgis, "I am touched, much, by what you tell me of the young Percy. . . . It's jolly for a youth to have that sentiment *pour quelqu'un* [for anyone]—but I wish I were a worthier object."[117]

During these formative years, divided mostly among London, Cambridge, and Windsor, Lubbock also developed an intense bond with Gaillard Lapsley, the classmate of Harry James's at Harvard who in 1904 became a Fellow and Reader in medieval history at Trinity College. It would seem that in Lapsley Lubbock at last found someone with whom he could freely discuss the torments of his closeted gay life. Whenever he could, Lubbock tried to escape from London to share time with his friend in Lapsley's private Cambridge lodgings, Fen Ditton. With Benson, whose homosexuality was more rigorously sublimated, Lubbock always had to be on guard. Having come to stay with his former tutor (after enjoying Lapsley's freer privacies), Lubbock remarked that "between Ditton & here one has to make a queer little adjustment of oneself, as you may well picture: it is a little difficult to remember at first that . . . I have to say, or that it is better to say, 'nailing good chaps' rather than 'sweet-looking boys'—and so forth—the result of which is you see that I can't quite let go of your hand."[118] Benson obviously was wary of such effeminate forms of speech—not to mention other queer idiosyncrasies—that he clearly discouraged. Some years before, when he and Lubbock had tried to sound out the respective depths of their emotional attachments, Benson observed, "I have a sort of feeling, in discussing this subject with him, that he has a kind of secret, hidden from me, a secret which others share, in the matter." Afraid that his own temperament might be too chilly (or repressed), Benson then acknowledged that

> [r]elations are not holy or solemn or awe-inspiring for me—only pleasant or unpleasant; and my tendency is to welcome in a congenial person very affably, and to the make the best of an uncongenial. But to P. L. and his school, this is a kind of emotional harlotry, I think. It was a deeply interesting conversation, but left me aware that friendship, etc., were for P. L. a series of deep thrills—exultations and agonies—while for me they are only like flying sunlight on a bright morning.[119]

Intensely jealous of Lubbock's affection, Benson clearly was hurt when his former student began to dote on Lapsley and other Cambridge tutors, such as Ollife Richmond, with whom he would journey to Italy in 1909. The closer companionship (and possibly physical intimacy) these other men offered Lubbock was something for which Benson could not compensate.[120]

Even though Benson was a lifelong bachelor and spent his entire career in the company of younger men, he seems to have been capable of a kind of chastity that the modern Vatican might well envy. A true student of the classics, his understanding of Greek love cherished the Platonic ideal, and he expected his students and fellow tutors to accept its sternest rigors. Those who fell short were ruthlessly chastised, if not to their faces, then in his astonishing private diary (forty-some volumes, running to more than four million words). Around 1912, for example, when Ollife Richmond began preying upon "the youngsters of the King's Choir School," Benson repudiated such open demonstrations of homosexual attraction. "He takes a strong sexual kind of interest in the attractive men," Benson scribbled, "and nothing else. . . . [He is] obsessed with a sort of perverted eroticism for anything young and fair. . . . It is the combination of sensuous motive with a kind of lofty priggishness."[121] When, after Benson's death, it fell upon none other than Lubbock to edit the diary for publication, the former student was appalled to discover that many of the most lacerating entries had been directed at *him*. Using a classic Jamesian metaphor, the pained editor told Lapsley, "One turn of the screw is also a surprise—to me—the reckless horrid way in which he apparently talked about me to people I hardly know—all noted down in the diary with a sort of *glee*—it's hard."[122] Needless to say, *those* passages—besides many others—did not find their way into print when *The Diary of Arthur Christopher Benson* appeared in 1926.

Lubbock's own confessions were seldom reckless; on the contrary, his surviving letters to Lapsley might almost be described as the quintessential Edwardian grammar of queer euphemism. (This is not surprising: to have written more plainly might have invited scandal, blackmail—even criminal prosecution.) If, as Benson had sensed, Lubbock kept hidden secrets, his former pupil also felt a deep need to disclose them to someone, and Lapsley clearly lent a sympathetic ear. After one of his later visits to Fen Ditton, Lubbock confided,

> I tumble back [to London] with a sense of gratitude to you which I can't tell you about properly because I can't go into all the reasons I have for feeling it. But I do just want to tell you that you have helped me more than you know, helped me to get some things straight in my mind that badly wanted straightening—so that with what look like & must be some rather black months in front of me I can go at them with a better spirit than I could have done otherwise. Thank you

& bless you for it, & be sure that I could have got such help from no one else, & that it was more real & more timely than I have ever perhaps got from anyone. I don't want to be dismal & don't mean to be—but these are difficulties that one has to tackle so very much alone that it sometimes gets frightening, & it is a relief to be able to put out a hand . . . to someone who *wird wohl verschwiegen sein* [i.e., to someone who will be able to keep a secret].[123]

With time, however (and perhaps some perceived relaxation of social taboos), Lubbock's confidences would become more revealing. When he made his first trip to Italy in 1902, the young disciple of Henry James approached the journey with an appropriately solemn agenda: this was his first opportunity to take in the artistic splendors of Florence, Venice, and Rome. Besides congratulating him "with all my heart on the great event of your young, your first, your never to be surpassed or effaced, prime Italiänische Reise," the Master also marveled at the plastic possibilities of youth. "It's a great event (*the* revelation) at any time of life, but it's altogether immeasurable at *your* lucky one," he enviously wrote. James knew it would be pointless to prescribe a specific itinerary for his young disciple: "[T]here would be no use whatever in my having 'told you what to do.' There wouldn't be the remotest chance of your doing it. The place, the time, the aspect, the colour of the light and the inclination of Percy Lubbock will already be making for you their own law, or better still, causing you to live generally lawless and promiscuous. *Be* promiscuous and incoherent and intelligent, absorbent, happy: it's your great chance."[124] A decade later, Lubbock obviously had taken that wisdom to heart. Writing Lapsley from Rome in 1912, he sketched a self-portrait of a man

rather hungry & sore & savage in his mind, sometimes, it can't be denied, but on the whole having & intending to have, in these next days & weeks, *the* time of his life, & not at present choosing (for what would be the use?) to look beyond it, where there is nothing so nice to be seen. This is an affected way of indicating that my solitude (which I get through well enough) is punctuated by opportunities for the company I most desire, & which I came here for.[125]

Some years later, after a particularly bleak—and lonely—Christmas (spent in Vienna, where he had come as a correspondent for the London *Times*), Lubbock must have poured out his soul in a letter that even Lapsley knew had to be destroyed. Its successor, however, fills in the silence. "I have been tempted to feel that I ought not to have written, even to you, as I did the other day," Lubbock began, "—but on the whole I reject the temptation as an unworthy one. I don't think anything is lost, & I am sure something is gained, by throwing the cupboard-door open for the right *one* person. It is shut again with a real feeling of relief that the knowledge of its contents has been shared, & shared by someone who is not horrified or frightened or bored by the spectacle—or made uncomfortable by it, as some of our dear friends would be!"[126] Lubbock's relief is palpable. It might almost seem as if he has rewritten James's harrowing tale of outing, "A Round of Visits" (1910)—a story terminated by suicide—to make possible a more liberating psychological outcome for himself.[127]

One dear friend who was *not* made uncomfortable by suggestions of homoerotic intimacy was Henry James, who took enormous vicarious interest in Lubbock's clandestine adventures. In the same New Year's letter to Lapsley, Lubbock noted that he had just received a "simply Gargantuan letter from Henry," obviously Rabelaisian not only in size but also in its queer (and exquisitely campy) sexual inquisitiveness. "As for me, alone & unhampered in a great foreign capital—his imagination makes great round eyes of delight & envy at the thought. I am to tell him *everything* when I get back; but he adds, 'Don't, I beseech you, however, forbear from any experience whatever by the fear or the possible shy scruple of having to tell me about it.'" "Really," Lubbock clucked, "isn't he *bad*? & isn't he lovely!"[128] No doubt Lubbock had whetted James's curiosity when, a few weeks earlier, he described his recent arrival in Vienna and told the Master that at last he was "doing what I ought really to have done long ago & never *did*—that is, achieve some living & working & collecting all by myself. The living may not be very high or the working brilliant—but at any rate the collecting has begun abundantly: a big bunch already of assorted acquaintances,—not the choicest rarities, I must say—but still new to *me*, & with many queer markings."[129] Not long after, when the Angel of Devastation was planning to snatch Lubbock up and whirl him across the Mediterranean for a tour of Algeria (already a Mecca for transgressive sexual indulgence), James teased Wharton about her talent for unbuttoning the straitlaced men in her company. "I find what you say about Walter B[erry] very interesting—as to the effect on him—his spirit—of his lapse of 'character,' so to speak; all the more that the recovery of that value, when it has lapsed, does take such a lot of doing. . . . You offer Percy a tremendous chance to let *his* lapse, don't you?—'over there at Algiers,' just when he is supposed to be building it up as hard as possible at Vienna (how pretty, though too scant & too few, his little Times articles are!)—but I do quite see everything go to pieces in the African dust-cloud."[130] When the Saharan dust had cleared, James's rather gloating prophecy had been fulfilled. On 13 April, Lubbock mailed Lapsley a photo-postcard of three nude Arab boys that carried this wry inscription: "The disconsolate are beginning to enjoy the distractions of travel."[131] (Of course, Lubbock took the necessary precaution of concealing the vaguely pornographic image in a letter envelope, away from the prying eyes of postal inspectors.) A few days later, Wharton described the scenic wonders of Tunis to Bernard Berenson as "a cauldron of 'louxoure' (as d'Annunzio says)": "one can't take two steps in the native quarter, the amazing, unbelievable bazaars, without feeling one's self in an unexpurgated page of the Arabian Nights!"[132] Deliberately circumspect, all of these Jamesian disciples and confidantes saved *their* unexpurgated pages for private conversation—making such occasional epistolary slips that much more revealing.

On their return from Algeria, Wharton and her party made their way up through Italy, sailing first to Naples and then (in her splendid motorcar) on to Rome and Florence. From there, Lubbock returned to his post at Vienna but not before being introduced to Wharton's friends in Fiesole, who were so lavishly domiciled at the Villa Medici and Villa I Tatti. Small wonder that Lubbock should have yearned for any chance to return and claim a share of such leisured magnificence. It had been in Florence some years before that Lubbock had intended to finish writing his first work of fiction—"a strange beautiful penetrating novel," he told Lapsley, "embodying sharp criticism of the extraordinary views women have about men. It ought to be called," he added with more than touch of misogyny, "'What no woman knows' (i.e., anything about men.)"[133] We can have few regrets that Lubbock apparently never completed this book; but, more important, he also began to worry at this time about his own dilettantism, especially because he had encountered so many other rather listless Britons, all with "artistic" pretensions, living cheaply—and unproductively—in various expatriate enclaves throughout Italy. What he found in Venice convinced him that, if an "artistic colony" was going to set up shop, "it should be the real thing—real art, professional, penniless, disreputable, furiously pederastic if it

likes, or as sober as it likes, anything, only *art*—not that frail little circle of cultivated amateurs, writing picturesque little poems & sketches & publishing them
in tiny books with broad margins . . . living on picturesquely narrow means,
philandering with gondoliers & thinking it romantic & pretty."[134] Concerns not
very different from these still dogged Lubbock during his later time in Vienna.
"Sometimes I wonder," he confessed to Wharton,

> whether I shall ever arrive at that minimum of facility which really is neces-
> sary if one is to get anything solid *done*. I am being fidgeted, rather, by the fact
> that though I pelt the Times with bright little chatty articles (written with what
> feverish brow-moppings!), & tho' they profess to like them, they never seem to
> find the occasion to print them—not that I should mind that if they would *pay*
> for them. The result seems to be that I must look out, I don't quite know where,
> for more strings to my bow—& with that my books, those beautiful books I am
> going to write, seem ever to recede.[135]

Unexpectedly—and unknowingly—the death of Henry James offered Lubbock
a compelling opportunity to allay these vocational anxieties. By identifying himself so completely with the Master, Lubbock found a calling that would subdue
his chronic professional indeterminacy, galvanize his wavering resolve, and
anoint him, unimpeachably, with custodial responsibility for the reputation of a
writer who had never shirked the most severe demands of the art he practiced.

Though gratefully applauded by Edith Wharton and the rest of James's inner
circle of acolytes, Lubbock's tenacious appropriation of the Jamesian mantle
did not sit well with some of his other contemporaries. H. G. Wells, who had
already perpetrated his savage parody of the Master in *Boon* (1915), was hardly
repentant when he inferred that Lubbock had used his influence at the *Times*
to refuse any notice of Rebecca West's acerbic (but still valuable) 1916 study,
*Henry James*. When his former mistress's book was snubbed, Wells fumed at
Hugh Walpole, "[N]othing I've ever written or said or anyone has ever written
or said about James can balance the extravagant dirtiness of Lubbock and his
friends in boycotting Rebecca West's book on him in *The Times Literary Supplement*. My blood still boils at the thought of those pretentious academic greasers
conspiring to down a friendless girl (who can write any of them out of sight)
in the name of loyalty to literature."[136] Even the ever-faithful little Bosanquet

found something to admire in the work. While conceding that West was "liable to very vulgar lapses" and wasn't "at all fundamentally sympathetic" to James, Bosanquet nevertheless recognized that there was "something to be said for her vigorous style," which, when appreciative, was very appreciative and accurate indeed.[137] Virginia Woolf, too, was disdainful of the cultish club of "devout Jacobeans" that had sprung up, like a weed in the graveyard, not long after the Master's death. When the (rather precious) poet Robert Trevelyan asked her if she wanted to join their exclusive clique, Woolf sneered at the idea. "Percy Lubbock & Logan [Pearsall] Smith play this very characteristic game," she confided to her diary, "of exquisite interest of course to Bob. They've counted 20, & Bob was seriously exerting himself to find a 21st. But I refused—with some vehemence at first thinking I was to be asked to subscribe to a memorial. Nothing so substantial; only an elderly cultivated game."[138] Five years earlier Woolf willingly had paid her five quid to have her name added to the list of James's British admirers on the occasion of the Master's seventieth birthday, but this was ancestor worship, something she could never countenance.

After some hesitation, Wells eventually allowed Lubbock to print the magnificent letters of remonstrance that a clearly wounded Henry James had written him after seeing himself lampooned in his erstwhile friend's parodic novel. Denying that James's fictions were in any sense true to life, Wells concluded in *Boon* that

> the only living human motives left in the novels of Henry James are a certain avidity and an entirely superficial curiosity. Even when relations are irregular or when sins are hinted at, you feel that these are merely attitudes taken up, gambits before the game of attainment and over-perception begins. His people nose out suspicions, hint by hint, link by link. Have you ever known living human beings do that? The thing his novel is *about* is always there. It is like a church lit but without a congregation to distract you, with every light and line focused on the high altar. And on the altar, very reverently placed, intensely there, is a dead kitten, an egg-shell, a bit of string.

With characteristic understatement, James confessed to Wells that he found this passage "very curious and interesting after a fashion—though it has naturally not filled me with a fond elation." Seeing that his own priority for artistic form never could be reconciled with the kind of didactic social agenda that drove so many of Wells's novels, James knew that their friendship had reached an end; but before he terminated it, the Master also wanted to make clear to Wells how empty and perverse *his* hollow philosophy of composition truly was. "It is art that *makes* life," James emphasized, "makes interest, makes importance, for our consideration and application of these things, and I know of no substitute whatever for the force and beauty of its process."[139] Lubbock was especially eager to include this epistolary exchange, because by then, having read thousands of James's letters, the editor realized that these particular documents had "a sort of historic literary value; as well as a unique biographical value for H.J.," for the author had nowhere else so concisely articulated his artistic credo. "There is hardly a single profession to compare with this in all the thousands of his letters I have seen," Lubbock told Pinker, who then used his influence with Wells (who was also a client of the agent) to recant his earlier prohibition and allow the editor to publish them.[140]

Lubbock hurried to finish his work in the spring of 1919, eager for a much-needed holiday in Florence. "There is now a wild projection of a fancy that I may spend the summer at the Medicean Villino at Fiesole," he happily scribbled to Lapsley, "—I rather reel at the thought—reeling *towards* it on the whole, however."[141] After meeting with Harry James in Paris, the editor reported back to Pinker that they "had two long & most satisfactory talks," but this was also in the absence of his manuscript, which had not yet been copied for the nephew's inspection.[142] When Harry finally had a fuller opportunity to review Lubbock's work—despite some crucial reservations (at which we have already glanced)—the family deputy was much relieved. "I have read enough to have the greatest confidence about everything which I haven't been through," he graciously told the editor.

> It seems to me that you have shown judgment and skill in selecting, and your introductory explanations are quite wonderfully happy and ingenious. Where you deal with family matters or with family relationships say, which it would have been natural to fumble over a bit, you have shot your bullet very straight into the bull's eye. It is a bullet of discreetly small caliber, but quite correctly placed. On this score on which you very likely expected suggestions, I have practically nothing to offer.[143]

Perhaps as a result of his wartime experience it was inevitable that Harry should have chosen such a martial metaphor to express his satisfaction, but comparing Lubbock's skillful execution to that of a marksman (or even an assassin) might betray the fact that the contest for control over James's legacy would continue to provoke aggressive impulses in those close to it.

The editor's introduction to the *Letters* and other various headnotes—so highly praised by Harry—provide the best evidence of Lubbock's almost seamless appropriation of James's aura. Written with a kind of detached majesty, these brief (but knowing) compositions owe their strength—and weakness—to this fact. By starting from the unquestioned assumption that no one else but James could write his own life, Lubbock inevitably concluded that only in his published work (and now these published letters) could we hope to find it. Transcending all the teasing irony of "The Figure in the Carpet" (1896), Lubbock was willing to brave the central question posed in that tale by the writer Hugh Vereker, who wonders whether the critic's chief occupation shouldn't be to discover "'the particular thing I've written my books most *for*. Isn't there for every writer,'" he says, "'a particular thing of that sort, the thing that most makes him apply himself, the thing without the effort to achieve which he wouldn't write at all, the very passion of his passion, the part of the business in which, for him, the flame of art burns most intensely?'"[144] The figure in James's carpet, as Lubbock perceived it, was the writer's solitary dedication to the craft he had mastered.

> Much as he always delighted in sociable communion, citizen of the world, child of urbanity as he was, all his friends must have felt that at heart he lived in solitude and that few were ever admitted into the inner shrine of his labour. There it was nevertheless that he lived most intensely and most serenely. In outward matters he was constantly haunted by anxiety and never looked forward with confidence; he was of those to whom the future is always ominous, who dread the treachery of apparent calm even more than actual ill weather. It was very different in the presence of his work. There he never knew the least failure of assurance; he threw his full weight on the belief that supported him and it was never shaken. That belief was in the sanctity and sufficiency of the life of art.[145]

Discovering those late letters to Wells gave Lubbock the keys to the Master's kingdom, enabling the editor's defensive exposition of James's artistic convictions to approach Shelley's *Defence of Poetry* in its lyric force. "It was absolute for him," Lubbock declaimed,

> that the work of the imagination was the highest and most honourable calling conceivable, being indeed nothing less than the actual creation of life out of the void. He did not scruple to claim that except through art there is no life that can be known or appraised. It is the artist who takes over the deed, so called, from the doer, to give it back again in the form in which it can be seen and measured for the first time; without the brain that is able to close round the loose unappropriated fact and render all its aspects, the fact itself does not exist for us. (*LHJ*, 1:xv–xvi)

If not exactly the unacknowledged legislator of the world, James surely was, for Lubbock, the unacknowledged legislator of the art he tirelessly practiced. In his edition of James's letters—and then *The Craft of Fiction*—Lubbock sought to legitimate the Master's proprietary claim to that jurisdiction.

The apparent absence of anything that might have caused Lubbock to question James's heroic detachment from the more prosaic realities of the artist's profession gave additional momentum to his hagiographic impulses. Unaware of the existence of the author's manuscript notebooks, and uninterested in the voluminous record of his (often grubby) day-to-day transactions in the literary marketplace, Lubbock could readily believe that James "put forth his finished work to speak for itself and swept away all the traces of its origin. There was a high pride in his complete lack of tenderness towards the evidence of past labour—the notes, manuscripts, memoranda that a man of letters usually accumulates and that shew him in the company of his work" (*LHJ*, 1:xviii).[146] Even though James's many bonfires had, in fact, consumed much of this collateral material, an unsuspectedly large cache of it survived, but in places (such as publishers' records—and Pinker's files, too) where Lubbock had neither time nor curiosity to look. Only by uncritically accepting the logic of James's own exclusions and erasures (so exquisitely allegorized in his various tales of writers and artists) could Lubbock consecrate—and appropriate—the Master's high authority.

Lubbock's intimate knowledge of the social and psychological prescriptions of the Edwardian closet powerfully reinforced his already instinctive biographical discretion. All of his books betray this. As Louis Auchincloss once observed, Lubbock's "method would be always pictorial" (one thinks how consistently the words *portrait, picture,* and *sketch* recur in his titles): he preferred to deal "with truth as it was outwardly presented or readily inferred; he made no pretense of opening closet doors or ferreting in desks."[147] The implied allusion here to the forbidden closet (in "The Jolly Corner") and the locked *secrétaire* (in "The Aspern Papers") only confirms Lubbock's oneness with the author of those stories, and whose deliberate reticence was most in demand when he was charged with editing the Master's letters. However fearful the family may have been about entrusting that job to someone outside its ranks, no one was better equipped to conceal whatever Jamesian secrets there were than someone who had been obliged to keep so many himself.

Through the summer months of 1919, Lubbock worked on the proofs of his edition in the splendid seclusion of the Villa Medici. In early September, Harry brought a set of them back to America on the SS *Rotterdam,* which was carrying him home to New York. What he read on board ship was enough to convince him that "these letters will become, in the history of English literature, not only one of the ½ dozen greatest epistolary classics, but a sort of mile stone—the last stone of the age whose close The Great War has marked. They are a magnificent commentary on the literary life of his generation," he told his sister, "and they're done in a style which will never be used naturally again. . . . These Letters will be the final, classic and magnificent manifestation of their kind."[148] Acknowledging the magnitude of Lubbock's achievement, the family, all the same, did not relax its vigilance; from Harry's hands the proofs were sent first to Alice in Cambridge (where Billy also read them carefully) and then on to California, so Peggy could preen them as well. Altogether, the four relatives compiled a fairly lengthy (and rather fussy) list of things to which they took exception: the repetitive nature of Uncle Henry's apologetic modes of address; his unflattering references to certain people that "might give a good deal of pain and add *nothing* to the picture of H.J."; the disproportionate inclusion of letters to Edith Wharton and Hugh Walpole; and a host of lesser quibbles.[149] Lubbock tried to allay the family's concerns, but without much success. "I have been very careful," he pleaded with Alice,

> to make sure I could defend explicitly (to myself!) every possibly doubtful case. And this applies, too, to the general question of the letters selected. I have asked

(& answered) myself, over each one, exactly *why* I included it—the answer is sometimes that I thought it intrinsically interesting, sometimes that it seemed specially characteristic, sometimes that it was *biographically* interesting (helping to link up the whole story).[150]

Squabbling over these details dragged on for months, Lubbock all the while insisting that the changes the family demanded were both unreasonable and unfeasible, since accepting their amendments—especially the deletion of entire letters—would disturb the continuous pagination of masses of type that already had been set up. Still needing to be diplomatic with the family, the editor could more openly voice his frustration to Pinker. "It is *now* too late to make any changes at all in vol. I," Lubbock maintained, "as I have passed the whole of it for press." Still unclear as to what, exactly, Harry was complaining about now, Lubbock had to question whether it was "worth while to delay the revision of vol. II in order to hear from him by letter . . . since the changes I could still make would only be the merest trifles. I can't upset the paging by omitting whole letters (if that is what he wants)—nor, between you & me, do I feel inclined to do so even if I could." Exasperated—and exhausted—Lubbock could only ejaculate, "It really is annoying that they couldn't have discovered these indiscretions sooner!"[151] Not until December were the proofs fully corrected and revised (more or less to everyone's compromised satisfaction). In almost every instance, Lubbock finally yielded to the family's wishes, though Harry reluctantly conceded that the editor's desire to conclude the edition with a letter to Hugh Walpole was a choice that he could live with. The two-volume set was published in England and America in early April 1920.

Reviewers on both sides of the Atlantic greeted *The Letters of Henry James* with almost universal acclaim. James Gibbons Huneker was just one of many who echoed Harry's advance judgment when he concluded, "These letter bid fair to become a classic in English literature."[152] The *North American Review* emphatically agreed. "For half a century Henry James poured himself out to his friends in letters that are matchless for their prodigal and eager flow of sympathy, their inexhaustible kindliness, their ample and exquisite tenderness, their beautiful generosity. These letters are priceless."[153] Virginia Woolf may have spurned membership in Lubbock's prim gentleman's club of idolatrous Jacobites, but she now had to concede his absolute fitness for the job at hand. "It would not be easy

to find a difficult task better fulfilled than by Mr. Percy Lubbock in his Introduction and connecting paragraphs," she affirmed on the first page of the *Times
Literary Supplement*. "It seems to us, and this not only before reading the letters
but more emphatically afterwards, that the lines of interpretation he lays down
are the true ones."[154] Here was a Henry James the world would long know: an
artist always in control of his powers, comfortably enmeshed in a thoroughly
cosmopolitan European milieu. Lubbock's overwhelming intention to erect a
monument to the Master had been realized, applauded, and acknowledged.

Producing such an imposing testimonial to James's human and literary
merits might have seemed absurdly premature in a country where most of the
writer's books were nowhere to be had. It was almost certainly Lubbock himself
who wrote the anonymous letter from "A Disappointed Reader" to the *Times
Literary Supplement* in 1919, complaining that James's works at that moment
were, practically speaking, out of print in Great Britain. "I do not think it can be
regarded as a very creditable fact," this disappointed reader began,

> that four years after Henry James's death his best and ripest works are only ob-
> tainable in England at practically prohibitive prices, and some of them, even at
> these prices, are not to be had. Apparently the old 6s. edition has been suffered
> to run out of print, and the *edition de luxe* costs 10s. 6d. per volume, or 21s. for
> the longer books. . . . [T]he only chance at present of making oneself acquainted
> with some of Henry James's best books is to see them at the British Museum.[155]

The situation in America probably was not quite as grim; still, Harry regretted that the different publishers of his uncle's novels "could not arrive at an
agreement permitting the manufacture and sale of a uniform edition at popular
prices which could be sold in single volumes."[156] With the New York Edition
(selective as it was) available only by expensive subscription, and all the other
ordinary trade editions scattered among so many different houses, marketing
the Master's books was hampered by competitive cross-pressures and the nag-
ging perception among his publishers that James's audience was too restricted
to warrant additional promotional expenditure.

Working in concert with Pinker, Lubbock at last persuaded Macmillan to
undertake a new complete and inexpensive edition of James's works. With the
*Letters* then in production, Lubbock immediately moved on to this complemen-

tary initiative of Jamesian monumentalism: *The Novels and Stories of Henry James* (1921–23)—in thirty-five volumes—would make any shelf (and probably some readers) groan. Initially, Frederick Macmillan assumed that the new enterprise would simply involve reissuing his firm's surplus sheets of the New York Edition in a cheaper binding. When Lubbock explained to him that the principal rationale for producing the new cheap series was to include works left out of the earlier edition, Macmillan expressed a certain disbelief. "I did not realize," he wrote Lubbock in surprise, "that *The Europeans, Washington Square, Confidence* and *The Sacred Fount,* as well as *The Bostonians,* were all omitted from the American edition."[157] Of course, there were many other omissions besides— fully half the shorter tales—and then the handful of stories that James had written after the Edition was published. Lubbock, loyal acolyte that he was, wanted to reprint them all—or, at least, all the shorter fiction that James himself had authorized for book publication while he was living.[158] For the rest, however, Lubbock was adamant about using James's revised texts: "any other course would be disloyal," he wrote, concurring with Pinker. James "would have been horrified by the idea that the unrevised form should be further disseminated," Lubbock believed, "& correspondingly pleased to think that the revision should be made generally accessible."[159] Harry was of a different mind altogether. "In view of the popular prejudice against the revised text," he urged that "this edition be made up in such a way as not to call attention to the fact that the revised text is used, by any more conspicuous announcement than may be required under the Copyright Act." Undeterred, Lubbock was proud to incorporate an acknowledgment in the advertisement that came at the back of each volume, declaring, "The text used in this issue is that of the 'New York' edition, and the critical prefaces written for that series are retained in the volumes to which they refer."[160] Lubbock could only have been disappointed in the younger James's willingness to capitulate to "popular prejudice," a prejudice that, as we know, Harry's late father, William, largely shared.

With guarded optimism, Macmillan went ahead with the project, hoping that its relative cheapness would attract buyers, even though Britain's postwar economy was far from brilliant. In its least expensive format, Lubbock's new edition made each of James's titles available for a mere three shillings six pence (less than a dollar a piece).[161] The *Times Literary Supplement* observed that, compared to the New York Edition, it would "be surprising if this double array of Henry James's fiction does not meet with a wider success than that issue did."[162] As the publication date neared, Lubbock eagerly told Frederick Macmillan that "the very newest literary generation shews signs of being a good deal occupied with Henry James, so I hope they will affect the sale."[163] But the new generation, if modernist in sensibility, was still terribly old-fashioned in its stingy preference for borrowing books instead of buying them. A year later the publisher reported, with regret, that "the reception of the new edition is so far rather disappointing." Still, he hoped that "things may be better when we get to the stories which have not been hitherto collected."[164] Conditions were not propitious, however, and Lubbock's heroic endeavor to expand the Master's posthumous readership largely failed of its aim.

Perhaps it was inevitable that, having expended so much time, energy, and devotion to the cause and memory of Henry James, Lubbock should have experienced a kind of psychic retrenchment when these years of unremitting (and depressingly unremunerative) labor came to an end. Having gone to spend much of the winter of 1921–22 with Edith Wharton in Paris, Lubbock sank into a depression that, to her, was baffling and alarming. Describing his long visit as "one of the most trying experiences I have ever undergone," Wharton confided to Lapsley that Lubbock's "gloom was unrelieved," his solipsism so complete as to "totally eliminat[e] the feelings of others from his mind." She and her other guests were "treated . . . to some six weeks of a morose & unbroken silence." To be alone with him was no better: whenever Wharton found him by himself, "he lifted that terrible *some-one else's* face," the sight of which gave her "a cold chill."[165] It might have seemed that the psychic demon of "The Jolly Corner" was abroad again, only this time the lurking doppelgänger was the Master himself. In reading and editing thousands of James's letters, republishing almost all of his fiction, and dissecting his methods in *The Craft of Fiction*, Lubbock had inhabited and identified with James so completely (and defensively)—all at the expense of his far from robust native ego—that completing those various projects left him spent and evacuated.

Fully to appreciate Lubbock's recoil from his Jamesian supersaturation, one need only look carefully at the two works of fiction he published soon thereafter. With different degrees of emphasis, both *Roman Pictures* (1923) and *The Region Cloud* (1925) are built upon the theme of discipleship. In both novels a protagonist who subordinates himself to the ostensibly compelling claims of art—or social mastery—is defeated by his overreaching identification with an older man, to whom he mistakenly has attributed some supreme virtue, the hallmarks of which are aesthetic superiority and cosmopolitan sophistication. Both tales are painful comedies of deflation in which the exalted figure of idolatrous affection is exposed, ultimately, as fraudulently unworthy of the hero's love. And in both, a barely sublimated homoeroticism distorts the protagonist's perception of his true relation to the venerated other, inviting him to mistake egotistical self-absorption for genuinely reciprocated affection.

In Lubbock's first novel, the relatively naïve anonymous male narrator looks up to his "precious Deering," another traveling Briton, as a kind of spiritual cicerone who will initiate him into the mysteries of modern Rome and help him avoid the abyss of philistine tourism toward which his female companions seem especially drawn.[166] "Deering *lived* in Rome," the narrator mentally sighs; "I had floated on the surface." Only too happy to be patronized, the narrator readily sloughs off his immature notions of taste to adopt those his friend recommends. "He delicately blasted whatever had appeared to me of interest and renown, he showed me the crudity of my standards. . . . And yet I was flattered, I was magnified by his fastidious irony; it brought me into a new world of mind and taste, more exclusive than my own" (13). Deering's intimate knowledge of the city brings other advantages, too. "He could lead me from the Trianon to the Vatican in ten minutes—as free of the one as of the other, no doubt; and he smiled naughtily as he admitted that his love of observation took him into many queer places" (38). Launched by Deering, the narrator proceeds (chapter by chapter) to assemble his sketchbook of Roman pictures—a Baedeker of social impressions, all traced with delicate irony—narrating his encounters with a humorous variety of British and European types, most of whom seem somewhat incongruous in their languid, Latin setting.

Years before, when Lubbock had come to Italy with his then companion Oliffe Richmond, he sent back a satiric vignette of the kind of people whom E. M. Forster recently had immortalized in *A Room with a View* (1908): "*Lor*," he exclaimed to Lapsley,

> the English who live at Florence—so desperately Italian, so solidly British. It seemed to me wonderful to be able, as so many of them are, to extract such fattening sustenance out of a diet of the view from Fiesole & the "charm" of the

place & the quattrocento & the rest of it. I can picture nymphs & sylphs feeding on such things by moonlight, & growing the more ethereal. But the Florentine Britons seem to champ at the delicate dish & wipe their mouths & take a nap & grow sleek as though after a heavy meal. How *do* they manage it? It is somehow as though rose-leaves *become* chops as they eat them.[167]

Changing his setting to Rome, in his later novel Lubbock maintains a similarly critical point of view, from which his narrator certainly is not exempt. As one of the few people who have commented on this book has observed, "[T]he 'I' in the story is made out to be quite as odd a specimen as any he meets. The commentary on people, either in short attacks quickly over, or in full-length reels of candid camera, is the most triumphant of innocent-sounding satire."[168] Nothing better confirms the narrator's "oddness" than the book's dramatic climax—a classic locus of homosexual panic, albeit comically rendered. Sharing an afternoon in an artist's studio with Miss Gadge, admiring the pictures and quoting lines from Browning to one another, the narrator (whose desire is all for the painter, Mr. Vickery, not for her) almost chokes when sentimental Miss Gadge begins to chant some lines from "Rabbi ben Ezra" to him.

> "Grow old along with me—" she intoned the lines in a hoarse and quavering wail; and I broke out on her with a passionate cry, though it remained unheard, over the depth of her misunderstanding. If a wish could have struck her in the face she would have reeled on the spot; but though I had struck her I couldn't have made her understand how completely she mistook my feeling. "It's not *that*," I might have burst out, "not in the least like *that*!"—and how should she have understood that my sudden interest in Mr. Vickery was larger and rarer and stranger than that of a "Browning-lover," even of one who could intone the chant of the Rabbi from end to end. (195–96)

Disentangling himself from Miss Gadge, the narrator at last meets up again with Deering, only now to see the extent to which his cicerone, "perverse and double-lived," has deceived him (220). Far from being a cosmopolitan *flaneur*, indifferent to the claims of genteel expatriate society, all along Deering has been taking up his station behind a Marchesa's samovar, dutifully serving tea (with his "Botticelli hands") to his aunt's guests in her "patched and tattered saloon"

(221, 218). (Much like one of James's characters, this relative, the Marchesa, had married an impoverished Italian nobleman.) The "Rome" to which Deering has enticed the narrator turns out to be as British as Devonshire, after all.

Reviewers of the novel were quick to note its many Jamesian echoes—the *Times Literary Supplement* even going so far as to assert that "if Henry James had not written, these scenes could probably never have been written. The niceties of reference, social and moral, draw one back involuntarily to the great explorer of such things; and now and then Mr. Lubbock has a phrase or an epithet which a little too decidedly recalls the master. Still, not less truly, the touch in this book is his own."[169] Judging from contemporaneous reviews, traces of the Master's hand were more evident still in Lubbock's next work of fiction, *The Region Cloud*. According to the *Saturday Review*, in that novel Lubbock "adopted from his master everything—the ethics, the subject, the point of view, the style, even the mannerisms."[170] What none of these reviewers perceived, however, is that both fictions more accurately might be seen as reflexes against James's influence: especially because in both books the images of the characters who most resemble James collapse into a kind of banal parody of him.

Suggestively enough, Lubbock takes the title of his second (and last) novel from Sonnet 33, Shakespeare's bittersweet testament of disaffection from his former lover.

Full many a glorious morning have I seen
Flatter the mountain-tops with sovereign eye,
Kissing with golden face the meadows green,
Gilding pale streams with heavenly alchemy;
Anon permit the basest clouds to ride
With ugly rack on his celestial face,
And from the forlorn world his visage hide,
Stealing unseen to west with this disgrace:
Even so my sun one early morn did shine
With all-triumphant splendor on my brow;
*But out, alack! he was but one hour mine,*
*The region cloud hath mask'd him from me now.*
Yet him for this my love no whit disdaineth:
Suns of the world may stain when heaven's sun staineth.

Ignoring the rather hollow consolation of the sonnet's concluding couplet, Lubbock inscribed lines 11 and 12 (italicized in the quotation) as his book's epigraph, emphasizing the poem's darker undertones of betrayal and abandonment. As we have seen, *Roman Pictures* glances at similar themes, but in the earlier novel they are overwritten with comic flourishes and self-deprecating irony. In *The Region Cloud*, however, the disciple Austin's infatuation with the all-too-Masterly painter Channon is much more starkly autobiographical, and the novel's characteristic mood, far from sprightly, approaches an almost gothic intensity. In an opening scene that echoes that of "A Passionate Pilgrim" (1871), the earliest of his tales that James included in the New York Edition, Austin first encounters Channon in the dining room of a country inn. Despite the attractions of French cuisine, the young man is distracted from "his wondrous meal" by his sudden recognition of the great man's presence at the other end of the room. In rapt attention, he sits with his elbows on the table to balance his chin and steady his gaze, "his great bright eye wide open to the morning."[171] (With the novel's Shakespearean epigraph on the preceding page, the borrowed metaphor here is not difficult to trace.) The tableau of what his eyes take in is so suggestive that it warrants full quotation:

> The man of honour sat perfectly still at his table facing the light of the side-window. Vulturine he almost seemed, with the sweep of thin grey plumage off his forehead and the high-pitched bone of his nose; he watched, he was vigilant in tranquillity, and yet he was absorbed, he was dreamful in alertness, as though he commanded so large and free a prospect that the lightest movement couldn't escape him anywhere, lost as he was in his inward visions. He sank his chin upon his hands, and the pressure thrust out his big underlip, and now he looked potent and immemorial like an image, like an idol brooding over long histories that nobody else remembered; but with power in him, too, to frighten an intruder, even a distant worshipper at the other end of the room, if he chose to use it. The ridge of his brow and the hollow of his cheek were acutely modelled in the whiteness of the light; the lines of his face were printed so plainly that you could read—you could have read the unknown histories in them if you had known the language. Everything was written in his face; not bluntly, not coarsely, but with swift and capable strokes—as though the hand of life, tracing his histories, hadn't faltered or fumbled over a syllable; so that the tale ran forward unbroken,

from his high forehead to his radiant eye, from the breadth of his cheek-bone to the sudden force of his chin. But the language was the difficulty, though Austin in the luxury of his intelligence might begin to think that *he* could almost understand it. These other folk, casual tourists and bagmen and such, they too looked inquisitively at that brilliant head; but they hadn't the eyes to take it in, not they. It was a sight for Austin, for no one else. (8–9)

Lubbock could easily have had Alvin Langdon Coburn's 1906 profile image of Henry James in front of him as he composed this paragraph, so strongly do his words reflect the features that the photographer's camera then captured.

Henry James, as photographed by Alvin Langdon Coburn in 1906. From *Men of Mark* (Duckworth, 1913). Courtesy of the Houghton Library (f Horblit TypPh 905.13.2938).

Austin's gaze, of course, is almost as powerful as that of its object: in fact, *his* fixed attention captures the eye of the other, who then walks down the length of the dining room to meet him; and from that point forward, the two men share an intimacy of intellect and feeling that jealously can admit no others.

As their relationship deepens, Channon's incomparable powers of psychological penetration (altogether Jamesian) allow him to intuit and almost effortlessly give voice to Austin's innermost desires and ambitions.

> "So, then, you are alone, you are hungry, you are insecure; and what about your ambition—is it still fairly hard and bright?—or do you find that squalor has bitten into it, dinginess invaded it, so that it isn't the lovely weapon it was when you took it in hand at first? But of course—you have answered that question already; so long as a man is certain in his mind that trash is trash his ambition has kept its shine. And some day accordingly the world will acknowledge that your ideas, your style, your newspaper-stuff, your books when they are written, have brought a new and real and indestructible fact into being—is that it?" (41–42)

Channon almost mocks the same dreary hallmarks to be found in Lubbock's dilettantish career—his "newspaper-stuff" and seemingly-always-unwritten books—especially as they must have seemed to James during the period in which he watched Lubbock scramble for his living. But soon their talk turns more serious, as Channon shares with the rapt disciple the chronicle of a consummate artist's slow self-discovery of his genius, a discovery that necessarily has isolated him from other men but has not extinguished his desire for the truest form of companionship: the shared fraternity of art. They are standing in a deserted moonlit square, when suddenly Channon turns to him and says,

> "My friend, ghost that you seem to me, I—I think I've found you; I never found you before." They stood squarely and looked at each other; but Channon had his back to the mounting moon, and it might have been only the quake in his voice that made Austin aware of the charged intensity of his face. An appeal, yes: not a command, not a permission, neither imperial nor condescending, but a call from a friend to a friend, an equal to an equal: this was the gesture of Channon's hand, once more, as he stretched it out to Austin. (49)

Soon after, when Austin is first admitted to Channon's private residence and gallery, tears irresistibly well up in the young man's eyes and begin to trail down his face.

> He was all alone in the middle of the shining floor, the hushed splendour of the place was around him, and that which flooded his brain was as sweet and as painful as love itself. "I am here—it is this!" Love isn't eloquent in words, it may be; but the lover knows the queer ache of desperation that is behind the poor plain words. (55)

The reviewer who noticed that "in the relation of the two men there is only the faintest suggestion of the motif of Dorian Gray" must have been politely tone-deaf, for the novel's depiction of Austin's homoerotic absorption in Channon is anything but subtle.[172]

The acolyte's infatuation is complete when he is installed as the great artist's private secretary, seeing to all the details of the painter's professional life: arranging his appointments with sitters and patrons, keeping his "little note-books and papers" (89). As Austin's quasi-religious instantiation with the Master advances, however, the narrative voice somewhat sardonically discloses considerable evidence of the Great Man's fraudulent nature. His Religion of Art turns out to be a Gospel of Philistinism, and the temple in which he practices it the very crossroads of Mayfair and the Exchange. His genius can be measured (and paid for) at a pound a minute. At last he confesses the truth to Austin point blank: "'The whole of my work is a witness to the fact that I'm vulgar—look at it!'" (190). This lesson of the Master is, indeed, the lesson of James's "The Lesson of the Master" (1888); but for Austin it is a lesson learned too late. To further the tautology, the novel's structure also betrays a lesson of the Master that Lubbock failed sufficiently to appreciate: his handling of point of view has the effect of diluting—rather than concentrating—the book's dramatic intensity. The very key to Austin's character is his acutely sensitive intelligence, which makes his blindness to Channon's (to us, increasingly obvious) vulgarity anomalous and dissatisfying.

If nothing else, the cruel inversions of this story and its predecessor suggest a writer struggling to make whole or reconcile violently competing elements of himself and his personal history. Just as important, as he was working on these books, Lubbock threw himself into a rather tempestuous affair with Adrian

Graham, a young painter—almost twenty years Lubbock's junior—who had been the first official war artist on the western front.[173] Most of Lubbock's close friends (and sometime lovers) were appalled by his infatuation—or, just as likely, by the indiscreet ways in which he betrayed it. Somewhat waspishly, Gaillard Lapsley suggested that for once Lubbock "had met someone in whom he was more interested than himself." Arthur Benson, just as hurt, sensed a wrongful disproportion in the outpouring of Lubbock's affection. "Howard Sturgis loved the Babe and H. James loved Hugh Walpole," he wrote in his diary, "—but neither H.S. nor H.J. were ever under any illusions whatever as to the Babe's or H. Walpole's intellect or character or superiority. It is a horrible dethronement of Percy's inflexible power of valuation."[174] Having gone to France with Graham early in 1924, Lubbock proposed that they visit Edith Wharton, who by then had purchased a home outside Paris, the Pavillon Colombe at St. Brice-sous-Forêt. "What a queer turn on the wheel!" she chuckled to Lapsley:

> Two or three weeks ago I had a line from Percy saying that he & a "young friend" were going to settle down at Arles to write & paint for several weeks on their way to Italy . . . two or three days later they turned up here, evidently very ready to be taken in. (You remember that Percy had sternly given me to understand that he would on no account favour me with his presence this winter!) Well—luckily I had room & gladly took them in. Percy was as radiant as a new bridegroom (somewhat in the same manner), & so conversible that the moments flew. The young man is decidedly intelligent, & made a pleasant impression. Mais c'est lui qui tend la joue [But he offers up his cheek for kisses], & Percy rather too visibly salutes it! It was all rather funny & pathetic.[175]

With James no longer there to ground all of their affections, and the cozy queer hospitality of Qu'acre but a fading memory (Howard Sturgis had died in 1920), the remaining members of Wharton's inner circle were drifting further apart—and not just geographically.

Wharton was especially taken aback by Lubbock's behavior because, just the preceding winter, she had watched (with ever-increasing dissatisfaction) his doting attentions to Sybil Scott at Villa Medici, from which Geoffrey by then had absented himself. Sybil, notorious for her fainting spells and seemingly perpetual bouts of sickness, readily availed herself of Lubbock's nursing companionship, in exchange for which, of course, he could live in otherwise leisured splendor. Even Graham's intimate company could not keep Lubbock long away from Florence. After leaving Wharton at Ste. Claire (her other residence, at Hyères, on the French Riviera) that spring, the two men went to Italy for a "perfect Venetian fortnight" (as Lubbock described it to Lapsley); just days after that interlude, however, Graham returned to London and Lubbock was back at Sybil's bedside in Fiesole.[176] Having seen this rival for her friends' attention snatch up Berenson first, then Scott, and now (possibly) Lubbock, Wharton was deeply suspicious of Sybil's motives. One only wonders what she thought if she happened to read Somerset Maugham's 1925 short story, "The Most Selfish Woman I Ever Knew"—an almost naked exposé of a hypochondriacal egotist who manages to outlast all of her various husbands, shamelessly lives off their inherited money, and also, like Sybil, has a daughter named Iris. Certainly, Wharton's feelings were not much different from those voiced by the story's narrator, who can't suppress his rage upon hearing that the woman's daughter is putting off her marriage so that she can continue nursing her delirious mother. "'I suppose it's never struck you as strange,'" he says to his target, "'that you're always strong enough to do anything you want to and that your weak heart only prevents you from doing things that bore you? . . . I think you're the most selfish and monstrous woman I have ever known. You ruined the lives of those two wretched men you married and now you're going to ruin the life of your daughter.'"[177] Maugham's—and Wharton's—premonitions would soon, in fact, come true.

Late in 1925, Percy Lubbock wrote Wharton from Fiesole, bemoaning the "strangeness and hardness of life" that forced him, helplessly, to witness the final breakdown of the Scotts' marriage. In the same mail, coincidentally, came Lubbock's new novel, *The Region Cloud*, with a promotional flyer, the language of which left Wharton gaping at the almost grotesque incongruity suggested by the juxtaposition of his letter and his book. After sharing her disgust with Lapsley (sensing that Lubbock really was just lying in wait for Geoffrey to be out of the picture), Wharton invited her correspondent to consider next a blurb she had clipped from the advertisement for *The Region Cloud*: "Two men, one at the full height of his power and fame and conscious of his genius; the other [Wharton's underlining] young and starved and critical and fastidious; they meet, and in this book is a picture of the year during which their alliance began and ended."[178]

Given all she had seen recently of Lubbock's emotional (and sexual) vacillations, the contrast was too unsettling. On the one hand, here was Lubbock (like Geoffrey Scott before him), a kind of heteronormative *manque*, clutching at Sybil's fathomless (but enviably rich) fatuity; on the other, here was Lubbock, the queerest of disciples, just the kind of sensitive young gentleman ("critical and fastidious") whom we find in so many of the Master's works. "Percy's book is indeed a strange product in the light of his private affairs," she confided to Lapsley. "I was told yesterday (via London): 'Oh, yes, Lady S. is divorcing Scott to marry Percy Lubbock.' It all makes me rather sick—for him."[179] That same winter, Lubbock accompanied Sybil on a trip up the Nile, where presumably she had gone for the benefit of the arid climate. When they returned to Florence, she immediately demanded a divorce from Geoffrey Scott (we've seen the peculiar way by which he complied with *that* request) and would wed Percy Lubbock several months later.

During his trip to Egypt, Lubbock's correspondence with his other acquaintances dropped off. Still, he managed to send Arthur Benson a rather curious missive (much like the clandestine one he had sent Lapsley years before from Algeria). "Percy is *hopeless*," Benson noted. "He sent me a p[ost] c[ard] to say he couldn't write—he was too much absorbed by the sight of pretty black boys & golden sands."[180] When Lubbock's engagement to Sybil eventually was made known, it would have been difficult for his closest friends not to have pause. As he was steaming aboard an ocean liner en route to Ceylon (where he and Sybil were to be married), Lubbock wrote an obviously pained letter to Lapsley, confessing the hurt that "the cackle of the so thoughtful & considerate world" had inflicted upon them. "Even with the experience of my many years I have been amazed by the amount of distress, real harm even, that people are ready to cause just by their inability *not* to cackle & chatter about things that don't concern them & of which they can't possibly know the truth."[181] Much of that cackle and chatter came from Edith Wharton, who was appalled by Lubbock's impending marriage. (Scorning what she considered Sybil's superannuated sexuality, she scoffed, "Oh these lubric grandmothers! They make me sick!")[182] When, three years later, Geoffrey Scott died penniless in New York, Wharton's bitterness was complete. Her relationship with Lubbock would never recover.

Painfully estranged from then on, Lubbock and Wharton still would spar for control of Henry James's memory. Wharton devoted many of the best pages of her 1934 autobiography, *A Backward Glance*, to her recollections of James, giving her a final opportunity to consecrate "a Henry that *no one* else knew . . . *the* Henry that we had," the beloved center of her once sacred inner circle.[183] Somewhat ironically, when she needed help recovering key facts and anecdotes about the Master (including the most famous one she repeated, the words James is supposed to have uttered at the onset of his first stroke: "So here it is at last, the distinguished thing!"), she was obliged to turn to Lubbock for assistance. But, alienated as they then were, she implored their (still) mutual friend Gaillard Lapsley to intervene on her behalf and ferret out the details. When Lapsley pressed him for answers, Lubbock rather wearily responded, "Yes, I can answer these two questions—but O dear me, how strange, how strange & sad that she shouldn't put them straight to me—& I answer them straight to her."[184] When, four years later, he read in the *Times* of Wharton's death, Lubbock again wrote to Lapsley, ruefully lamenting the years of silence that had kept her confidences from him. "It means to me the closure of so much," he sighed, "—even though so much *had* been closed; or rather perhaps it means, quite differently, the re-opening of everything: of all the old days, and all the delight and the laughter and the charmed interest that was in them."[185]

In the memorial volume, *Portrait of Edith Wharton*, which Lapsley (as her literary executor) commissioned Lubbock to compile, the Master's remaining custodian tried sincerely to recover the feeling of those old days, canvassing Wharton's broad acquaintance for chronicles of friendship and treasures of anecdote and then artfully stitching together the responses he received into a very readable book. No doubt remembering Lubbock's dutiful service to James, Lapsley first had imagined that his friend would (more narrowly) edit a collection of Wharton's letters; but Percy persuaded him to consider a different kind of volume. "I should say," Lubbock urged, "that she never really got herself into her letters, never really talked in them with the sound of her voice, never brought one her actual company in her letters: as for instance (in their so different ways) H. J. did, and Howard [Sturgis], and A. C. B[enson]. Or rather she did at times, but only in times and circumstances of entire privacy, where there could be no question of publication."[186] In the rest of his response to Lapsley, Lubbock outlined exactly the kind of book he would eventually compile, although Sybil's perpetual ill health and the scourge of the Second World War (during which the Lubbocks were obliged to seek refuge in Switzerland, where Sybil died in 1943) prevented him from completing the project for another decade. Inevitably, Lubbock would remember Wharton as herself the quintessential Jamesian subject—gilded by wealth and blest with "skill, grace, intelligence, all of the best, flashing across to meet this Europe on the highest terms, any terms she pleased—she had only to make her own." But with his instinct for a fine phrase, ever so slightly barbed, he summed her up by saying that "she was herself a novel of his, no doubt in his earlier manner."[187] In this contest of two Jamesian disciples, Percy Lubbock would have the last word. Wharton's literary reputation would be shadowed by this patronizing judgment for decades to come, her works always viewed as lesser versions when compared with those of the Master.[188]

# Modernist Ventriloquism

## *In Memoriam*

Henry James's decision to become a British subject, just months before he suc-
cumbed to a series of strokes, had a profound and lingering influence upon
the modern debate about his proper place in literary history. Almost all the
significant works of James criticism in the first decades after his death in 1916
voice contentious arguments about the author's national allegiance and identity and the possibly debilitating effect that expatriation had upon his aesthetic
development. Already anticipating this reaction, James's lifelong friend William Dean Howells had wanted to forestall—or even preempt—the question
of deracination by writing a definitive estimate of the Master, a tribute that
he would call "The American James," explicitly to emphasize the writer's national fidelities. The invitation to write such a commemorative essay came less
than a week after death had claimed his friend, and Howells was eager to seize
the opportunity afforded to him. The two writers had shared almost a lifetime
of literary fraternity—dating all the way back to Howells's arrival in Cambridge, whence he had come (in 1866) to assume the assistant editorship of the
*Atlantic Monthly*. "No one knew James as I did," Howells wrote to the editor of
*Harper's Monthly*; and he promised that a substantial essay ("biographical, personal, critical") soon would follow. Howells saw no reason why the magazine
shouldn't advertise his contribution immediately. His close friendship with
Samuel Clemens had enabled him to complete a similar work (*My Mark Twain*,
1910) not long after that writer's death; why should anything prevent him from
doing the same kind of eulogistic tribute now for the other American author he
so deeply admired? "I will write you such a paper as I wrote about Longfellow,
about Lowell, about Holmes," Howells urged—"and better." Perhaps embarrassed by his own exuberance, the author then added a cautionary postscript
to his reply, requesting that the magazine avoid specifics and simply say that
something from him would "appear in a forthcoming number." Still, Howells
clearly wanted his audience to understand that he acknowledged a special kind

of duty to Henry James. "I should like to have it heralded," he said, "because people will naturally expect something of the kind from me, and perhaps wonder why they do not get it."[1]

When he sat down to memorialize James, however, Howells encountered unexpected difficulties. Writing about *this* subject proved much more problematic than eulogizing those earlier New England worthies—all pillars of the Brahmin establishment—whose cultural status then seemed beyond dispute (and therefore easy to affirm). With James the case was different. The Master's wartime renunciation of his American citizenship, however nobly inspired by a desire to attest "the force of [his] attachment and devotion to England and to the cause for which she [was] fighting,"[2] still was an act that Howells found hard to stomach. The bitter experience—and then memory—of Britain's neutrality during the Civil War had long since soured Howells's view of England (in almost all of his novels, characters of British descent are represented as pretentious cads or society snobs); even an honorary degree from Oxford, awarded in 1904, could not pacify his deeply ingrained Anglophobia. When rumors of James's intention to become a British citizen first reached him, Howells was rather stunned: the prospect of his friend's denationalization cut to a kind of democratic nerve. "Are you ready to join with James in renouncing Wilson and swearing fealty to King Jorge?" the somewhat shaken writer asked another of the Master's oldest American friends; "or don't you believe he's done it, or means to?" While acknowledging that James's situation was different—he had lived in England for so long—Howells refused to qualify his own democratic allegiance to the republic he still fiercely loved. "Nothing could persuade me," he flatly said, "to bow the knee to e'er a crowned head of them all."[3] America's later entry into the war made it easier for Howells to sympathize with James's motives, but in the spring of 1916 he still could not easily reconcile them with either official US policy or public opinion, which had long been suspicious of James's patriotism. When Harper's refused to pay the much-inflated price (twenty-five hundred dollars) Howells had demanded for his essay, the author seemed almost grateful for the excuse not to finish it. "I doubt now whether I shall ever write the paper," he confided to his editor—"certainly if I do it will not be immediately."[4]

In fact, Howells had made a running start on the article (he said as much when he wrote to name his price for it) but then laid his manuscript aside. Four years later, when Lubbock's two-volume edition of James's letters appeared, Howells once again felt an obligation to commemorate their friendship, and he began to write a notice of the *Letters of Henry James* for the "Editor's Easy Chair" column in *Harper's* that still carried his venerable byline. One short month after Lubbock's edition arrived on his desk, however, Howells was dead. A partial draft of this review was later found among the author's papers, however; and when Mildred Howells published the *Life in Letters of William Dean Howells* in 1928, she included this document (together with what the author had begun of "The American James") as a kind of appendix to her second volume—a fitting coda, as she must have felt, to honor her father's long-standing friendship with a fellow writer. The text of the "Easy Chair" essay she printed, however, deliberately concealed Howells's conflicted response to his subject, as careful study of the manuscript will confirm. A full transcription of the author's draft will give the best visual evidence of the extent to which Howells was compelled literally to overwrite his first critical impulses in order to suppress a kind of recriminatory nationalism that kept spilling from his pen. Comparing Howells's much-made-over draft for his intended review of the *Letters of Henry James* to the sanitized text circulated by Howells's daughter (see pages 113–116), we can see that unintended (and even seemingly willful) errors of transcription—and the deliberate omission of its most curious final sentences—give the published text a chummy atmosphere of fraternal harmony that the manuscript does not consistently attest. Again and again, for example, Howells must suppress initial phrasings that serve to accentuate—rather than qualify—James's essential foreignness to America. Howells first concedes, for example, that James had an unabashed "love of alien ideals," but then he mutes this to say instead that "foreign conditions and forms" were objects of his friend's "adoration." If at first James "grew more English" ("in the course of his long life in England"), Howells revises this to insist—to the contrary—that in all James's time abroad "he did not grow less American." If America rejected James, "it must be owned," Howells first wrote, "that he paid us back in kind"—an unsparing allegation (with its retributive first-person plural pronoun, *us*) that the author then crossed out. Even more revealing are the last two sentences of the draft (suppressed altogether by Mildred), which call attention to "the sense"—as Howells delicately puts it—of James's "oddity." Howells's stammering approach to that coded word for homosexuality nevertheless conveys the unusually physical quality of James's epistolary manner of address and his own struggle to understand it. James seems forever to be clasping his friends (all of them male) "closer and closer . . . more and more personally and publicly." This cumulative rhetoric of intimacy rattles the reviewer, who finds it all "a strange exhibition to say the least." (And this after Lubbock, at Harry's insistence, already had omitted the more extravagant salutations!) If nothing else, we can safely say that Howells's daughter exhibited a custodial instinct much akin to that of the Jameses. The Master's officially sanctioned memory was faithfully reiterated in her pages.

Many other writers shared Howells's commemorative impulse, and, less encumbered by conflicted feelings, they were able more quickly (and surely) to compose and publish their tributes to the Master. One of the first—and best— was written by the indefatigable Arthur Christopher Benson, who, somewhat remarkably, had five thousand words ready for the *Cornhill* within a week after James's death. Benson's memories of James went back more than thirty years, and from them he culled some that would become staple material for later biographers: James as the stately proprietor of Lamb House, whose speech was as finely crafted as an "impassioned soliloquy," yet unpremeditated, welling up "out of a reservoir of fancy, emotion and language which seemed inexhaustible." Possessing, too, a large bundle of James's letters, Benson found it irresistible to quote from them. "If there be a wisdom," James had written to him, "in not feeling, to the last throb, the great things that happen to us, it is a wisdom that I shall never either know or esteem. Let your soul live—it's the only life that isn't on the whole a sell." In this correspondence, stretching over decades, Benson also discovered the same "sense of growing freedom and controlled exuberance" that, with increasing age, characterized the Master's private conversation. (The earlier letters, Benson felt, were "serious and a little ceremonious"; but in the later ones, "the epigram melts out, to be replaced by the far finer and deeper gift of metaphor,—never simile, but a hidden image tinging the sentence with colour.") Lubbock's edition of the Master's letters, four years to come, would offer ample evidence in support of Benson's claim.[5] Indeed, the publication of the *Letters of Henry James* provided the occasion for several of his other close friends and disciples—Bosanquet, Gosse, Wharton—not merely to offer their own personal testaments but also to advance particular claims as privileged custodians of the Master's memory.[6]

"Editor's Easy Chair." Left column: The typographical symbols and devices indicate the author's deletions and interlinear emendations. A subscript caret within brackets ([∧]) at the end of a phrase indicates the end of material inserted interlineally; at the beginning of a phrase it indicates the beginning of material inserted interlineally when Howells did not write a caret. Manuscript from William Dean Howells Papers (MS Am 1784.16 [6]), by permission of the Houghton Library, Harvard University. Right column: Text from *Life in Letters of William Dean Howells*, ed. Mildred Howells, 2 vols. (Garden City, NY: Doubleday-Doran, 1928), 2:394–97.

## Manuscript

*Editor's Easy Chair*

[1] ~~Probably s So strangely~~ The Letters of Henry James which his biographer, Mr. Percy Lubbock has ~~put~~ [∧]lately[∧] put together and ~~so massively~~ put forth in two massive volumes holding well a thousand pages form a literary document of ~~unequaled ch~~ [∧]a[∧] nature and character which we should ~~look~~ [∧]seek[∧] far ~~and~~ ∧to find and[∧] fail to find the like of. The reason is that there ~~never~~ has been but one Henry James, and that he ~~wrote in~~ poured himself out in letters such as no other man knew how to write or could help writing. They are addressed to ∧half[∧] a hundred or a hundred different men and women, mostly English but more largely American than most Americans might think, though Americans of European texture and color, but alike in the ~~European~~ civilization which we share ~~with~~ surpassingly with the English and ~~then very sub~~ far [∧]incomparably[∧] less with the French. ~~It is~~ ∧These letters form[∧] the report of English life in an inalienably American soul, for American was what James remained through all the perversities of his expatriation, and his ~~love of~~ adoration of ~~alien~~ ∧foreign[∧] ~~ideals~~ ∧conditions and[∧] forms; and he throws himself into them with ~~a passion~~ [∧] an ardor[∧] of ~~friendship, of~~ sympathy ~~of passion~~ which ~~are~~ [∧]is[∧] of the same ~~sincerity~~ [∧]quality[∧] whomever ~~they the [gloss] letters address, whether old or young, akin or~~ he wishes to win ~~by his appeal~~ to his embrace. The range of his ~~correspondence~~ correspondents is every age and

## Text from *Life in Letters of WDH*

*Editor's Easy Chair*

[1] The letters of Henry James which his biographer, Mr. Percy Lubbock, has lately put together and put forth in two massive volumes holding a thousand pages form a literary document of a nature and character which we should seek far to find, and fail to find, the like of. The reason is that there has been but one Henry James, and that he poured himself out in letters such as no other man knew how to write or he could help writing. They are addressed to half a hundred different men and women, mostly English but more largely American than most Americans might think, though American of European texture and color, but alike in the civilization which we share surprisingly with the English and incomparably with the French. These letters form the report of English life in an inalienably American soul, for American is what James remained through all the perversities of his expatriation, and his adoration of foreign conditions and forms, and he throws himself into them with an ardor of sympathy which is of the same quality whomever he wishes to win to his embrace. The range of his correspondents is of every age and he

he greets them all with the same effusion in which there is no question of his ~~aff~~ sincerity.

[2] The letters begin with those addressed to ~~the his~~ written to his father and mother and his ~~brothers~~ from his repatriation in Paris after his exile in America where he came to his literary consciousness and mainly continue ~~to~~ through the forty years of ~~the~~ his home in England, where he did not succeed in becoming English, even by the formal renunciation of his nationality. This may be said with no cast of censure, for James was American to his heart's core to the ~~death~~ day of his death. He may ~~succeed~~ have made the English think him English; he may have made himself think so; but he was never anything but American, ~~th and~~ though by early ~~educat~~ sojourn and schooling he was French. He renounced us because he was rightly ashamed of our official, never our national, neutrality in the world's self-defence against Germany, an attitude which we now all feel so grotesque and contemptibble, and must remember with ~~self-~~loathing. Of course we must ~~feel his~~ regard his means of saying so, of doing so, as ineffectual, but it was not the less ~~sincere~~ [^]unselfish[^] and self-sacrificial.

[3] It at least enlarged him to the fellow~~ship~~ citizenship of the largest ~~and and~~ civilization in the world and enabled him to clasp in the same ~~same~~ ardor ~~of the~~ this [^]civilization in the[^] same embrace with the Americanism which he could not really undo in his nature.

[4] In his very interesting and interested study of James's nature and character, Mr. Lubbock who edits his letters, has not been able ~~to search~~ search [^]quite to make[^] him out, for some very simple reasons. ~~He fails to~~ [^]One of these is that he[^] ignores the ~~simple reason~~ [^]cause[^] of James's going to live abroad which was that he was a sick man who was less a sufferer in Europe than in America. He was better in Paris than in Boston where he was always suffering and when his

greets them with the same effusion in which there is no question of his sincerity.

[2] The letters begin with those addressed by the writer to his father and mother and his brothers from his repatriation in Paris, after his exile in America where he came to his literary consciousness and mainly continued, through the forty years of his homes in England where he did not succeed in becoming English, even by the formal renunciation of his nationality. This may be said with no cast of censure, for James was American to his heart's core to the day of his death. He may have made the English think him English; he may have made himself think so; but he was never anything but American, though by early sojourn and schooling he was French. He renounced us because he was rightly ashamed of our official, never our national, neutrality in the world's self-defence against Germany, an attitude which we now all feel so grotesque and contemptible, and must remember with loathing. Of course we must regard his means of saying so, of doing so, as ineffectual, but it was not the less unselfish and self-sacrificial.

[3] It at least enlarged him to the fellow-citizenship of the largest civilization in the world and enabled him to clasp with the same ardor this civilization in the same embrace with the Americanism which he could not really undo in his nature.

[4] In his very interesting and interested study of James's nature and character, Mr. Lubbock, who edits his

brief French sojourn became his English life of forty years ~~the~~ it was not mainly because he was better in England, but it was more and more largely so. The climate was kinder to him than ours; and the ~~country was~~ life was kinder than his native ~~air~~ [^]life[^] and his native land. In fact America was never kind to James. It was rude and harsh, unworthily and stupidly ~~so~~ so, as we must more and more own, if we would be true to ourselves. We ~~own to~~ ought to be ashamed of our part in this; the nearest of his friends in Boston would say ~~he~~ they liked him, but they could not bear his ~~literature~~ [^]fiction[^]; and ~~they were not aware that that their personal liking on these terms was an insult from people~~ [^]and the people, especially the [^^]women ~~of the~~[^^] ~~smaller Boston scattere~~ conscious[^] of culture, especially women, ~~in places where opinion~~ [^]throughout New England, ~~and the~~[^] ~~out in country places where opinion was formed, he had~~ [^]he had sometimes[^] outright insult. At the same time ~~he~~ ,his work anomalously[^] found ~~the gr~~ favor with editors who eagerly sought ~~his work for all~~ [^]it in all[^] the leading periodicals. ~~The case was very anomalous, and it It~~ The ,case[^] was not ~~very~~ different in England when he went to live there except that the ,popular[^] ~~dislike was not united nor the so outrage~~ [^]and the editorial[^] rejection and contumely[^] ~~were not[^]~~ which met it ~~at home~~ ,were neither so ~~noisy~~ vicious nor so generous.[^] But a public grew up in England such as never grew up in America, ~~if not more~~ and made England more ~~home~~ like home to him. [^]It was fine[^]

[5] ~~It must be owned that he paid us back in kind, and dealt as though in terms~~ in him, ~~and sweet that h~~ that he was able to use him to the conditions, and it is fine that in the course of his long life in England that ~~grew more English~~ he did not grow less American. There is a tenderness in his remembrance of ~~A~~ America which ~~indeed~~ does not appear in his ~~cor~~ [^]printed[^] ~~frequent~~

letters, has not been able quite to make him out, for some very simple reasons. One of these is that he ignores the cause of James's going to live abroad which was that he was a sick man who was less a sufferer in Europe than in America. He was better in Paris than in Boston where he was always suffering and when his brief French sojourn became his English life of forty years it was not mainly because he was better in England, but it was more and more largely so. The climate was kinder to him than ours, and the life was kinder than his native life, and his native land. In fact America was never kind to James. It was rude and harsh, unworthily and stupidly so, as we must more and more own, if we would be true to ourselves. We ought to be ashamed of our part in this; the nearest of his friends in Boston would say they liked him, but they could not bear his fiction; and from the people, conscious of culture, throughout New England, especially the women, he had sometimes outright insult. At the same time his work unanimously found favor with editors who eagerly sought it in all the leading periodicals. The case was not very different in England when he went to live there except that the popular rejection and contumely which met it were neither so vicious nor so general. But a public grew up in Europe such as never grew up in America, and made England more like to him. It was fine [5] that he was able to use him to the conditions, and it is fine that in the course of his long life in England he did not grow

criti ₍^₎public₍^₎ printed criticism of us, but
which abounds in these letters which address
ₐthemselves₍^₎more to more Americans friends
than to English friends, and when the ₐcivic₍^₎
change, very interesting and began to work itself
out in him it was without a moment of rancour,
but never ceased from a from a fine reluctance,
tacit or relu explicit. He was deeply wounded by
our unworthy ridiculous endeavor for neutrality
where there could not be neutrality and he did
not live to witness the generous abandon that
contemptible policy. Almost w Word by word
he renounces his birthright, with self-question
with ruth, with self-compunction and ₍^₎grief₍^₎
but never with doubt of the only course ₐhe
saw₍^₎ open to him; and if our later ultimate but
still tardy embrace of the heroic part seemed to
leave him without justification that was an unfair
appearance.

[6] The These letters of this unparalleled papers
which address themselves to this friend and that
with with ₐunvarying an₍^₎ intimacy and affection
and intimacy which alone does not alone does not
vary in them. They may vary vary in from person
to person to person; but they do not vary in the
vary in the desire to clap/ clasp the friend the
friend closer and closer, to greet him with greater
and greater intima more and more closely more
and more personally and personally publicly.
It is a strange exhibition to say the least, on the
part of a being who will strike most of his new
acquaintance at the first ₐpersonal₍^₎ encounter th
as the most withdrawn. His work He writes to his
br father, his mother, with a sort of jovial burly
burliness, which seems almost grotesque, and of
a kind with the general shouting familiarity with
the rest of the letters, and must confirm them in
the sense of his oddities oddity.

less American. There is a tenderness
in his remembrance of America which
does not appear in his public printed
criticism of us, but which abounds in
the letters which address themselves
to more American friends than to
English friends, and when the change
began to work itself out in him it was
without a moment of rancor, but never
ceased from a fine reluctance, tacit
or explicit. He was deeply wounded
by our ridiculous endeavour for
neutrality where there could not
be neutrality and he did not live to
witness the abandonment of that
contemptible policy. Word by word
he renounces his birthright, with ruth,
with grief, but never with doubt of the
only course he saw open to him, and
if our ultimate but still tardy embrace
of the heroic part seemed to leave him
without justification that was an unfair
appearance.

[6] These unparalleled papers
address themselves to this friend and
that with an intimacy and affection
which alone does not vary in them.
They may vary from person to person;
but they do not vary in the desire to
clasp the friend closer and closer, to
greet him more and more personally
and publicly.

We find a somewhat different commemorative impulse among the modernist avant-garde (most notably T. S. Eliot and Ezra Pound), who acknowledged their debts to James in special numbers of London's *Egoist* and New York's *Little Review*. Perhaps even more so than Howells, both Eliot and Pound, expatriates themselves, felt a defensive need to emphasize the Master's essential Americanness, thereby to affirm their intrinsic affinities with him. Eliot contributed two brief essays to these journals. The first bore the rather solemn heading "In Memory," but even as he eulogized the Master, Eliot insisted that no one "who is not an American can *properly* appreciate James." When Eliot suggested that James's "being everywhere a foreigner was probably an assistance to his native wit," an audible trace of self-justification reverberates in his judgment. Again, when remarking upon certain similarities between Turgenev and James, this former midwesterner slyly noted, "There are advantages in coming from a large flat country which no one wants to visit," advantages that his two predecessors— and, by extension, Eliot himself—enjoyed.[7] The poet's letters also confirm the extent to which he understood his own conquest of London in Jamesian terms. Just a few months after his two commemorative essays appeared, he wrote to his mother about various social and literary triumphs, concluding, "I really think that I have far more *influence* on English letters than any other American has ever had, unless it be Henry James." ("All this sounds very conceited," he admitted, "but I am sure it is true.")[8]

When Eliot famously asserted that James "had a mind so fine that no idea could violate it,"[9] he may have been indebted to Ford Madox Ford, who had expressed a very similar insight in his earlier 1913 study of the Master, the book through which *he* first laid (rather presumptuous) claim to that writer's special legacy. Ford had observed that, in contrast to so much British and American fiction of his time, James's work was rigorously devoid of moral or political intentions. "Mr. James alone," Ford wrote, "in this entire weltering universe, has kept his head, has bestowed his sympathies upon no human being and upon no cause, has remained an observer, passionless and pitiless."[10] Eliot's even more profound appreciation of this quality in James anticipated the underlying premise of his own most seminal critical essay, "Tradition and the Individual Talent," published shortly after his two pieces on James. Taking the concept of the artist's impersonality to a much more exacting level, in "Tradition and the Individual Talent" Eliot would insist that "[t]he emotion of art is impersonal. And the poet cannot reach this impersonality without surrendering himself wholly to the work to be done."[11] Eliot learned his lessons (from the Master) well.

In "The Hawthorne Aspect," Eliot's second piece of homage, the poet sought just as emphatically to ground James in a specifically American tradition. "The really vital thing, in finding any personal kinship between Hawthorne and James," Eliot wrote, "is what James touches lightly when he says that 'the fine thing in Hawthorne is that he cared for the deeper psychology, and that, in his way, he tried to become familiar with it.'" This, for Eliot, was crucial because only through the probing exercise of "the deeper psychology" could these two novelists "grasp character through the relation of two or more persons to each other," a technique in which they differed significantly from any other British or European contemporary. "Hawthorne and James have a kind of sense," Eliot could feel, "a receptive medium, which is not of sight. Not that they fail to make you *see*, so far as necessary, but sight is not the essential sense. They perceive by antennae; and the 'deeper psychology' is here."[12] James, then, becomes the writer Hawthorne might have been, if only he had been afforded James's more cosmopolitan opportunities—the point being that Eliot would confirm the expatriate logic of this tradition not merely by becoming a British subject (as did James) but more significantly by appropriating James's notions of tradition and culture in his own critical practice. When the occasion presented itself for Eliot to define those terms, the best he could do was to refashion the Master's notorious catalogue of all the things missing from American life—the "terrible denudation," as James called it in his biography of *Hawthorne* (1879), implied by the absence of a State, a sovereign, a Church, an aristocracy, ivied ruins, a political or even a sporting class.[13] For Eliot, accordingly, culture embraces "all the characteristic activities and interests of a people," and his own enumeration of them—"Derby Day, Henley Regatta, Cowes, the twelfth of August, a cup final, the dog races, the pin table, the dart board, Wensleydale cheese, boiled cabbage cut into sections, beetroot in vinegar, nineteenth-century Gothic churches and the music of Elgar"—provides exactly the kind of solidity of specification that the Master so highly valued, giving by way of contrast even a rather demotic concreteness to the abstract absences of James's list.[14]

A similar fondness for the piling up of data is certainly a hallmark of the energetic overview of James's career that Ezra Pound contributed to the *Little Review*. Having girded his loins by, apparently, reading almost the entire canon in the two years after James's death, Pound was determined to give his readers "a Baedecker to the continent" of the Master's prose, a more-or-less chronological run-through (or "Shake Down," as he called it) of a staggering number of titles. Much like Eliot, Pound attempted to unshackle James from the petty forms of criticism that could only see and ridicule his limitations of style and subject and, instead, to refocus attention where it properly belonged. "What I have not heard," Pound urged, "is any word of the major James, of the hater of tyranny; book after early book against oppression, against all the sordid petty personal crushing oppression . . . the rights of the individual against all sorts of intangible bondage. The passion of it, the continual passion of it in this man who, fools said, didn't 'feel.' I have never yet found a man of emotion against whom idiots didn't raise this cry." At the same time, Pound also belabors the provincialism of the early James, echoing the lamentations of *Hawthorne* while transferring them, generationally, to effect his own modernist exemption from such a charge. For a poet saturated with ancient philology, James's "innocence of the classics," was nothing to boast of. "If James *had* read his classics," you can almost hear Pound tapping the ruler, "he would not have so excessively cobwebbed, fussed, blathered, worried about minor mundanities." Without such learned restraint, James too often was tempted, in Pound's view, to strive for exaggerated effects—giving pleasure, that is, but offering "amusement" in the form of "seeing cocoanuts hurled at an aunt sally." At supreme moments James, too, could be *il miglior fabbro* (the better craftsman), but Pound was not shy about pointing out perceived (or misperceived?) signs of weakness. *The Spoils of Poynton* he finds "detestable"; *The Princess Casamassima* is but an "inferior continuation of *Roderick Hudson*"; *The Wings of the Dove* and *The Golden Bowl*, so excessively overwritten, are "caviare not part of the canon (metaphors be hanged for the moment)." We certainly need not agree with Pound—yet it is hard to ignore (hard even not to admire) the audacity of some of his particular judgments. They were, indeed, *Instigations*, the title of the 1920 book in which he collected them.[15]

Even more emphatically than Eliot, in these fist-pounding paragraphs Pound also insisted upon James's unrenounceable Americanness. "No English reader," he chided, "will ever know how good are his New York and his New England; no one who does not see his grandmother's friends in the pages of the American books." Perhaps most surprisingly, Pound found exactly the words that Howells had struggled to utter—or at least commit to paper—in defense of James's ineradicable patriotism. "No other American," he claimed, "was of sufficient importance for his change of allegiance to have constituted an international act; no other American would have been welcome in the same public manner. America passes over these things," Pound lamented, "but the thoughtful cannot pass over them."[16] These energetic assertions caught the attention of at least one bedazzled reader. In the November 1918 issue of the magazine, a woman from Brooklyn wrote in to say, "The Henry James number is a great eye-opener to me. I never knew there was so much in the man."[17] Pound, who at one point confessed that his inspiration for mounting and editing the special issue most likely had struck him in a "moment of lunar imbecility," must have been pleased.[18]

## Passionate Pilgrim—or Pariah?

Running in tandem—and very much at odds—with these early moves to canonize James were other critics who wanted to discredit the criteria advanced by the Master's disciples for the validation of his cultural capital. Those who came to bury James, not to praise him, were just as eager to monopolize the Master, but they were intent upon hoisting him up as a target for parody and ridicule rather than placing him on a pedestal as a figure worthy of emulation or hero-worship. James had never been difficult to spoof—for decades his work had been fodder for literary jokesters and flag-waving editorialists (as Martha Banta graphically has shown).[19] But once he was dead (and the hagiographic outpouring from his more devoted followers had begun), a more serious line of attack came from writers who gave short shrift to the Master's preoccupation with aesthetic form and deplored his presumed detachment from, or indifference to, a deeper range of social life and experience. As the style of James's fiction became more tortured and convoluted, so, according to this view, did his themes become more tenuous—a deadly disproportion to which such critics could not be reconciled.

As we have seen, H. G. Wells mercilessly lampooned the vacuity of James's subject matter in *Boon* (1915); but neither could he refrain from chastising the Master for his ridiculous verbosity. "'Having first made sure that he has scarcely anything left to express,'" Boon avers, James

"then sets to work to express it, with an industry, a wealth of intellectual stuff that dwarfs Newton. He spares no resource in the telling of his dead inventions. He brings up every device of language to state and define. Bare verbs he rarely tolerates. He splits his infinitives and fills them up with adverbial stuffing. He presses the passing colloquialism into his service. His vast paragraphs sweat and struggle; they could not sweat and elbow and struggle more if God Himself was the processional meaning to which they sought to come. And all for tales of nothingness. . . . It is leviathan retrieving pebbles. It is a magnificent but painful hippopotamus resolved at any cost, even at the cost of its dignity, upon picking up a pea which has got into a corner of its den."[20]

Far less clownishly, Rebecca West ramped up the attack a year later in a very incisive critical study of James. Almost anticipating Van Wyck Brooks's thesis of deracination, West alleged that James's reverence for Arnoldian "culture" and the past—what "Europe" represented to him so luxuriously—encouraged "a fundamental fallacy" that perverted his understanding of contemporary life and society, so much so that he betrayed "an almost Calvinist distrust of the activities of the present." (Bosanquet's spirited defense of James becomes more understandable when we see it as a response to this earlier charge of a want of social consciousness.) "He never perceived," West alleged, "that life is always a little painful at the moment, not only at this moment but at all moments; that the wine of experience always makes a raw draught when it has just been trodden out from bruised grapes by the pitiless feet of men, that is must be subject to time before it acquires suavity. The lack of this perception matters little in his early work but it is vastly important in shaping his later phases." Such a divorce from reality could only result in the solipsistic world of *The Sacred Fount*, a book that West rather shamelessly (mis)represented as typical of James's maturity. "With sentences vast as the granite blocks of the Pyramids and a scene that would have made a site for a capital he set about constructing a story the size of a hen-house."[21] After such knowledge, what forgiveness?

More than a decade later, E. M. Forster would resuscitate (and recirculate) Wells's parodic denunciation of James in *Aspects of the Novel* (1927), but only after giving his own eviscerating analysis of *The Ambassadors*. While conceding that "the beauty that suffuses *The Ambassadors* is the reward due to a fine artist for hard work," Forster then specifies at what cost and "sacrifice" such beauty is achieved. "So enormous is the sacrifice," Forster continues, "that many readers cannot get interested in James," and he proceeds to explain why. If, as Forster thinks, James cannot write a novel unless, as a precondition, "most of human life has to disappear," the deleterious consequences of his method become painfully obvious, especially with respect to the characters who people his imagination. "They are incapable of fun," Forster writes,

> of rapid motion, of carnality, and of nine-tenths of heroism. Their clothes will not take off, the diseases that ravage them are anonymous, like the sources of their income, their servants are noiseless or resemble themselves, no social explanation of the world we know is possible for them, for there are not stupid people in their world, no barriers of language, and no poor. Even their sensations are limited. They can land in Europe and look at works of art and at each other, but that is all. Maimed creatures can alone breathe in Henry James's pages—maimed yet specialized. They remind one of the exquisite deformities who haunted Egyptian art in the reign of Akhenaton—huge heads and tiny legs, but nevertheless charming. In the following reign they disappear.[22]

Readers of Forster's novels would not have been surprised by such harsh judgments. In *The Longest Journey* (1922), Agnes Pembroke tells Rickie Elliot that she and her brother had been trying "to read out a long affair by Henry James" ("recommended [by Percy Lubbock, one suspects] in 'The Times'"). "'There was no doubt it was very good,'" Agnes admits, "'but one simply couldn't remember from one week to another what had happened.'"[23] Despite the memorable imperative enjoined in *Howard's End* ("only connect"), James was an author with whom Forster could not sympathetically link up.

Quite unwittingly, one supposes, Percy Lubbock provided powerful ammunition to James's harsher critics both through his narrow selection of the Master's letters (tilted in favor of the later years) and through some of his own editorial commentary.[24] With all his diplomacy, Lubbock had tried to present the question of James's expatriation objectively and dispassionately; but he was also forced to concede that the "decision to settle in Europe, the great step" of

James's life, though inevitable, "was none the less a decision for which he had to pay heavily, as he was himself very well aware." His apologia for the Master's sometimes rarified subject matter was also expressed in terms that critics easily could turn against James. Lubbock felt obliged to acknowledge that the world with which James sought to identify himself "was a small affair, by most of our measurements. It was a circle of sensibilities that it might be easy to dismiss as hypertrophied and over-civilised, too deeply smothered in the veils of artificial life to repay so much patient attention. Yet the little world of urbane leisure satisfied him because he found a livelier interest, always, in the results and effects and implications of things than in the groundwork itself." "With much that is common ground among educated people of our time and place," Lubbock had to grant, James "was never really in touch"; therefore, admittedly, "much of the ordinary consciousness was closed to him." One of Lubbock's broadest (and most startling) generalizations—"Henry James's genius opened and flourished in the void"—could have been the opening salvo for any anti-Jacobite still sharpening his fangs.[25]

The critic who would best exploit Lubbock's revelations and disclosures was Van Wyck Brooks, who laid out his damning assessment of the Master in *The Pilgrimage of Henry James* (1925). As a complement to his earlier study of Mark Twain (which bemoaned that writer's abandonment of the frontier in favor of the polite society of Elmira and Hartford, with which his true genius was not compatible),[26] Brooks used a similar logic when he took up the case of Henry James. By leaving the United States, Brooks argued, James had alienated himself from the true wellspring of his native talent and denied himself the opportunity to rank, ultimately, with the world's greatest novelists. "'The silent spirit of collective masses,'"—Brooks quoted from Renan's eulogy of Turgenev—"'is the source of all great things.' The great writer is the voice of his own people: *that* was the principle, the principle of which every European novelist of the first order had been a living illustration, and James had been too intelligent not to perceive it." Building his case from a tissue of (mis)quotations from James's work (especially the recently published *Letters*), Brooks nevertheless constructed a seemingly persuasive account of James's inner psychological conflicts and urged that his later fixation with questions of form was a kind of compensatory aesthetic, a brittle substitute for the more human qualities of the earlier novels and tales. In the later work the characters are intensely curious about each other, but what, in the end, do they or we come to know about them as human beings? Turning the tables on the Master, Brooks then offered a parodic inversion of the list of American deficiencies from *Hawthorne*, this time cataloguing all the things that were absent from the characters of James's later fiction:

> A dim visual image—no heart, no mind, no vitals. No interests, no attributes, no activities, no race, no philosophy. No passions, ambitions, convictions: no local habitation—scarcely a name. They collect rarities, objects of beauty, objects of price, animate and inanimate; they become aware of other people as insubstantial as themselves; they drift in a confused limbo that knows no dimensions. They are made, as William James observed, "wholly out of impalpable materials, air, and the prismatic interferences of light, ingeniously focused by mirrors upon empty space."[27]

Such deliberate imitation of James's style is the best evidence of the continuing compulsion to appropriate his critical aura.

Even in a period that was frequently hostile to James, a certain number of more academically objective studies devoted to him and his work also began to appear. Much more unobtrusively than Brooks, critics like Joseph Warren Beach, Pelham Edgar, Cornelia Pulsifer Kelley—and, to be sure, an as-yet-unknown scholar by the name of Leon Edel—published their variously discriminating appreciations of James, even though their books largely were drowned out in the popular press and restricted to very small circulation. In his truly pioneering (1918) study, Beach, for example, already had wrestled with the problem of James's social deafness, the apparent absence of "a larger social consciousness" in his fiction. "Many will be found to declare that no literature—perhaps no art of any kind—can be truly *great* in our day that is lacking in this essential element," he conceded. But Beach also recognized that James deliberately had sidestepped the more overt aspects of political and economic life. "It is idle," he concluded, "to speculate on the greater social significance he might have had with a wider social horizon. He gave us a thorough and beautiful rendering of what he *knew*; and that, I must believe, is the one thing required by art."[28] Edgar, too, offered a reasoned vindication of James's supposed limitations, holding steadfastly to the high ground of culture. "Since Matthew Arnold," he wrote in the Master's defense, "no thinker has been more fully aware of all the implications that are involved in the idea of civilization, and, as with Matthew Arnold, his fastidiousness has incurred the hostility of precisely those readers whose enlightenment was most to be desired."[29] Even though Kelley's study of James's early development never transcended the bane of its origin as a rather tedious doctoral dissertation, her work at least had a kind of scholarly competence that Brooks's sorely lacked.[30] The author of *The Pilgrimage of Henry James* baldly confessed that readers familiar with the Master's work would "observe that many phrases and even longer passages from his writings" had been incorporated in the text of his book, "usually without any indication of their source." Brooks claimed that he "resorted to this expedient" because he knew of no other way to convey "with strict accuracy at moments what he conceives to have been James's thoughts and feelings."[31] Far from achieving "strict accuracy," such pervasive wrenching of language from its original and proper context could only result in radical distortion, cleverly concealed.

Even though many critics immediately had repudiated Brooks's thesis and his slipshod methodology, *The Pilgrimage of Henry James* became a kind of critical gospel until the so-called James Revival after the Second World War. The other academic rebuttals had too little purchase and too small an audience. As one reviewer remarked about Pelham Edgar's pioneering biographical study, "[W]e assent to all Professor Edgar's judgments but while we assent we yawn—and secretly yearn for the perverse, provocative heresies of Van Wyck Brooks."[32] The *New York Times* had to agree. "It is very difficult, not to say impossible, to accept Henry James as an American novelist," that paper opined: "his is not an American reaction to the American scene."[33]

Worse yet, the influential cultural historian Vernon Louis Parrington crudely redacted Brooks's image of James in his monumental three-volume *Main Currents in American Thought*, a work of "Progressive" history that would hold sway in American colleges and universities for at least a generation. Even though Parrington never lived to complete the final volume of his trilogy, we can easily assume that he would have had nothing complimentary to say about James, whom he dismissed in his preliminary outline sketch as a "self-deceived romantic, the last subtle expression of the genteel, who fell in love with culture and never realized how poor a thing he worshipped." Following Brooks's lead and logic, Parrington damned James for seeking out "other lands, there to refine a meticulous technique, and draw out ever thinner the substance of his art."[34] Some of Parrington's reviewers even delighted in his gross disproportions. As one of them jibed, "If six times as much space is devoted to the financial manipulations of Jay Cooke as to the life and work of Henry James, it is because the author *is* throughout primarily concerned rather with the economic and political life of America."[35] That, ostensibly, was a subject to which James was utterly, abjectly, foreign.

In much the same vein, Wyndham Lewis conceded that while no one "of the last hundred years, writing in English, is more worthy of serious consideration than Henry James," he also regretted that this same writer was "by force of circumstances, led to conceive of art as a disembodied statement of abstract values, rather than as a sensuous interpretation of values, participating in a surface life."[36] As the effects of economic collapse reverberated in the 1930s, James's supersubtle fry easily could seem parasitical, effeminate, overdone. Like a good Frenchman, André Gide found a gastronomic metaphor to express his literary frustration with the Master. "England has never sinned up to the present by too much good cooking," he wrote, acknowledging that James was indeed "a master-cook. But, as for me," he went on, "I like precisely those great untrimmed chunks that Fielding or Defoe serves us, barely cooked, but keeping all the 'blood-taste' of the meat. So much dressing and distinction, I am satiated with it in advance; he surpasses us in our own faults."[37]

The stock market crash of 1929, followed by the economic catastrophe of the Great Depression, made it even more difficult for readers and scholars to see James as anything more than a prisoner of the leisure class he was claimed to champion. The major critical work of the decade was C. Hartley Grattan's family biography, *The Three Jameses*, in which H. J. Jr. ranked a rather distant third in order of importance. Unlike his father (surfeited with utopian socialism) or his brother William (never detached from the here and now), the younger James, Grattan claimed, "was beguiled by the 'happy few' and it was with them that he threw his lot." Viewed from this vaguely Marxian angle, James's literary achievement could only seem pernicious. "In concentrating his attention upon highly complicated representatives of a highly specialized social group," James "brought the interest of his stories to the narrowest possible point," Grattan insisted. From the moment that James became convinced that "leisure class life in a complex society was the highest expression of human living . . . it was only a question of time until he would end up by writing so baroque a fiction as *The Golden Bowl*."[38] By the 1930s, the Fabian sniping of Rebecca West had effloresced into a kind of frontal assault on the remnants of James's claims for canonicity.

In that decade, the Master's posthumous reputation had reached something of a turning point. The most celebrated of the high modernists seemed eager to embrace his commitment to form—or at least to exempt him from their wholesale dismissal of Victorian taste. While Arnold and Emerson, guardians of the faith, were keeping watch upon the glazen shelves,[39] one by one volumes of Henry James were coming down from them, finding their way into the hands of at least an influential group of discriminating readers. Still, even T. S. Eliot had anticipated that James would "probably continue to be regarded as *the* extraordinarily clever but negligible curiosity" (a judgment made even more bitter by his use of the definite article).[40] More popular arbiters of literary opinion, such as Brooks and Parrington, did their best to make that label stick, using the deplorable example of James to confirm their suspicions that effete gentility had betrayed the virile, democratic mainsprings of American culture.

## *The Art of the Novel*

Eventually, other (and saner) voices would speak, not just to rebut such arguments but also to reaffirm the modernist endorsement of James. The most important of them would be heard in another special "Henry James" number of an influential literary magazine—the April 1934 issue of *Hound & Horn*—the appearance of which gave distinct momentum to the recuperation of James's literary standing. The idea for dedicating an issue of the journal to the Master was spawned, serendipitously, by the unexpected discovery—and sale at auction—of James's preliminary Scenario for *The Ambassadors*. That remarkable document was purchased by Bernard Bandler, one of *Hound & Horn*'s principal backers, who then gave it as a wedding present to A. Hyatt Mayor, with whom he shared editorial responsibilities. (This was "the only act of generosity I ever subsequently regretted," Bandler later said.) Lincoln Kirstein, who had founded *Hound & Horn* while still an undergraduate at Harvard, decided that James's "Project of a Novel" would be prime material for the magazine, so he approached another confirmed Jacobite, Edna Kenton (1876–1954), and invited her to edit James's typescript for a special number he was planning for spring 1932. Never shy about asking, Kirstein also wrote to a brilliant constellation of literary figureheads—Edith Wharton, Bernard Berenson, T. S. Eliot, Ezra Pound, and Gertrude Stein, among others—soliciting personal reminiscences and particular reflections on the subject of the Master's expatriation. Kirstein's ambitious agenda for the issue could not be realized on these extraordinary terms, and its publication was consequently delayed; but when it did at last appear, *Hound & Horn* could still be proud of the milestone the "Henry James" number represented.[41]

The opening salvo in the special issue came from Marianne Moore, who, as if to confront Brooks and Parrington at the gate, descanted upon "Henry James as a Characteristic American." Basing her argument largely upon quotations from James's letters and his autobiographical volumes, Moore concluded by insisting, "Family affection is the fire that burned within him and America was the hearth on which it burned." Most American of all was that idealism that, everywhere in James, was "willing to make sacrifices for its self-preservation."[42] In her own contribution, Edna Kenton tried to settle the tiresome question of James's citizenship once and for all, alleging that "the tears shed over [James's] so-called life-long struggle between countries must strike us as slightly mawkish. Life is a struggle, wherever we are. But Henry James *was* 'between' countries. There lay his subject and his relation to it, and there was his home." To hang the albatross of expatriation around his neck was simply to indulge a lazy critical cliché.[43]

This special number of the magazine featured other memorable items (aside from the abridged scenario for *The Ambassadors*): Edmund Wilson's soon-to-be-classic essay on "The Turn of the Screw" and Newton Arvin's "Henry James and the Almighty Dollar," an eloquent rebuttal to short-sighted leftist critics who wrongly claimed that the author merely had pandered to a decadent bourgeoisie. But, as an extension of the modernist recuperation of James,[44] nothing here figured more prominently than R. P. Blackmur's expository essay "The Critical Prefaces," his analytical overview of James's theoretically minded introductions to eighteen volumes of the New York Edition. Even though some early notices of the Edition had remarked on the significance of these compositions,[45] the Prefaces remained inaccessible to many people because of their peculiar bibliographical fate, embedded as they were in a series of books (twenty-four in all) that very few were willing or able to purchase. James himself had recognized that, collected together, the Prefaces ought "to form a sort of comprehensive manual or *vade-mecum* for aspirants in [the] arduous profession" of novel-writing. "Still," he admitted to his friend William Dean Howells, "it will be long before I shall want to collect them together for that purpose and furnish *them* with a final Preface."[46] What Blackmur wanted to do, then, was to fulfill James's latent intention, to assemble his texts *ad seriatim* and supply that final Preface. He accomplished the latter by sifting through the Master's frequently digressive and always sinuous expository paragraphs, selecting out important subjects, and thereby providing a kind of schematic index to key topics about which James had dispersed his insights. After providing the reader with an overview of major themes to be found across the whole of James's commentary (such as "The Relation of Art and the Artist," "The Relation of Art and Life," "The Plea for Attention and Appreciation," and "The Plea for a Fine Central Intelligence"), Blackmur then refined his provisional analysis to offer a subject list of more specific topics ("The International Theme," for example) and narrative techniques (such as "Foreshortening"), commenting on the artistic principle at hand while directing the reader to specific locations where James discussed each of them. To illustrate by way of example how this approach could further our understanding of James's fiction, Blackmur then proceeded to offer a close reading of the Preface to *The Ambassadors* and to demonstrate that the novelist's rigorous intention "to employ only one centre and to keep it entirely in Strether's consciousness" made it necessary for him to complement his design for the book through the use of *ficelles* and other indirect forms of representation.[47] Quentin Anderson surely was right when he said that Blackmur's thirty-odd pages constituted "a tribute to his author almost as extraordinary as James's prefaces themselves."[48] Blackmur, better than anyone else, had perfected the act of modernist ventriloquism.

Blackmur's interest in James dated to the summer of 1921, when someone directed him to the Cambridge Public Library with the suggestion that he read something by the Master. Just seventeen years of age, a high school dropout (but desperate Harvard wannabe), Blackmur checked out *The Wings of the Dove* and immediately came under the spell of James's prose. Starting the novel in the heat of midday, he finished it before midnight. "Long before the end," he tells us, "I knew a master had laid hands on me. The beauty of the book bore me up; I was both cool and waking; excited and effortless; nothing was any longer worthwhile and everything had become necessary."[49] The Jamesian cadences of Blackmur's prose are hardly accidental; Denis Donoghue has said that the critic's early embrace of James was nothing less than an "addiction."[50] Curiously enough, in its rather wayward character, much of Blackmur's early professional life can almost be seen as a shabby replica of James's own. Struggling to find a career in letters (despite his absence of formal training), Blackmur at various times tried his hand writing novels, poems, and plays—never with much success. Scribner's rejected both of his stillborn novels, works that Blackmur's biographer contends are the surest sign of his entrapment by the Master. In these utterly derivative compositions, Blackmur "was James without the spendthrift talent," paralyzed by "his misplaced allegiance."[51] Fortunately, the young writer could follow surer instincts in literary criticism, and, through the decade of the 1920s, he began to publish a series of incisive essays on modernist poetry in various highbrow little magazines. It is indeed a sign of his extraordinary critical gifts that, with not even a high school diploma in his academic portfolio, Blackmur eventually was appointed and promoted to the rank of full professor in the Department of English at Princeton. No less a figure than Edward Said has eulogized him as "the most patient and resourceful explicator of difficult literature produced in mid-twentieth-century America."[52]

In 1934, however, with no published book to his name, Blackmur was hardly recognized outside the restricted circle of readers of *Hound & Horn* (a journal sometimes referred to by savvy insiders as the *Bitch & Bugle*). Drawing a meager salary from that magazine (which itself was about to go under), Blackmur was chronically desperate for money; snared in genteel poverty and caught up with literary aspirations, he resembles any number of James's protagonists, those sorry and struggling artist-figures whose negotiations with the world so often come to ironic conclusions. Even to write his essay on the Prefaces, Blackmur was indebted to the Scribner publishing house for lending him a set of the New York Edition: those twenty-four plum-colored volumes were certainly beyond the modest reach of his very occasional paychecks. Coincidentally, though, his contacts with Scribner's also prompted him to suggest to the firm that James's ultimate hope for the Prefaces be fulfilled by their bringing out a separate volume in which all of those compositions might be collected for the first time. "I have been reading and working over James' Prefaces long enough now to become permanently fascinated and permanently assured of the value of that fascination," he told a senior editor in January 1934. "I therefore want to ask again, what I know has been suggested many times before, whether Scribner's might not consider publishing these Prefaces together in a single volume moderately priced." Blackmur confessed a selfish motive, too: the piece he was writing for *Hound & Horn* would serve admirably as an introduction for the book, and he was very much in need of the money. "However Scribner's may feel about such a project at the moment, I am sure that eventually the thing will have to be done," he insisted. "The things do make as much of a classic, and I think really a more substantial one, as Arnold's *Essays in Criticism*, and almost, I feel now (because of their greater eloquence), as much as the *Poetics* [of Aristotle]."[53]

Despite the eloquence of this appeal, Blackmur's letter got a rather cool response from Scribner's, who found it difficult to believe that such a book could find a market in the depths of the Great Depression. Here the paradoxes begin, for if the volume could be published at all, its best chance (in Scribner's view) would be as an expensive novelty item for James collectors and connoisseurs. Notwithstanding, Blackmur avidly sensed and seized the opportunity, telling the firm that he would "feel deeply honoured" to supply "an analytical and informative introduction" for such a book—"(besides, God knows, taking up whatever pennies there may be in it as so much, not manna, but absolute bread and butter)."[54] Within a month, Blackmur delivered a copy of his *Hound & Horn* article to Scribner's, again urging the project forward. Still, the publishers were reluctant. Admitting that Blackmur's essay "would be of very vital concern to all lovers of James," these, the firm went on to say, "are nevertheless a small number" and, moreover, "a number which has decreased rather than the opposite, in recent years."[55] Immediately, Blackmur fired back, claiming that he knew fifty people who would buy the volume in an instant—not to mention a bookseller in Connecticut "who would push it fresh and living down the throats of all his customers."[56] Even with that delicious prospect, Scribner's held back, revealing that profits from the sale of just one or two sets of the New York Edition annually were more lucrative to the firm than taking on the risk of publishing the Prefaces separately. Besides, doing that "would rob the New York Edition of one of its most attractive features": the fact that only by buying the complete set could one secure the Prefaces. At the end of another six weeks of badgering from Blackmur, Scribner's flatly turned the project down. "The simple fact is," they said, "it just isn't possible, as we see it, to publish a work of this character under present conditions."[57] Good-bye *Art of the Novel*.

What made them change their mind? Surviving archival evidence does not point to a simple answer. The unsung hero of the James revival, however, might well have been a lowly English professor at Northwestern who was also corresponding with Scribner's at this time, complaining about the difficulty of getting James's books (especially the revised texts of the New York Edition) into the hands of his students and even asking permission to cut mimeograph stencils of some of the Prefaces in order to make those documents available for his classes. "Have you ever considered the possibility of reprinting all the prefaces in a single volume?" he earnestly inquired. "I should immediately add the volume as a required text in my course in literary criticism, as would many other teachers in that field. I cannot see how such a volume would cut down the number of potential purchasers of the New York Edition, and the publication would help Henry James and you."[58] Such a letter, together with Blackmur's appeals, did not exactly constitute a deafening chorus of supplication; still, it must have struck a note somewhere, if only to reverberate as a faint jingle in Scribner's pockets. The prospect that a market for James might extend beyond the limited one of connoisseurs (together with the looming fact that copyrights on the Prefaces would shortly expire) eventually persuaded the publishers to reverse their decision. Blackmur accepted an outright payment of one hundred dollars for his introduction, and *The Art of the Novel* was published in November 1934. Twenty-five years later, with the James Revival going stronger than ever, Scribner's brought out a paperback edition, and, with a gesture of graciousness not often seen in publishing, the firm sent Blackmur a five hundred–dollar bonus, acknowledging that the "modest but steady success of the book" had been helped greatly by his introduction.[59] With characteristic wit Blackmur responded, "Thank you very much for the check which accompanied and gave so elegant a sauce to your letter. . . . It makes it all the more pleasant to remind myself that for once I can be right in saying I told you so."[60]

The more immediate reaction to the appearance of *The Art of the Novel* was largely favorable, and the book enjoyed a better sale than Scribner's had anticipated.[61] With the global economy mired in Depression, many critics (not surprisingly) still had reservations about James's rarified subject matter; but even the rather grudging reviewer for the *New York Times* acknowledged that the "very fact that the James prefaces can, two decades after the passing of their author from the scene, find publication as a separate volume . . . is, in itself, an evidence of the vitality of the principles contained in them."[62] The evolution of a genuinely popular market for James's work would not mature for several decades, but with his most theoretically sophisticated criticism now more widely accessible, James's stature among influential writers and intellectuals could begin its canonical ascent. R. P. Blackmur further assisted in that trajectory by contributing a major chapter on James to the *Literary History of the United States* (1948) and, later, when the paperback revolution was going full tilt, by providing introductory essays for a series of cheap reprints brought out by Dell Publishers. In 1940 he had also planned—and promised—to complete a book-length study of James for New Directions (appropriately enough, the volume was to be part of their Masters of Modern Literature series). Not very pleasantly, Blackmur took a substantial advance (one thousand dollars) from James Laughlin, but he pocketed the money and never delivered the manuscript.[63] Whatever his later derelictions, Blackmur's role in bringing out *The Art of the Novel* was the crucial first step in securing James's modern reputation, a step made possible by appropriating the role of the Master himself and fulfilling the deferred prophecy conveyed in that 1908 letter to Howells. James's "plea for Criticism, for Discrimination, for Appreciation" at last could be heard, his voice made resonant by tracing his method and performing, as Blackmur wrote, "an act of criticism in the sense that James himself understood it." It naturally followed, then, that "our own act of appropriation will have its difficulties, and we shall probably find as James found again and again, that the things most difficult to master will be the best."[64] And so they have ever been.

# 4

## The James Revival

### *Documentary Monumentalism*

Slowly, but inexorably, a shift in critical opinion had begun. A truly seismic event would register in 1943, the centennial year of James's birth, when Harvard professor F. O. Matthiessen first applied for permission to examine the vast trove of family documents that Harry recently had bequeathed to the university.[1] Before the decade was out, Matthiessen would author or edit five full volumes devoted to the Master—*Henry James: Stories of Writers and Artists* (1944), *Henry James: The Major Phase* (1945), *The James Family* (1947), *The Notebooks of Henry James* (coedited with Kenneth B. Murdock, 1947), and *The American Novels and Stories of Henry James* (1947)—an outpouring of Niagaran proportions, not merely launching but confirming and accelerating the wholesale revival of interest in James and his work. Only Matthiessen's tragic suicide in 1950 ended his effective—but undeniably productive—monopoly of the field.

Up until the time that Matthiessen's application to consult the James manuscripts was approved, at best a very small number of other scholars had ever seen or worked with them. For more than a decade, the family papers had lain in storage in the basement of Harvard's Widener Library, but only the select few upon whom Harry had bestowed his necessary blessing had access to them. Preeminent among this elite group was Ralph Barton Perry, a former student of William James's and (by then) professor of philosophy at the university, who had been chosen by Harry to compile a full-scale life-in-letters biography of his father. For that monumental two-volume work, *The Thought and Character of William James* (1935), Perry would be honored with the Pulitzer Prize for Biography. At Perry's urging, Harry also allowed Austin Warren to consult a smaller portion of the family manuscripts, enabling him to complete a well-regarded biography of his grandfather, *The Elder Henry James*, the year before.[2] Somewhat later, having received Harry's permission to assemble an edition of James's dramatic works, Leon Edel also would gain access to the family archive, since several of the Master's working play scripts remained among his posthumous papers. (Edel's curiosity led him much further afield, and he took advantage of his days and hours in the basement to scour many other source materials not immediately relevant to his proposed subject of research.) These three men were the lucky few. Not many others were even aware of the archive's existence, and those who somehow got wind of it were denied permission to see what it contained.[3]

Once he had at last completed his edition of William James's letters, Harry, too, distinguished himself as a writer of others' lives. In 1923 he published an admiring biography of Richard Olney, the bellicose secretary of state who served during the second presidential term of Grover Cleveland. Unlike his father, who had been profoundly antagonistic to nascent American imperialism, Harry was much more sympathetic to Olney's muscular interpretation of the Monroe Doctrine, particularly when he asserted in 1895 that the United States "was practically sovereign on this continent" and demanded that Great Britain renounce its claims in a border dispute with Venezuela.[4] Previously, as Cleveland's attorney general, Olney had persuaded Cleveland in 1894 to authorize the use of federal troops to break the Pullman strike in Illinois, a local company dispute that had shut down much of the nation's rail traffic after Eugene Debs and the American Railway Union extended the labor action to any railroad that carried Pullman palace cars or sleeper coaches. In that case, too, James had vindicated Olney's sweeping assertion of executive power on behalf of the national interest, even though such action had resulted in widespread violence, leaving dozens of workers dead or maimed.[5] Similarly predisposed to exercise tightfisted control, Harry found in Olney a biographical subject who not only shared his own fundamental instincts but, just as bracingly, was not afraid to act upon them. Olney may have been "a hard-thinking, accomplishing," even "ruthless being," but these very qualities were what Harry seemed most to admire in him.[6]

Olney had been trained in the law at Harvard (like his biographer), and that established seat of cultural power also continued to elicit Harry's ongoing interest. Elected by fellow alumni in 1920 to the first of two successive seven-year terms as a member of Harvard's Board of Overseers, Harry became deeply involved in the governance of his alma mater and welcomed his role as a guardian of the institution's venerable reputation. This investment in the life (and history) of the university would lead Harry to chart the career of Charles William Eliot, the Harvard president—already a legend—who transformed the school during his remarkable forty-year tenure (1869–1909) from a provincial college into a modern research institution. James's two-volume chronicle of Eliot's life, published in 1930, was awarded the Pulitzer Prize the following year and would remain the standard biography for decades to come.[7] Even that usually acerbic pundit, H. L. Mencken, gave the book a modest thumbs-up. If Eliot "was not really great, then he was nearly so," the Sage of Baltimore acknowledged: "Mr. James has made an interesting book about him, and deals with him honestly and sensibly."[8] Like another famous Baltimorean before him, Edgar Allan Poe, Mencken certainly was no friend of the "Frog Pond"; but Harry's meticulous account won from this redoubtable critic a measure of respect even for an arch-Bostonian like Eliot.

Not insignificantly, as Harry was working on both these projects, he was granted exclusive access to certain primary sources that were pertinent to his subjects' careers and life histories; each biography included a copious supplement of documentary evidence previously unavailable to other researchers or the broader public. While he was writing the Eliot biography, Harvard even reserved a special room in the library for the biographer's sole use and "provided facilities without which it would have been impossible" for him to complete his manuscript.[9] Recognizing the extraordinary value of such ideal research conditions, Harry sought to re-create and extend them—in a highly restricted, even jealous, way—to the particular individuals whom he deemed competent to handle materials in the James family archive. It fell, then, first to Perry (and his tireless assistant, Betty Aldrich) to inventory and catalogue the James papers: together they sorted and sifted thousands of documents, arranging them in orderly files, condensing masses of material into reasonably searchable categories and biographical subsets, for which they then prepared separate indices and handy sets of briefs. With this vast body of manuscripts at his exclusive disposal, Perry then set out to compile his definitive study of William James, seeking to expand upon the documentary record already established in Harry's edition of his father's letters by "giving to the public selections from the great mass of correspondence, lecture notes, diaries, marginalia, and other manuscripts" locked away in the depths of Widener.[10] In Perry's two hefty volumes, hundreds of previously unpublished letters were made available for the first time; most were written by members of the family (especially William, Henry, and their father), but Perry also included reciprocal parts of the correspondence (where these survived) from many other notables, including Ralph Waldo Emerson. As one reviewer quipped, Professor Perry "lacked nothing" for his task "but a pair of scissors."[11] Somewhat more charitably, John Dewey simply stood in awe of the riches Perry's volumes brought forth: "the wealth of materials, in records of personal contacts and of ideas, is so vast that anything like an adequate review is out of the question," he wrote.[12] Almost all the other notices of Perry's work were inclined to agree.

One of the more curious details about Perry's *Thought and Character of William James* is the copyright notice printed on the verso of the title page. Even though Perry had spent five years researching and writing these two large volumes, his work was copyrighted in the name (very conspicuously printed) of HENRY JAMES. It might seem anomalous that such a monumental undertaking should have been, essentially, a work for hire (Perry was certainly no ordinary hack); but such were the strict terms upon which Harry had insisted. In an arrangement not unlike that made with Percy Lubbock years before, the professor would get a fixed flat fee for his labor, and all future royalties from the sale of his work would be paid to the James estate. Harry's measure of control was not merely fiduciary. He frequently consulted with Perry and freely advised him about editorial policy for his forthcoming opus. With respect to material that would overlap with documents previously (mis)quoted by Uncle Henry, for example, Harry insisted that "the thing to do was to use the text of my father's letters as he wrote them, not as tinkered in the *Notes of a Son and Brother*, and to use what it seemed necessary or important to use regardless of its being published in the *Notes of a Son and Brother*."[13] What Harry intended was a monumental act of biographical supersession—accomplished, if not by sheer weight and volume (though these were considerable), then by the reassertion of a kind of textual integrity that Uncle Henry had been incapable of preserving.

Complementing his obvious relish for biography, Harry also dedicated himself not merely to consolidating but also to enlarging the trove of family papers that had come under his direct control after his mother's death in 1922. Already for his edition of William's letters Harry had solicited material from dozens of people, coupling his invitation with a request that each correspondent consider freely donating his manuscripts to the larger collection that, eventually, he planned to give to the Harvard library. Similar appeals went out to Uncle Henry's epistolary acquaintance. In 1927 Harry laid out his intentions—and specific custodial priorities—in a very revealing letter written to Lucy Clifford. "When I came a few years ago," he explained,

> to take the measure of the collection which had then gathered in my hands I saw that it was so rich and interesting that it entailed a certain responsibility. And since then, little by little, I've been getting it into order, weeding out what had better not be preserved, ordering what ought to be. . . . In the end I shall place the whole lot in the manuscript archives of the Harvard University Library—the whole lot of those that it seems right to preserve.[14]

Once again, the contradictory symptoms of what Jacques Derrida has diagnosed as "archive fever" betray themselves in the family consciousness: a compulsion to record and preserve shadowed by a competing desire "to burn the archive and to incite amnesia."[15] To appreciate just how deeply seated such conflicting impulses resided in Harry's archly conservative temper, we can return to the youthful diary he kept on his first visit to Lamb House in 1898. From that small stapled pamphlet, otherwise continuous, Harry ripped out a single leaf; but on the page immediately following this traumatic lacuna, he wrote, "I have begun at last by saying things here that must be for my own perusal only. And yet, strange to say, I still feel conscious of a possible future audience. I can imagine keeping this quiet all my days, but can equally not refrain from imagining that after my death the whole world will be eager to read it. I should find it hard to disappoint *them* by ordering it to be destroyed."[16] Obviously unafraid of incurring such disappointment, Harry *did* destroy an unknown quantity of material from the family archive—far beyond his single diary page—documents that he felt later researchers should not uncover.[17]

Already very much an insider after his two terms on the Board of Overseers, in 1936 Harry was tapped to join the Harvard Corporation (the ultimate finals club), the nonelective and self-perpetuating body that has always had the last word in the university's most sensitive areas of academic and financial administration. From the start, then, Harry would have had intimate knowledge of Harvard's plans to construct a new rare book and manuscript library—the first of its kind in the country—a formal proposal for which was first circulated in 1938 by Keyes D. Metcalf, the newly appointed director of the university library. Opened in 1942, the Houghton Library was equipped with what was then state-of-the-art technology for preserving (and securing) its precious holdings: air conditioning and precise humidity control, restricted access to materials, vast new stretches of dedicated shelving space, as well as rigorously enforced reading room policies to safeguard against possible theft or damage. Knowing that such a facility, the crown jewel of the university's sprawling library network, would soon be ready surely quickened Harry in his resolve formally to bequeath the family archive to Harvard. There the James papers would be maintained with all the prudence—and vigilance—such a cultural treasure justly deserved.

While he had been contemplating this gift for more than a decade, Harry also had been formulating sweeping—and very conservative—guidelines for the use of *all* manuscript materials in the university's possession. Having inherited his father's scornful mistrust of "The Ph.D. Octopus,"[18] Harry already had determined that undergraduates or students for higher degrees should be prohibited from consulting the James materials. "The news that the papers are in the Library seems to have got abroad," he regretfully wrote a college librarian in 1930. "One of these applicants, who has just called on me, has left on my mind the impression that she may have applied for permission when she herself was in the Library. If you are bothered with this sort of thing, as I am, it may be a convenience to you to know that under no circumstances do I give permission to go into or use the family papers, to students or candidates for doctors' degrees."[19] This long-standing apprehension was further amplified when Harry had occasion to read a rather digressive article, "Personal Papers in the Harvard Library," in the pages of the *Harvard Alumni Bulletin*. The author of this piece was obliged to acknowledge that, besides the issue of cost, the difficulty in collecting letters was also "directly traceable to the delicate question of ethics," noting that a prominent bookseller had recently brought out a book in which the first chapter was entitled (all too ominously), LETTERS THAT WE OUGHT TO BURN. (The Jameses, as we've seen, were themselves not always above such scruples, Harry being no less incendiary than his forebears in the matter.) "To make public the confidences of other people seems to be a breach of faith," this article continued, "and giving letters to a library appears, at first glance, much like offering them to anyone who cares to read them." Making that possibility even more lurid to Harry was the author's casual observation that "large collections of personal correspondence . . . will undoubtedly supply future editors and candidates for the doctor's degree with a great deal of virgin material."[20] Much alarmed by that prospect, Harry strenuously objected to what he could only think of as a kind of pillaging or exploitation of others' private communications. Why should anyone donate family papers to the library, he pointedly asked, if such bequests would then simply become "a midden heap in which anybody is free to scratch around for such flints and bones as he can find"? To his own rhetorical question, Harry had a ready imperative answer: "Manuscript collections are not to be treated," he flatly declared, "for the sake of students or anyone else, as Christmas pies into which Jack Horners may stick their thumbs to pull out plums."[21] In close collaboration, then, with Metcalf, Harry (ever the lawyer) drafted the somewhat forbidding "Application for the Examination of Manuscripts," the document that for decades has been the first piece of paper anyone entering the Houghton Library has been required to sign: a legal contract restricting the patron's use of material and specifically prohibiting any publication thereof without an additional appeal for the express consent of the university.[22]

With respect to his own gift of family papers, Harry was determined to be even more explicitly tightfisted. "Unless clear reason for an exception appears," he insisted, "no student at Harvard or elsewhere shall be permitted access to these manuscripts and papers or be supplied with copies or extracts." Moreover, anyone wishing to publish anything from the archive would have to seek permission from a select committee of three Harvard faculty, including representatives of the Departments of Philosophy and English, who would vet the applicant's credentials and the seriousness of the researcher's project. Only with the committee's unanimous consent could an investigator go forward.[23] Certainly while Harry was alive (and for some time thereafter), Harvard followed these stipulations to the letter, which is the reason that Matthiessen, despite his rank as a full professor of history and literature, was obliged to apply for permission merely to examine manuscripts that were part of his own university's library collections.

Wartime construction problems delayed the opening of Houghton until February 1942, just two months after Harry effected the formal transfer of ownership of the family archive to Harvard. The centennial of William James's birth had just lapsed (he was born on 11 January 1842), but Henry James's anniversary would fall within the boundaries of the coming academic year, and the university seized that occasion to mount a major exhibition that would celebrate (and advertise) the addition of the family archive to the library's manuscript holdings. Anticipating that event, which Houghton would sponsor during the month leading up to the actual centennial date (15 April 1943), the head librarian of the rare books and manuscripts collection, William A. Jackson, persuaded Matthiessen to offer Harvard's first course on Henry James—in itself something of a landmark—that same spring semester. Somewhat embarrassed by the fact that the library's existing catalogue was rather thin, Jackson immediately went on a spending spree, hoping, as he told Harry, to fill in "a great many gaps in Harvard's Henry James collection, both in his own works and the books about him."[24] Jackson also began a very aggressive campaign to locate significant collections of James's letters that were still in private hands, wanting to acquire them for the library—if not as outright gifts, then at least as possible loans to enhance the planned exhibition. When the library's doors opened for that event, the Harvard *Crimson* noted (with typical undergraduate inattention to the niceties of English idiom), "The outstanding feature of the exhibition is the presentation of many of the extremely rare James's manuscripts."[25] Besides displaying handsome first editions and unique items relating to James's theatrical years, the Houghton exhibition called attention to that fact that "in the James Papers recently given to Harvard are over 1600 letters from James and nearly a thousand written to him. The collection gives ample proof, if proof were needed, both of the charm of his epistolary style and warmth of his friendships."[26] Knowing such letters were there was one thing; seeing (or publishing) them, another.

Wartime shortages affected not only Harvard's building plans but also its curriculum and teaching faculty, many of whom were recruited for military service. In 1942–43, F. O. Matthiessen was one of the few men left on campus with any claim to competence within the field of American literature, so he would have been an almost inevitable choice to teach the proposed course on Henry James. In his magisterial *American Renaissance* (1941), Matthiessen had taken certain cues from T. S. Eliot to chart a kind of genealogy of moral inquiry, beginning with Nathaniel Hawthorne, continuing through Henry James, and culminating in Eliot himself; and he certainly appreciated the extent to which the modernists seized upon James's preoccupation with the formal coherence of a work of art and transformed the Master's obsession into a distinctive aesthetic credo.[27] But, unlike the figures of the American Renaissance (Emerson, Thoreau, Hawthorne, Melville, and Whitman), all of whom were united, in Matthiessen's view, by "their devotion to the possibilities of democracy,"[28] James was an artist whose social and political values would challenge this critic's powers of sympathetic identification and interpretive acumen. That a left-wing critic, almost single-handedly, could produce a fivefold monument to the Master—in spite of Matthiessen's considerable personal reservations about that writer's more conservative tendencies and priorities—testifies quite powerfully to the continuing need to shape and control the meaning of James's literary legacy.

That Matthiessen should have led the vanguard of the James Revival when he found so much to criticize in his subject's want of social consciousness is one of the enduring paradoxes of modern literary history.[29] Teaching Harvard's first course on the Master certainly did not make him a immediate convert: Matthiessen had a hard time just keeping up with his weekly preparations, which often seemed to him a decided chore. In a long series of letters to his lover and longtime companion, the painter Russell Cheney, Matthiessen revealed his conflicted response to James, alternating between modest enthusiasm and a kind of deprecating tolerance. From the very beginning, Matthiessen was working at a disadvantage. "I keep woefully behind in my reading of James," the professor freely confessed, "and will finally be reduced to doing much of it between lectures." In early February, Matthiessen reported that the "James course is launched, though I waver back and forth continually in the degree of my interest in him. He certainly is not someone I'm instinctively with all the way like Melville." To make matters worse, the instructor's institutional responsibilities seemed incessantly to multiply (especially with so many of his colleagues leaving for the war): always more committee meetings to chair and attend, "and in the meantime," Matthiessen joked, "I'm supposedly reading all of Henry James." By the time the Houghton exhibition was mounted, Matthiessen had almost reached the breaking point. "I'm up through *The Spoils of Poynton,*" he told Cheney, "and on the verge of the three big novels. I continue to alternate between admiration and satiety. I guess it grows even clearer that I don't want to do an extended job on James. One revealing symptom is the joy with which I rush back to Shakespeare on the alternate days."[30] Once the headlong pressure of the semester was over, however, Matthiessen seems to have been able to recalibrate his priorities, for he immediately began writing a series of valuable essays on James, including those that eventually would cohere into his pivotal monograph, *Henry James: The Major Phase*. His "extended job" on James was really just beginning.

Perhaps the most crucial exercise that Matthiessen assigned his Harvard students that spring was to have them compile and analyze the extensive substantive variants between the text of the first published edition of *The Portrait of a Lady* (1881) and that which was printed in the New York Edition (1907). Their dutiful spadework gave Matthiessen all he needed to write his now classic essay on Jamesian revision, "The Painter's Sponge and Varnish Bottle," which first appeared as an appendix to *The Major Phase*. Before that, Matthiessen reflected his abiding interest in the visual arts in another essay, "James and the Plastic Arts," his contribution to yet another watershed "Henry James" number, the autumn 1943 issue of the *Kenyon Review*, edited by Robert Penn Warren.[31] And the *Partisan Review* first printed his introduction to the 1944 New Directions anthology, *Stories of Writers and Artists*.[32] These preliminary exercises laid the way for Matthiessen to focus on the three great novels of James's later period—the major phase, as he would memorably call it.

In his book of that title, Matthiessen sought definitively to redeem the Master from the disproportionately influential criticism of Philistines like Brooks and Parrington, who reductively had condemned the expatriate artist for cutting himself off from his native land and whose works, in consequence, declined to become (at best) "the frustrated gestures of 'an habitually embarrassed man.'" Having had access to James's manuscript notebooks, Matthiessen found in them all the proof he needed of James's ever-increasing technical sophistication—evidence that utterly refuted Brooks's hackneyed thesis of "flight, frustration and decline." Such discoveries prompted Matthiessen to reclaim and redefine the essential meaning of James's legacy and to reposition him securely within a specifically American literary pantheon. Where Brooks and Parrington most egregiously had erred was in ignoring the formal virtuosity of the writer's imaginative vision and focusing instead on a superficial census of his (supposedly limited) range of characters and the kinds of situations they could comfortably inhabit. "The separation between form and content simply does not exist as the mature artist contemplates his finished work," Matthiessen warned. "That separation is a dangerous short-cut taken by critics, and its disasters are written large over the history of James's reputation."[33] More than any other critic, Matthiessen worked almost tirelessly to repair such damage.

Whatever reservations Matthiessen still held about James's politics, having access to Harvard's newly acquired archive of family materials proved irresistible to him as a means of rehabilitating the Master's reputation. Recognizing the crucial importance of James's manuscript scribblers, Matthiessen enlisted the help of another Harvard colleague, Kenneth Murdock, to edit and publish them. On his own, Matthiessen culled through masses of autograph letters (Perry's two volumes on William James had only skimmed the very best of these), and from them and other sources he compiled *The James Family*—"a particular kind of biography," as he described it, "the biography not of an individual but of a family, and of a family of minds." Through the voluminous documentary archive of this remarkable kinship group, Matthiessen asserted that "we may feel that we have gained a fairly full index to American intellectual history from the time of Emerson to that of the first World War."[34] From 1944 to 1947, with astonishing speed and regularity, the various parts of Matthiessen's massive quintumvirate were delivered from reputable presses, widely reviewed, and welcomed as hefty harbingers of a genuine cultural watershed: the James Revival.

## *Partisan (Re)views*

That phenomenon cannot, of course, be attributed to Matthiessen alone. Historical variations in an author's cultural capital are always readily apparent in retrospect, but targeting exact pivot points in reputation (or assigning their causes to a specific agent) too radically simplifies the interplay—often fortuitous—of literary, social, and economic determinants. Already sensing that the James centennial might reawaken popular interest in the author, Maxwell Perkins, the legendary editor at Scribner's, thought that some kind of commemorative anthology might find success; but who would be the best man to edit such a work? Perkins turned to the Master's nephew for advice. "I should first of all consider Edmund Wilson myself," the editor wrote, "—though he is a hard man to work with in some respects—very uncompromising. And between ourselves, he is difficult in money matters. Another possibility is Richard Blackmur, but he too would, I think, present difficulties." Harry confessed that he knew little about either of them and instead recommended another candidate, still quite obscure: "*Leon Edel* by name, Jew, born in Canada, educated at McGill and at the University of Paris. . . . He is a great H.J. admirer, very discriminating, and I think definitely more scholarly and competent than any of the other younger people whose writing about H.J. happens to come under my eye. He is quite unknown; very meticulous."[35] Scribner's eventually shelved the idea (the American Book Company had beat them to the punch by issuing a compact volume of "representative selections" from James),[36] but in this simple exchange of letters we can see a portent of impending change: new actors soon would begin to stake their claims to Henry James, abetted by the interest of publishers who saw new commercial opportunities in the prospect of his revival.

Leon Edel had first corresponded with Harry in 1928, at which point the Canadian graduate student was just beginning his research into James's *années dramatiques*. When in Lubbock's edition of correspondence he encountered for the first time documents that testified quite powerfully to his uncle's disastrous experience with the English stage—especially James's bruised response to the debacle of *Guy Domville* in January 1895—Harry felt that the publication of such letters might result in renewed interest in James's plays. Fearful lest a work like *Guy Domville* fall into the hands of scurrilous pirates, Harry hoped—as early as 1919—that Lubbock might be persuaded to secure the copyright in James's surviving playscripts by editing them for book publication.[37] While nothing immediately resulted from this flurry of interest in James's largely forgotten dramas (as far as anyone could find out, the only surviving copy of *Guy Domville* was locked away in the Lord Chamberlain's office), an unprecedented context had been established for Harry to receive more willingly an appeal—from a total stranger—for bio/bibliographical information about the playwright. (As we have seen, others who made serious inquiries were not so fortunate and typically were turned away empty-handed.) Before Edel completed his graduate work at the Sorbonne, he also had the opportunity to meet Harry in Paris, securing in that interview the executor's permission to incorporate quotations from James's manuscript letters and playscripts into his thesis work, which, by long-standing custom, eventually would be published in France. Two research essays were then required as the French equivalent of a doctoral dissertation, and when those two slender volumes appeared—one written in French (*Henry James, les années dramatiques*), the other in English (*The Prefaces of Henry James*)—Edel immediately sent copies of them to Harry, not merely to express his gratitude but also to lay future claim to the dramatic material, which he hoped to edit and publish later. Duly impressed by Edel's intentions and professional credentials, Harry answered him quite cordially and had words of praise for his two essays. "I think you have done in each of them a very judicious and discriminating piece of work," he wrote approvingly. "I have always regarded what might be called my uncle's theatre phase as having been insufficiently understood, and underestimated with reference to its importance. But you make an even stronger case than I would have anticipated and I think you make it convincingly." Edel's analysis of the Prefaces to the New York Edition was equally commendable. "I know of no more sensible treatment of the prefaces than this of yours," James told him. "Very few people seem to read them studiously."[38] Through personal contact and these gestures of academic reciprocity, Edel had made a major stride in winning Harry's (and the family's) confidence.[39]

With the Depression worsening, however, Harry was not persuaded that the time was right for an edition of James's plays. Knowing that the actress Elizabeth Robins was about to publish a memoir about her life in the theater (a book that would also include her correspondence with his uncle), Harry thought the reception accorded to that volume would give a better estimate of the market's interest. Before committing himself in any way to Edel, Harry also wanted first to consult a trusted adviser. To Percy Lubbock he sent copies of their recent correspondence (as well as Edel's formal publishing proposal), seeking advice but also giving Lubbock the first option to edit the plays himself. "Of course," Harry obligingly wrote, "if you yourself cared to do something of this kind I wouldn't for anything encourage Leon Edel or anyone else to try it." Lubbock, now ten years removed from the Master (and otherwise engaged as Sybil's devoted caretaker), demurred, but not before giving Edel an approving nod. "It is good of you to keep the job open for me," he responded; but, having also received a copy *Les années dramatiques* from its author, Lubbock acknowledged that Edel was "far more familiar" with that aspect of James's life and work, and, besides, he felt that the younger man had paid his dues. "I think he deserves it," Lubbock concluded.[40]

Later that year, Harry gave the young scholar permission to compile an edition of his uncle's plays, a task that unwittingly launched Edel's career as James's biographer and would-be superintendent of materials that could testify to the contours of the author's life. With a certain prophetic irony, Edel addressed these two related concerns in his early review of C. Hartley Grattan's *The Three Jameses: A Family of Minds* (1932) and Elizabeth Robins's epistolary memoir of her stage career, *Theatre and Friendship: Letters from Henry James to Elizabeth Robins* (1932).

Edel complained that by giving us a "family of minds," Grattan was merely scratching the surface of "a rich, fine field for the biographer." Likewise, Robins's volume, while charming because of the new personal documents it brought to light, still left many questions unanswered: "Only the initiated," Edel warned, would appreciate the "biographical values that lie between the hills and valleys of James's prose." The full story of James's obscure "dramatic years" was yet to be told, he suggested: the actress's memoirs left that necessary task "but half done."[41] Edel himself *had* told it, of course, but his narrative was imprisoned in a French-language dissertation; still, he now had the family's go-ahead to collect James's plays and preface them with a work he had already largely written.

Progress was slow, however, because Edel encountered for the first time the problems intrinsic to textual editing. James had published some of his unproduced plays in two volumes of *Theatricals* in the mid-1890s; others had appeared in long-lost periodicals; and still more were extant only as scripts retained by actor-managers or playbooks deposited at the Lord Chamberlain's office in London. Assembling and collating all the available versions of these scattered documents were formidable and necessarily time-consuming tasks; meanwhile, as the Great Depression lingered, Edel struggled to find continuous employment, in and out of the academy. Winning a Guggenheim Fellowship to concentrate on the play project allowed Edel to visit Harvard for the first time in 1937, where (with Harry's permission, of course) a literal sea chest of documents was opened for his inspection. "I have spent my first day at the Widener Library," he happily reported back to Harry, "and it has been most illuminating. I see already that I will find here the solution to most of the elusive problems that have troubled me these past few months in connection with the plays."[42] At that point, Ralph Barton Perry's work with the archive was mostly finished and Matthiessen's was hardly begun (he may not even have known yet of its existence): Edel was in sole and privileged possession. Ironically, having so many new resources at his disposal only made the editor's job more difficult: hundreds upon hundreds of letters were there, as well as previously unknown dramatic scripts and the closely written manuscript notebooks that Alice and Peggy had retrieved from Lamb House after Uncle Henry's death.[43] Reading and transcribing so much material from James's difficult hand took much more time than Edel had reckoned. When his fellowship support ended, Edel was obliged to resume his newspaper work, further impeding progress on his collection of James's plays.

America's entry into the Second World War and the demands of military service pushed things back yet again. Rather much to his surprise, Edel was drafted into the ranks of the US Army in 1943; but (not unlike Harry James before him) he welcomed military service as a means of distancing himself from a failed marriage. ("Becoming a soldier was an act of colossal avoidance," he would later confess.) With his bilingual facility and experience in journalism, Edel was an obvious candidate for the army's Psychological Warfare Division, and he followed up the rear of the D-Day invasion force that bloodily made its way toward Paris. Once the French capital was liberated, Edel worked as a "media soldier" for the Office of War Information; but, never one to neglect an opportunity, in his off-duty time Edel hunted down aging survivors who had known (and corresponded with) James—most notably Morton Fullerton—many of whom presented the eager biographer with bundles of letters that he transcribed for future use.[44] He also notified Harry of these discoveries, hoping that Harvard (and/or the family) would want to purchase such documents to supplement the Houghton archive.[45]

Meanwhile, back in America, with the observance of the Henry James Centennial acting as a catalyst for revival of interest in the Master, Matthiessen and a handful of others were moving forward, hedging in on what (all too briefly) had been Edel's exclusive territory. "It seems hardly fair," Matthiessen confessed to Edel (whose conscription was still several months away), "that, in the light of your long concern with this James material, it should be [Kenneth] Murdock and myself who are editing his Notebooks instead of you. However, the present Henry James, who has, as you know, long since restricted this material, has now given us his permission, so there we are."[46] The perceived injustice was not lost on Edel, who now became anxious that his favored position with respect to the archive was in jeopardy. Prying for more details, he queried another member of the English Department for information. With his infallible instinct for the invidious, Harry Levin taunted Edel with the prospect of his Harvard colleagues getting first crack at the family papers. "Doesn't the Houghton collection entice you?" Levin teased, blandly adding that "Matthiessen's designs on James are more immediate than mine" and further remarking that New Directions was planning to celebrate the centennial of the Master's birth with "a collected volume of the stories about art."[47] Such news only rubbed more salt in the tender flesh of Edel's wounded pride, since he himself had lobbied vigorously for that job and now was being superseded by a rival.[48] Getting a draft notice—instead of a book contract—was not what the ambitious journalist had in mind.

By the summer of 1943, Edel was sidelined by the army and would soon be shipped off to Europe. At just that moment, Matthiessen was getting down to work. With the James papers now open to him, his various critical and biographical projects began to take shape; and by the time the war ended, they would begin, *ad seriatim*, to appear. Reviews of Matthiessen's *The Major Phase* were largely favorable (the *New England Quarterly* went so far as to proclaim that "jacobolatry" was "in the air"),[49] and in retrospect one could almost say that the modern James Revival dates from its publication. Appreciative of the book's merits, but deeply envious of its author's opportunities for taking advantage of sources long hidden from view to document the vital link between James's otherwise disastrous experiment as a playwright and the formal structure of the late fiction, Edel admitted to Matthiessen,

> I suppose if I were more vain than I am, I would feel a certain chagrin that you should have beaten me to the story of how HJ fitted the dramatic key into the narrative lock. But I have the satisfaction of having made that point in my Sorbonne thesis 13 years ago, and in any event I did have my chance but delayed the edition of the plays, so I can only blame myself. In any event I suspect that the edition of the plays (which is still a valid project) will be enhanced by what you have done and by the current "boom."

Edel tried very hard to compliment his rival but then could not resist suggesting that "in one sense you had it easy"—by which he meant that all the manuscripts had simply been placed in front of him, while Edel himself had had to labor to track down elusive sources—besides pointing out certain "obvious" errors that Matthiessen had committed in transcribing James's difficult penmanship. "I dont know whether there is anyone beside myself," he proudly admonished, "who could (after 15 years of practise) give you the most positive check on such pitfalls—HJ's erratic handwriting."[50] Not much collaborative energy would be lost between these two.

Matthiessen had made no secret of his plans. In due succession, he brought out a series of books that laid bare most of the contents of the venerable sea chest to which Edel first had privileged access: first *The American Novels and Stories of*

*Henry James,* including the "Notes for *The Ivory Tower*" and other titles long since unavailable (1947); then the weighty anthology *The James Family* (1947); and, at last, *The Notebooks of Henry James* (coedited with Murdock, 1947). Matthiessen had also told Edel that, once the war was over, he hoped to edit a volume of James's early letters, "mainly the correspondence with his family" (he anticipated) "and with Grace Norton and other American friends—in other words, the part of his correspondence that was least represented in Lubbock."[51] Before Matthiessen could strike gold with that, too, as soon as he was back in the United States, Edel tried to shove past him. Having resumed his work on the volume of plays, Edel told Harry that he was also working on a biography that would "set at rest the fruitless and quite irresponsible speculation about the novelist's life which has characterized so much of the criticism that has been written in recent years." Besides that, he proposed editing "a volume of letters that would supplement the two Lubbock volumes. I have in mind a volume devoted exclusively to letters which shed light on Henry James's work. Such a volume would be complementary to the notebooks. My special claim for such a task is that I have in my possession many such letters copied from collections in England and France."[52] Significantly, Harry, who had always been somewhat suspicious of Matthiessen's leftist politics, began to tilt in Edel's favor. "Everybody who owns a fountain pen seems to be planning to dig or cull something out of the H. J. papers in the Harvard Library," he only half-facetiously wrote. "If the Library has to say 'there must be priorities' it would not surprise me to see a picket line thrown around it carrying banners inscribed 'Harvard Unfair to James-Researchers.' So I would not delay long about informing and consulting the Library about any projects you are nursing."[53] F. O. Matthiessen was no stranger to picket lines—he was a founding member (and immediate past president) of the Teachers Union at Harvard, a group that often sparred with university president James B. Conant and the Harvard Corporation[54]—and this implicit jab emboldened Edel to devise a strategy for outmaneuvering his rivals.

Following Harry's advice, Edel immediately wrote to William A. Jackson, the assistant librarian of Harvard College in charge of rare books and manuscripts, to "stake a claim," as he put it, for the unpublished letters. Since Harry had already indicated his willingness to Jackson for Edel, Matthiessen, and Murdock to have priority in the use of the family papers, the library was ready to enforce it. Jackson warned Edel, however, that such priority could not be extended unduly: "if the person who has it delays, without any reasonable excuse, for too long a period of years," he made clear, "we will then have the right to say that if within a reasonable time he does not produce the book we cannot hold the material for him any longer." Edel assured him that producing a volume of letters would be nothing compared to the volume of plays, since there would be no complicated matters of transcription or collation. One wonders what Jackson's reaction would have been had he known that Edel would not finish his edition of James's letters for another thirty-seven years?[55]

Despite repeated efforts to secure an academic position, Edel still had to support himself as a freelance journalist; but even with his outsider status he maintained certain advantages over his ivy-walled competitors, especially insofar as he could quickly reach a much larger audience of influential readers. In late autumn of 1947, Edel published an almost derisive review of Matthiessen's *The James Family* in the liberal New York newspaper *PM*. Clearly irritated by any claims that the Harvard professor made for his work as biography, Edel pointedly reminded his readers how few of Matthiessen's pages represented his own labor. "Matthiessen has ended up with an anthology which he baptizes biography," he chided. "And, in his effort to mold his anthology to biographical ends, he has found himself tightly squeezed by both *genres*. And the pay-off is that the publishers, overlooking the fact that more than three-quarters of the book is from Jamesian pens, offer it, on the dust jacket, as a biography by Matthiessen 'together with selections' from the Jameses." Edel then went so far as to impersonate the Master himself, chastising Matthiessen for his ill-informed confusion:

"Dear, delightful young man, you cannot have biography and anthology at the same time. *Voyons donc*, if it is biography it is not anthology, and if it is anthology then it is not biography.

"The biographical process, to my mature vision, involves a particular detachment, calls into play the great stewpot or crucible of the imagination, of the observant, recording, studying, researching and interpreting mind. The anthological process, if I may put it thus, is quite another matter. It is the gathering together in a book of someone else's flowers of prose or verse culled here and there by the anthologist and displaying *his* taste, *his* prejudice, *his* feeling. We may not agree with *his* choice, but then it is not we who are doing the choosing."[56]

Matthiessen, who was conducting a seminar in Czechoslovakia at the time, presumably was out of the newspaper's range, but Alfred A. Knopf forwarded a copy of Edel's notice, and it provoked an obviously wounded response. "Do you think it's fair," he demanded,

> to make it sound as though the publisher and myself were trying to palm the book off as something it isn't, in your sentence beginning "And the pay-off,?" (Incidentally, a most un-Jamesian expression) For I say as explicitly as possible what the book actually is, and even if three quarters—or more—are by the Jameses, that leaves an ordinary-length book by me, if one is forced to judge such matters by elementary arithmetic.

Other lacerations went deeper. Acknowledging that a reviewer was entitled to adopt a tone of superiority to an author, Matthiessen still felt that *he* was owed something better, especially since he had befriended Edel and allowed him to see an advance copy of both *The James Family* and the transcriptions of the *Notebooks*. He bluntly said,

> I would not [have] expected it from you,—in such remarks as what "close readers" of HJ's fiction will find, or in your regretting of my acceptance of the "catch-phrase," "family of minds." To me that phrase means no more than what gave this family its greatest distinction was its varied play of intellect, a fact as obvious to me as that HJ is one of the most objective writers of fiction on record.

The unkindest cut of all, though, was the ventriloquized rebuke from James himself. "What I really resent," he fumed,

> and what I suppose has dictated this response is your message from "The Master." I am not *dear*, nor *delightful*, as I am sure you will agree when reading this. Nor, Leon, are either you or I any longer *young*. So why not write the definitive biography of HJ for which you have the equipment, and not criticize me for not doing something that I never set out, or pretended to do?[57]

Ever wedded to his own reductive version of Freudian psychology, Edel answered by conceding that "I seem unconsciously to have indulged in a certain amount of self-aggrandizement at your expense."[58] Even if this apology was sincere, one doubts that Matthiessen ever could quite forgive the slight. Whether it discouraged him from continuing his work with James is something we can never know, for Matthiessen tragically committed suicide less than three years later. His anticipated edition of James letters was never completed—at least not by him.

If Matthiessen was stung by Edel's notice, members of the James family were more favorably impressed. Billy James, who had befriended Edel since the mid-1930s, happily accepted the reviewer's logic. "What you say," he wrote, "concerning the difference between biography and anthology is so true that it makes me wish that you rather than the good Mattie had been the biographer. Perhaps something of that order may still come from you."[59] Something of that order was indeed coming from Edel, and in a quantity that seemed always to multiply. Seventeen years after first proposing it, Edel's edition of *The Complete Plays of Henry James* appeared under Lippincott's imprint in 1949. Its massive impression of definitiveness helped Edel win his first academic appointment in 1950 as a visiting professor at New York University; three years later, the completion of what would be the first volume of his biography of James encouraged NYU to give him a full-time position at the rank of associate professor. Published to generally wide acclaim, *Henry James: The Untried Years* (1953) consolidated a kind of transfer of power from Harvard (from which Matthiessen was now three years absent) to Edel himself, although that university's control of James's manuscripts necessarily involved the biographer in a kind of triangular relationship with surviving members of the James family and those formally in charge of the archive. Edel's cozy relationship with Billy James ensured the continuation of his favored status after the death of Harry James in 1947. Long impressed by Edel's deep understanding of his subject, Billy even expressed to him the wish "that no one but you were allowed to write about Uncle Henry!"—a desire that Edel himself seems to have shared.[60]

## From Archive to Industry

Besides the five volumes produced during what Edel would later refer to (rather patronizingly) as Matthiessen's "brief and busy excursion into James,"[61] the decade of the 1940s witnessed the appearance of many other titles that would help resuscitate the Master's readership and serious critical interest in his work. The

American Book Company's *Representative Selections* anthology (1941) had been aimed primarily at the college market; but from the centennial year onward, commercial publishers also brought out several other collections that sought to (re)generate interest in James among a broader, less specialized audience. First came *The Great Short Novels of Henry James* (Dial Press, 1944), edited by Philip Rahv; then Modern Library published *The Short Stories of Henry James* (1945), edited by Clifton Fadiman; F. W. Dupee brought together a catholic range of critical viewpoints in *The Question of Henry James* (Holt, 1945); and, across the water, Simon Nowell-Smith scoured a wide swath of biographical source material to compile *The Legend of the Master* (Constable, 1947), a highly entertaining anthology of verbal snapshots. Very quickly, the publishing arena was becoming crowded and competitive—so much so that even the *New Yorker* would print two satiric little stanzas announcing "The Henry James Boom." This modified limerick took a few quick jabs at the men whose editorial labors were propelling the resurgence of interest in James (Matthiessen, Fadiman, Rahv, and Dupee), by suggesting that each of them was, in essence, riding the coattails of the Master. In the first stanza of the poem, each of the anthologists pompously advises James, "You will never be known in the temperate zone, unless you are known through me." Still grimly aware of his perpetual unsalability, the Master gets the last word (and line) of the poem, as he fires back a most unJamesian rebuke: "Listen, you guys . . . I'll never go down with the toughs in this town through collections by you of *me*!"[62]

While some publishers harbored reservations similar to those of this snide poetaster, a rising tide of reprints nevertheless seemed likely to lift the Master's boat. James's works, the earliest of which were lapsing into the public domain, especially appealed to fledgling houses—such as John Lehmann and Rupert Hart-Davis in England, and New Directions in America—that were eager to add distinctive cachet to their modest lists.[63] Rather quixotically, perhaps, James Laughlin at New Directions even contemplated a complete reissue of all of James's fiction. But, more soberly, he began with Matthiessen's *Stories of Writers and Artists* (1944) and *The Other House* (1948), edited by Edel, though he was also anticipating a volume from R. P. Blackmur to add to the Makers of Modern Literature series.[64] Blackmur, as we know, never completed that project, but he, too, shared Laughlin's fond ambition for getting all of James back into print. After the close of the Second World War, Blackmur tried to persuade Scribner's to issue a complete, moderately priced edition of James (similar to what Percy Lubbock had done in the 1920s with Macmillan in Great Britain), but the publisher looked stubbornly at the bottom line. A senior editor at the firm admitted that while Blackmur's "idea for a complete, moderate-priced edition of Henry James" made "a strong appeal to me personally, I doubt very much whether it would be a practicable publishing venture. There has been, as you say, a revival of interest in James, but it seems to be largely among the literati, and while a great deal is written about it, and the name of Henry James features once more, prominently, in reviews and in the press, the resultant sales, even of the few volumes re-issued, have been small."[65] Such market pessimism did not deter Scribner's from reissuing *The American Scene* in 1946 (with an important new introduction by W. H. Auden); and theirs was just one of more than thirty titles that would appear in a census of James reprints published from 1942 to 1949.[66] Momentum certainly seemed to be building for what Rupert Hart-Davis liked to call "The Boom," and he, among others, willingly embraced James and certain key players (notably Edel) who were largely responsible for it.[67]

Many of these new editions featured critical introductions authored by sympathetic critics who felt obliged to correct a fundamental misperception of the Master that still carried over from the heyday of Brooks and Parrington. Once derided in the *New York Times* as an author whom it would be impossible to consider as an American, James was now extended a generous welcome by that same paper when the bulk of his "American" novels and tales were collected. "The revival of Henry James is a phenomenon as surprising to his devotees as it is to his detractors," the *Times* observed, noting (in 1947) that "in the last three years more of his work has been reprinted in this country than in the entire quarter of a century following his death in 1916." Brushing aside the ghost of Brooks's James, the reviewer (Philip Rahv) was obliged to testify that, "for a writer who, as the legend goes, was enamored of old-world privilege and by no means aglow with belligerent fervor in dealing with the national ideals, the work collected in this volume is astonishing in that it shows us to what an extent James was able to express creatively the meaning and quality of American life."[68] The Allies' recent victory over Fascist totalitarianism also worked to open up new avenues of perception about James's relevance to the current moment. "It is only now," Alfred Kazin shrewdly sensed, "that we are beginning to realize that James, whose career was such a lesson in devotion to his craft, honors us in America far more than we have honored him. For we know that the real meaning of a democratic society lies in what it makes of its freedom, and that the ultimate meaning of freedom, when illustrated in art and thought, lies in its service to the full development of the individual person. James, whose lifelong struggle to remain unimpeachably himself has been so important to the newer American writers, helps us to realize that today."[69]

These self-conscious efforts to reclaim the Master in a specifically American tradition did not, of course, discourage others from making broader appeals for James's artistic resurrection. If, in the depths of the Depression, Granville Hicks easily could dismiss James as a "fugitive" from *The Great Tradition* of American letters because, regrettably, "he needed the sanctions that an established class could lend to his individual tastes and activities,"[70] F. R. Leavis could just as easily instantiate James in *his* configuration of *The Great Tradition* of the English novel by aligning his moral seriousness with that of Jane Austen, George Eliot, and Joseph Conrad. Polemically averring his preference for James's earlier works, Leavis deplored the "cobwebbiness" of the late novels. So far from constituting any kind of "major phase," those novels betrayed, in Leavis's view, an artist too much divorced from the felt life of the world around him. If there was going to be a James cult, at least it should genuflect before the proper idols: masterworks such as *The Portrait of a Lady* and *The Bostonians*. Whatever Leavis's reservations—and he was honest enough to admit them—he still insisted that James's distinctive greatness could not be denied. "His registration of sophisticated human consciousness is one of the classical creative achievements," Leavis affirmed with stalwart assurance: "it *added* something as only genius can."[71]

While the views of the ever-idiosyncratic Leavis were somewhat anachronistic, what most of the other new champions of the Master wanted to emphasize was James's modernity. As Philip Rahv testified, "The reputation of Henry James has grown immeasurably since his death in 1916, and he is now generally regarded by discriminating readers as America's greatest novelist and a master of modern prose belonging to the company of Proust and Joyce."[72] Even Clifton Fadiman, whose flatulent critical pronouncements often make one wince, was able to see "that James, for all his limitations, is wonderfully near to us; that he is a modern writer, to be ranked with Joyce, Proust, Mann, and not a nineteenth-century writer at all."[73] To some purists, Fadiman's middle-brow approach to James (reflected, too, in his choice of tales for the Modern Library

anthology) was bound to be disappointing,[74] but whatever his want of discernment, his role as a popularizer should not be underestimated. Radio and televi-
sion carried his voice and name everywhere, and his imprimatur on the works
of Henry James only could have helped their sales.

Jonathan Freedman has noticed that many of the critics at the center of
the James Revival—Fadiman, Trilling, Rahv, Edel—were of Jewish descent.
For these second-generation sons of Jewish immigrants, Henry James's value
as cultural capital was doubly important, because in championing the Master,
they found a vehicle by which to assimilate themselves into the then still highly
restricted ranks of American higher education. As Freedman argues, "Henry
James was at once an embodiment of traditional high culture and a figure from
it with whom they wrestled as they made their way into its precincts." If that
underlying ethnic imperative encouraged someone like Lionel Trilling to reinvent Henry James as a Jew—the perpetual outsider, the modern alienated
consciousness, "a detached moral witness bearing knowledge of the horrors of
history and social life" but "one who erects from that alienation a stance that
endures"—it also reinforced an equally powerful need (particularly acute in
Edel) to monopolize him.[75]

By the late 1940s, then, critical and popular interest in the Master was
sharply rebounding. "What one wouldn't give," Peggy James sighed to her
brother Billy, "if Uncle Henry could have sat at the centre of all this appreciation of him!"[76] The Henry James Revival—as Paul Rosenfeld christened it in
1946[77]—assuredly must be recognized as one of the great watersheds in the
history of modern taste. One cannot fully understand its significance, however,
without also acknowledging the possessive instincts that drove the cultural
agents who were central to it. For all the key figures involved, as Hilton Kramer
has suggested, "their own literary aspirations were felt to be implicated in the
rehabilitation of a writer who, in the reach of his aesthetic ambition and his
remarkable consistency in realizing it, might serve as a model of future achievement."[78] In 1918 T. S. Eliot predicted that Henry James would always remain a
literary curiosity. By 1950 the Master had become an industry.

# 5 The Legend of the Bastard

## *Policing the Archive*

Even though Percy Lubbock's 1920 edition of *The Letters of Henry James* was greeted with almost universal acclaim, not everyone was satisfied or pleased with what those two volumes revealed—or didn't. "Are not the friends of Henry James inclined to be a little too solemn when they write about him," one writer asked, "perhaps feeling that they must rise to the occasion and put on their best style, as though he had his eye on them and would be 'down' on any lapses?" Lubbock's monument to the Master was almost too imposing: admirably as he had done his work, "the editor," to this skeptic, seemed "just a little bleak . . . wearing the grave face of the historian and mindful never to become familiar."[1] The American novelist Robert Herrick also sensed that "the too discreet Mr. Lubbock" somehow had been obliged to make sure that James's real nature should "not by any inadvertent slip be allowed to become known to the inquisitive public."[2] To the contrary, some members of James's family (even though they had had an opportunity to censor Uncle Henry's letters) were chagrined by what they found in the published volumes and felt that Lubbock had been lax in discharging his editorial responsibility. Harry's mother despaired over what she felt were repetitious outpourings (especially the writer's extended apologies for resorting to dictation, sending letters typed by his amanuensis rather than written by hand) and the disproportionate inclusion of correspondence to certain people (notably Edith Wharton) whom she disliked. "I wish that we had done the letters with paid help," she lamented, "so that the final *yes* was ours."[3] Later, when certain rumors started filtering back to her, Alice complained even more bitterly. "I am more and more impatient with Percy Lubbock's work," she said; and she urged Peggy and Harry to prepare a "better edition" that would supplant and displace his. "I feel as if I have failed of my trust," she fretted. For all the editorial excisions made by James's relatives and Lubbock's instinctive reticence, the published volumes could not allay the family's most morbid anxiety. "People are putting a vile interpretation on his silly letters to young men," Alice lamented: "Poor dear Uncle Henry."[4]

Thankfully, Alice never saw a copy of *What Percy Knew*, a pornographic parody of the Master that had been written some years before. The work's pre-amble offers an adequate glimpse of its contents:

> The scene is a Gentleman's Library. A small company, select, is assembled. One gentleman, somewhat elderly, stands bending near the fire, his head parallel to his knees. Another gentleman, younger, stands behind him, unbent. The trou-sers of both gentlemen lie gathered about their ankles.[5]

This Master is about to get a very pointed lesson, with a bevy of chosen aco-lytes as witnesses. (Other contemporaries, such as Max Beerbohm, had sati-rized James's obsessive sexual curiosity, but seldom with such a queer turn of the screw.)[6] As a young man, the author of this ribaldry had corresponded with Oscar Wilde when that writer was imprisoned in Reading Gaol (1895–97) for "gross indecency"; he certainly knew something about the underground world of Edwardian homosexuality. How widely this fragment of gay persi-flage circulated is unknowable, but its very existence (and the fact that it was written during James's lifetime) adds a certain resonance to the family's fears. Discouraging such inferences—or even speculation—became an insistent pre-occupation for the Jameses, and restricting access to the author's unpublished correspondence seemed the surest means of exercising control over the Mas-ter's posthumous reputation.

Whatever reservations the family had about Lubbock's two-volume edi-tion of James letters, they reasonably assumed that through its publication they had discharged their formal obligation to curious posterity. It was not long, however, before other recipients of James's epistolary outpourings ex-pressed the desire to publish letters in their possession. One such request came from the British novelist E. F. Benson, then the occupant of Lamb House, who, after his brother's death in 1925, wanted to commemorate Arthur Christopher Benson's long friendship with James. Without much hesitation, Harry relaxed his vigilance and gave permission (much to his later regret); he certainly must have assumed that his uncle's letters to the son of the Archbishop of Can-terbury could only have been blamelessly circumspect. He was unprepared,

then, to encounter in print such highly charged passages (laced with suggestive double entendres):

> Why aren't you here to take a good Devonshire walk with me? I hang over a
> green garden and a blue sea from a big balcony where I smoke solitary ciga-
> rettes. There would be room on the balcony even for your inches or cigarettes,
> even for Apollo's lips. (HJ to Arthur C. Benson, from Torquay, 5 Aug. 1896)

> I am divided between 2 sensations—panting for to-morrow p.m. and blushing
> for all the hours of all the past days. I ought to have acknowledged your beauti-
> ful letter (after your last being here,) about—about everything. But I have been
> so taken up with living in the future and in the idea of answering you with
> impassioned lips. . . . I can with utter ease procure myself to be transported [to
> join you]. I shall *come*—"that is all you know—and all you need to know." (HJ
> to Arthur C. Benson, from London, 16 Jan. 1896)[7]

To these (and many others) Harry's reaction was swift and negative. On the fly-
leaf of the copy he had received ("with thanks"!), the nephew scribbled crossly,
"When E. F. Benson asked me for permission to use Uncle Henry's letters to his
brother . . . I thought he was proposing to incorporate them in something about
his brother and consented. Behold what he's done!"[8] With this lamentable precedent before him, the nephew became more determined than ever to censor or
prohibit unwarranted publication, especially when the documents in question
were, as he frequently euphemized, "trivial." He justified himself to Lubbock
with this argument:

> One reason for trusting you with the delicate task of editing a couple of volumes
> and for rejoicing when they have been done the way you did them, is that one
> can say, "Let those volumes stand." Of course, I don't say that nothing unpub-
> lished is ever to be printed hereafter, but most of these people who want to print
> now are merely reaching out for a few shillings or ministering to their own van-
> ity. What they have in the way of letters is usually not the kind of thing that any
> friend of Uncle Henry's would select as doing him any sort of justice, and—in
> short—I trust that you will agree with me.[9]

"Lately almost everybody whoever received a letter or two from my uncle seems to have conceived plans for publishing them," he complained to one supplicant. "The effect is not happy."[10] Minimizing embarrassment to the family was Harry's foremost priority, and henceforth he was determined to erect safeguards that would ensure that only competent and mature researchers would have access to materials still under the James's control.

Before long, Harry was approached by another correspondent—a man who had not merely one document or two in his possession but seventy-eight: Hendrik Christian Andersen (1872–1940), the Norwegian-American sculptor whom James first met in Rome in 1899 and to whom he sent probably the most ardent letters in his vast epistolarium. Andersen's professional career had been doomed by his predilection for gargantuan subjects (as James himself grimly had prophesied), and he had continued to live and work in Rome only through the devoted generosity of his widowed sister-in-law, Olivia Cushing, whose vast fortune enabled the sculptor to build the Villa Helene as a home and studio for himself and his unsalable monstrosities.[11] By the 1930s, hard pressed for money, Andersen hoped to publish his James correspondence in an illustrated volume called *Letters to an Unknown Artist*: a potentially profitable exercise in self-pity.

Andersen reasonably could have nursed his ambition for this project, because he had known—and corresponded with—many Jameses besides Henry for decades. If not exactly an intimate of the family, he was certainly no stranger. In 1901 William James had come to his Roman studio and, more so than his brother, found much to admire in the sculptor's work. "The figures are really glorious," William commented, "ideally significant of human nature before its eating of the fruit of the fatal tree."[12] Olivia Cushing's marriage in 1902 to Andersen's ill-fated brother, Andreas (who died less than a month after exchanging vows), established another family tie, as she was also the sister-in-law of Edward Holton James (1873–1956), one of the Master's nephews. (He had married Olivia's sister, Louisa Cushing, in 1899.)[13] When Billy James and his family came to Rome in the 1920s, they, too, were frequent guests at Villa Helene, and Andersen struck up a friendly correspondence with this fellow-artist and his wife, Alice Runnells James. It was to them that Andersen first announced his intentions (in his barely literate way) in the summer of 1933. "I am busy composing a fourth fountain in the basement of our house," he wrote,

> which is the only cool place to work in these hot days, and in the evenings I write and hope to finish the introduction to a little volume Uncle Henry's letters to me, that like all his letters have a charm and beauty rich in sentiment and feeling. I often wish I had some tallented and sympathetic person to help me in this work, and my other writings, that need a clever man or woman to put into bookform; if you know of a rich person who is willing to work for Art's sake with a big plate of spaghetti as recompense, pin wings on their back and let them, or one, fly over.[14]

At Christmastime, Andersen was still at work on the volume, confident that he had something in his possession that no one else could match. "These letters are entirely different in sentiment from those already published," he confided to Billy and Alice, "and it is for this reason that I think it would be desirable to publish them."[15]

If at first Billy did not take Andersen quite seriously, he now felt obliged to enlighten him about the delicate question of copyright in Uncle Henry's unpublished manuscripts. "My brother Harry," he advised,

> was named as executor in the wills of both my father and my uncle Henry, and his consent is required for the publication of letters. It seems strange that letters to you, from anyone, should not be, quite simply, your property to publish or not as you pleased. But, legally, the writer of the letters, or his descendants, still have some rights over the publication of such material. I am sure of this because I know of several cases in which Harry *withheld* his consent to let people publish what they saw fit. So I beg you to write to Harry, and, if possible, to send him what you propose to publish.[16]

Perhaps because the documents themselves, in Andersen's view, revealed such a profound spirit of generous encouragement, he could not imagine why any other member of the James family would suppress their publication. "The letters in question," he reiterated, "throw a new light on the noble and beautiful spirit of Uncle Henry which I feel should not be disregarded or lost to the world." ("I must confess," he nervously added, "that, after preserving them for so many years, I do not care to have them destroyed.")[17] Far from destroying them, Andersen (with the help of a much more competent assistant) made several typescript copies of all but one of the letters; and in November 1934 he sent one set of duplicates to Harry with his formal request for permission to publish them.

Harry's quick refusal (a three-page, single-spaced masterpiece of Jamesian understatement) stunned, but did not completely deter, Andersen. At length, Harry had tried to make Andersen understand that, far from unique, the letters he had received from his uncle were similar to many already in print (only the recipient's vanity, he discreetly intimated, exaggerated their importance). Having come to regret other exceptions he already had made with regard to publication of Uncle Henry's letters (especially those to A. C. Benson), Harry felt that stricter prohibitions now were necessary. "The seventy odd letters that you sent me," he admitted, "would make quite a book. A publisher, especially in these days, would consider it very cautiously" (presumably because of the documents' thinly veiled homoeroticism). Though anything like full publication was out of the question, as far as Harry was concerned, he did suggest that some smaller portion of the letters—those in which James had voiced his admonitory strictures about Andersen's lifeless statues—might warrant circulation; and he proposed that some more competent person ("in whose taste and judgment I would have confidence")—Lubbock, perhaps, or Desmond MacCarthy—compile and edit such a selection.[18] Knowing that Andersen surely would reject this sly—and unmistakably humiliating—alternative, Harry craftily found a way of keeping the correspondence underground. As expected, Andersen bristled at his suggestions. "I am not prepared," he replied, "—as you yourself anticipated—to submit the letters to anyone, no matter how competent he may be, for selection and editing." It would hardly be fair, moreover, "to publish the adverse opinion of so eminent a man as Henry James without publishing also the appreciative letters I have received."[19] Such a profound stalemate would result in an equally profound silence.

Before letting the matter drop completely, Harry further suggested that Andersen send him the original letters for safekeeping. "I have a very large manuscript collection of my Uncle's correspondence which I have deposited in the Harvard College Library," he explained, "and which I shall leave in care of the University with certain restrictions designed to protect it from being pawed over, quoted and exploited except for definite literary and historic purposes and by really competent scholars or critics."[20] Andersen demurred, however, and the ultimate disposition of his James letters would become a pivotal event in the later history of the family's jealous custodianship of the Master's legacy.

Though Andersen never published his James letters, he did begin to draft a kind of biographical introduction to them. This fumbling scrap uncannily reads like a précis of Lubbock's *The Region Cloud*, the testimony of a fawning unknown artist at the feet of a venerated Master. "The following letters," he began,

> were written by Henry James during the latter period of his life, when he had reached the zenith of his fame, and they continue almost up to the time of his death, giving a vivid picture of his wonderful many-sided personality and broad sympathies. They show him in a variety of moods—gay, critical, sympathetic— and gradually darken with the passing of the years until, weighed down by sickness, old age and the tragedy of the World War, he laid down his pen for ever.
>
> The friend to whom these letters were written—myself—was an American sculptor of Norwegian origin, many years younger than himself who, when the correspondence began, was waging in a Roman studio the bitter, hand-to-hand fight for recognition which is the lot of so many artists at the beginning of their career.
>
> My first meeting with Henry James took place in my damp, sunless studio in the Via Margutta, that melancholy yet hallowed street, haunted by memories of the past. A warm friendship immediately sprang up between us—he a mature man, his feet firmly set on the highroad of success, and I a poor and unknown artist working from dawn to dusk in my efforts to give material form to the visions which filled my heart and soul.[21]

In addition to the letters, Andersen had another object to consecrate his relationship with the Master. In 1908, he had sculpted a marble portrait bust of James, from which several bronze castings also were made. When the Houghton Library began to assemble materials in various media for the 1943 Henry James centennial exhibition, the curator inquired about notable artworks that might complement their display of the Master's books and manuscripts. "There is an excellent bust by Derwent Wood," Harry sharply replied, "a terrible one by somebody else whose name I don't remember."[22] Harry knew that other artist's name very well, but he was determined to suppress any evidence of Andersen's connection to his uncle or the family. Very quickly the others closed ranks. A few years later, when Simon Nowell-Smith was trying to compile a catalogue raisonné of representations of the Master in the plastic arts, he asked Billy for help in identifying a bronze bas-relief that he had heard of but could not locate. Billy tried to ward him off by joking that the piece was negligible and not worth mentioning. Nowell-Smith ultimately gave up on the project, but not before telling Billy how he would have handled this particular entry. "As for the bronze," he said, "I should like to know the name of the artist. I am proposing to make the merest allusion to it in my article, probably in the form—'A bas-relief in bronze by . . . once existed, but it became the target of family criticism & the suggestion that it was worth preserving was shot down by James's great nephews.'"[23] Nowell-Smith got the genealogy wrong but the sentiment right (Harry and Billy were only one generation removed from Uncle Henry, not two).

Portrait bust of Henry James, by Derwent Wood. By permission of the Trustees of the Boston Public Library.

Portrait bust of Henry James, by Hendrik Andersen (1907). Courtesy of the Library of Congress.

Keeping Andersen (and his letters) shrouded in secrecy was hardly possible forever. Leon Edel had been told about this correspondence years before and was refused access to the material by Andersen himself; but that only would have whetted his already avid curiosity.[24] Andersen had never been shy about boasting of his connections with famous people: surely others knew that Henry James, for a time, had been his friend. When Andersen died in 1940, he bequeathed the Villa Helene—and all his unsold statuary—to the Italian state (his fondness for Mussolini may also have explained the Jameses' later disavowals of him), making provision for his foster sister, Lucia Lice, to have possession of the property for the rest of her life. As Lucia Andersen's resources dwindled, she found it necessary to sell off some of the contents of the villa, including valuable documents and autographs that were still among Hendrik's papers. In 1953 she sent a set of duplicates of the Henry James material to Frederick B. Adams Jr., the director of the Morgan Library in New York, hoping to entice his interest in purchasing them. Unable himself to judge their significance, Adams turned to Leon Edel for advice. "These are extremely personal," he told Edel, "but I don't know really how much they tell us about James."[25] For his part, Edel was hugely gratified in being able, at last, to see the transcripts (the letters to Andersen would loom very large in the later volumes of his biography).

Word of the letters began to spread—partly, one has to suppose, because of their undeniably amative nature: the intensity and freedom of expression that James used when writing to Andersen are not found elsewhere in his voluminous correspondence. Leon Edel was not the only Jamesian with an interest in these documents; nor was he alone in having the necessary instincts to find them. Right after the war, when John Lehmann launched his Chiltern Library of classic reprints, an eager young man in the publicity department volunteered to handle all the James titles on their proposed list.[26] For the next decade or so, at least in Britain, Michael Swan was to Henry James what Leon Edel had long wanted to become: a trusted authority and editorial mainstay leading the James Revival. Swan edited no less than a dozen volumes for Lehmann and other publishers; and, also a biographer on a much smaller scale, in 1952 he produced a compact volume on James that anticipated many of Edel's psychological insights but without the latter's Freudian trappings.[27] In 1953 Swan would publish a study of James and H. G. Wells (based on their unpublished correspondence); five years later, Edel and Gordon N. Ray would imitate—and supersede—Swan's work by editing their longer compilation of documents and commentary.[28] Edel sniffed that his rival's "devotion to James perhaps exceeds his devotion to historical fact."[29] But if Swan was something of a dilettante, he was also something of a detective: for it was he who first succeeded in finding James's letters to Andersen and who first brought them to public awareness.

In 1954 Swan had embarked on "a quest for the Italian traces of Henry James." He traveled to Florence and Rome, visiting sites that stirred imaginative association with so many of the Master's works and hoping, too, to find anyone who had known James, because he was planning a program of biographical interviews for the BBC and had brought recording equipment along. While in Rome, Swan acted on a tip he had received and paid a visit to the Villa Helene, where Lucia Andersen welcomed him, his questions, and his tape recorder. After visiting Andersen's studio and seeing all the groups of "Michelangelesque bodies, fifteen feet high or more, writhed in shining plaster," Swan then inquired about the sculptor's relationship with Henry James and the letters he had received from the Master.[30] The imperfect transcription of his interview with Lucia reads like a page from "The Aspern Papers":

[L. A.]: But they must have been sold in America. I'm sending them to him [Frederick B. Adams of the Morgan Library]. Because he wrote to me that he had a client and I told him . . . sell them at auction. I can show you the letter.

[M. S.]: Oh, I'd *love* to see . . .

[L. A.]: To see the letter?

[M. S.]: The Henry James letter[s], the original[s].

[L. A.]: Ah yes, the original[s]. I have the original[s] . . .

[M. S.]: Could you give permission to use those James letters?

[L. A.]: Well, it won't do any harm will it?

[M. S.]: No, no, I don't think so, but I mean we'd have to have your permission.

[L. A.]: You can go in the other room and you can go through some.[31]

"As far as I knew," Swan later wrote, "no one had ever seen this correspondence"; "Percy Lubbock, who edited the two volumes of James's letters, had never so much as heard of the existence of Hendrik Christian Andersen."[32] Immediately recognizing the unique significance of the material, Swan wrote a very discreet article about James and his "heroic young master," but he could not arrange for its publication until after the Andersen letters had been sold in America.

A minor bidding war ensued when the letters were put up for auction by Sotheby's. William A. Jackson at Houghton had hoped to fetch them for the James collection at Harvard, but he was smartly outbid by Clifton Waller Barrett, the "20th-century literary Maecenas" whose appetite for bibliographical curiosities was matched only by the considerable reaches of his personal fortune.[33] "The Sotheby price on the Andersen letters was ridiculous," Jackson complained. (For fifteen hundred dollars, one might have thought that Barrett snapped up a bargain.)[34] "They were much overcatalogued and some one must have been disappointed when he got them."[35] Jackson may not have known who outbid him, but Leon Edel was in on the secret. For some time Edel had made it his business to track the whereabouts of James manuscripts, because, as he worked on his biography of the Master, his top priority was monopolizing access to primary source material about Henry James. When in 1960 Barrett deposited the Andersen letters with the Special Collections division of the Alderman Library at the University of Virginia, Edel made sure that his friend gave him exclusive privilege to consult or quote from them. "As you know," he explained, "I am completing the life of Henry James . . . and between 1962 and 1966 there will appear four volumes of James's letters edited by me, to be published by the Harvard University Press." Having devoted many years of work to these enterprises ("with the full knowledge and approval of the James estate"), Edel was anxious that his work be protected from others whose research he could only think of as poaching. With that in mind, he urged Barrett to take "whatever steps may be necessary to restrict the material at the University of Virginia so that my priorities in this material might be protected until the works I have under way are published."[36] Edel's expected timeline for the completion of these projects may have been wildly optimistic, but his appeal was nonetheless successful, and the archive at Virginia was sealed for years to come.[37] Edel had perfected this strategy years before, when Harry first conferred priority upon him in the use of the James Archive at Harvard. But the unexpected appearance of James's letters to Andersen in 1955 greatly increased his exclusive leverage.

Michael Swan's former employer had been forced to close his publishing house in 1952, but John Lehmann went on to found the *London Magazine* two years later, and in that venue Swan first made portions of the James-Andersen correspondence public. Even though his discussion of "Henry James and the Heroic Young Master" hardly sensationalized its subject, the excerpts from letters he published did indeed reveal an author writing (as he maintained) "at a pitch of emotion rare in his letters or his works." In a headnote to his article, Swan claimed that he had received permission from the James estate to publish these documents, but their appearance occasioned a minor firestorm involving literary agents, publishers, and lawyers on both sides of the Atlantic.[38] If Swan's piece had appeared only in Lehmann's rather highbrow literary periodical, the family might not even have been aroused. But when Billy James saw Uncle Henry's letters splashed across the pages of *Harper's Bazaar*, his indignation was immediate. "I am outraged by publication of HJ letters in Harpers Bazaar," he fumed,

—letters which Harry had refused permission to publish and which are headed by the caption "By permission of the James estate." It is easy to see why Harry refused publication. The rather extravagantly endearing forms of address give fuel to the Freudian critics and the eloquence of HJ's condemnation of Anderson's [*sic*] artistic insanities throws the whole correspondence into the realm of the trivial and absurd.[39]

Through the estate's literary agent, Paul Revere Reynolds, Billy wanted to press charges and sue for damages, but *Harper's* laughed off the claim. "You've got a suit," Reynolds assured Billy, but "my lawyer . . . doesn't think you'll ever recover anything like what it would cost to get into litigation. My hope is that *Harper's Bazaar* will make some offer of settlement although of course the damage is done and there's nothing very much we can do about it."[40] Billy bitterly resigned himself to the situation, but he never wanted to see anything like it happen again and was quick to tell Edel that, more and more, he was "harassed" by people who wanted to quote from his uncle's manuscripts.[41] Edel realized that the anxiety provoked by this not-quite-surreptitious publication would be very useful in allowing him to tighten his grasp over other manuscript letters. By setting himself up as an ally of the family in defense against such publishing scoundrels, Edel found the crucial vehicle for perpetuating his archival priorities, and he never hesitated to remind James's successive literary executors of that supposed fact.

Just as fortuitous—if less potentially salacious—had been the hasty publication in 1953 of two minor articles based on fragments of James's correspondence with Vernon Lee. Billy James much regretted having given permission to two young scholars who made use of newly discovered James letters in their local college library (Colby). When Edel pointed out—in print—that the inferences they drew from this evidence were clearly erroneous, he also took the occasion to lay out a rationale for his own priorities. "HJ letters," he flatly told Billy,

> should never be published unless the person seeking to do so can put them into proper context and show a valid reason for their appearance, explain the nature of the friendship and see what was going on between the person writing and the person receiving the letters. HJ's epistolary situation is perhaps one of the most complicated in literary history, as you know. There were thousands of letters and many he considered the "mere twaddle of graciousness." When a letter is diagnosed as being "twaddle" it certainly should not appear in print, unless a good scholarly reason exists. Without proper editing and explaining these letters do seem curious and often over-elaborate, and I think that was why your brother vetoed so many of them and ringed the Harvard collection with such judicious safeguards. This said, I realize that very few persons outside myself can really put these letters into proper perspective, since I alone have read thousands and so can balance and weigh them against each other.[42]

Billy, for one, was grateful to be thus armed. "Your letter . . . supplies me with perfectly stated reasons for turning on the red light in future," he eagerly replied, adding in a later letter that Edel (through his "verdicts") happily had equipped him "with phrases which are invaluable to me when it comes to refusing [other] applicants. I feel just as you do about it but I haven't the language!"[43] Restrictive synergy of rare force resulted from barely concealed self-interest on Edel's part and protective family scruples on James's.

## Dr. Edel and Mr. Hyde

Almost from the time he began researching the Master, Leon Edel did his best to cultivate cozy relations with people who still had unpublished James letters in their possession. In the late 1930s, with support from the Guggenheim

Foundation, he traveled extensively in the United States and abroad, tracking down documents and making transcriptions—some of which are now the only copies extant—as he began to compile what would eventually become a ten-foot shelf of loose-leaf binders (ninety-seven in all) containing twenty thousand pages of typescripts, photocopies, and miscellaneous notes relating to James's correspondence.[44] When his edition of the *Collected Plays* at last was published in 1949, Edel resumed his biographical research, formally announced his favored status as James's authorized historian, and solicited owners of unpublished letters to make those materials available to him.[45] Not infrequently, Edel later would serve as the crucial intermediary between the owners of documents and the repositories (especially Houghton) or private collectors (such as Barrett) that desired to acquire them. After he had made transcriptions for his own use, Edel would tip off his favorite confidantes about such batches of letters, especially when those in possession of them were desperate for money, or otherwise eager to sell. In exchange, Edel typically stipulated that materials thus acquired be reserved for him, inaccessible to other library patrons, even after shelf-list numbers had been assigned to the manuscripts and evidence of their existence had been entered into the public catalogue. Grateful for his assistance in the acquisitions process, most buyers obligingly enforced these restrictions, acknowledging that Edel had become the veritable Bernard Berenson of Jamesiana, a uniquely privileged expert who commanded their obedient deference.

At Harvard, almost every important addition to the original family bequest of James papers was treated this way. Anticipating one such acquisition, Edel promptly wrote to William A. Jackson, "I want to be sure that if the letters arrive suddenly at the Houghton, my offices in the matter be recognized to the extent that they not be made available to other scholars until I have had a chance to study them more closely."[46] In 1960, Noel Perrin published a clever piece in the *New Yorker*, humorously ruing his own dashed hopes for writing a graduate dissertation on the Master—a plan that was foiled when the collection of James letters he had first discovered in England (and wanted to write about) was appropriated by Edel the Ubiquitous. Having been interrupted in his work, the narrator of Perrin's feuilleton returns two years later to his old college at Cambridge and immediately goes to see his former tutor, who was the nephew of George and Fanny Prothero (close friends—and frequent correspondents—of

James's). "'Do you remember those letters of my aunt's that you catalogued?'" the tutor asks him.

> I nodded dumbly.
>
> "They've gone to America," he said, laughing as if it were some kind of joke between us. "Leon Edel—do you know him?—has carried them off to New York. I believe he's considering them for a new collective edition in—ah—'the works.' Your countrymen are certainly tireless scholars, ha-ha."[47]

Perrin apparently could afford to make light of his own academic misfortune, but many other aspiring scholars could not. The letters to the Protheros, like so many other caches, ended up at Harvard, with Edel once again acting as the privileged agent of acquisition. At all the other major repositories, the pattern was the same. When, for example, Rupert Hart-Davis sold James's letters to Hugh Walpole to the Harry Ransom Humanities Research Center in Texas, Edel wanted his usual stipulations enforced. "Do you think you could write to the man you dealt with at Texas," Edel pressed Hart-Davis, "and say that you hope they will recognize my priorities in the Henry James letters in the Walpole Collection granted me long ago both by you, as Hugh's executor, and by the James Estate? Some such letter might pave the way for my requesting recognition of my priorities in the material they now own."[48] After Yale's Beinecke Library acquired the invaluable archive of James B. Pinker, Donald Gallup also agreed to enforce the same restrictions, telling Edel, "I am glad to know of the arrangement which you have with the Estate concerning publication of letters and shall certainly see that the rules are followed in any future use of James material."[49] For decades, successive curators at Harvard respected what Edel euphemistically called his "priorities" in the James papers, obeying the precedent first set down by Harry in 1947. Over time, Edel's privilege became a kind of unwritten law, and the library effectively gave him a private veto over any requests it received for permission to publish manuscript material. "We will remember your prior claim," Edel was assured early on, "and give them nothing unless you agree to it."[50]

As research librarians whose mission, ostensibly, was to foster serious scholarship, Jackson and his successors were sometimes discomfited by the anti-intellectual nature of the restrictions they were obliged to enforce. When, for example, a microfilm of the playscript of *Guy Domville* was loaned to a faculty member at the University of Kentucky, Jackson had to enjoin the recipient not to make it available to his students. "Oddly enough," Jackson explained, "the James collection was given to Harvard with the express provision that no graduate students be allowed to use it for work on their theses. I can assure you that this is a somewhat embarrassing restriction for us, but we are powerless to alter it."[51] Harvard's embarrassments would only multiply as, over time, serious researchers (especially younger ones) were turned away from its resources or denied permission to publish from them. On occasion, Edel's peremptory monopoly even may have encouraged sympathetic staffers to help some hapless scholar by suggesting ways of evading the counterintuitive restrictions they were supposed to enforce. When Millicent Bell, for example, was first researching James's complex relationship with Edith Wharton, that writer's papers on deposit at Yale (including James's letters to her) were still under seal. In the meantime, Harvard had acquired what remained of the typescript copies of the Master's correspondence that Percy Lubbock had used to prepare his 1920 edition of *Letters*; those to Wharton had survived the depredations of German officers who had occupied Lubbock's Italian villa during the Second World War and who then used many of his papers—including roughly half the James letters—as fireplace kindling. William A. Jackson brought the Lubbock typescripts to Bell's attention and encouraged her use of them; moreover, since these were not technically original manuscripts, the onerous James restrictions did not apply, allowing her (with the library's permission) to quote from them. Without access to these materials, Bell never could have written her pathbreaking study, *Edith Wharton and Henry James* (1965). Edel, needless to say, was greatly perturbed whenever such breaches or lapses occurred; and when they did, whatever librarian was in charge could expect a quick rap on the knuckles. By the middle of the 1960s, after a series of what the biographer could only think of as perfidious encroachments on his exclusive domain,[52] Edel yearned for Harvard to enforce even more restrictive policies on his behalf. "What I'm thinking," he wrote to the Houghton librarian,

is that I have perhaps taken in the past too liberal a view of the whole matter. The Mark Twain papers have been tightly sewn up from the first, as you know. You can probably name other instances. The deed of gift of the James papers to Harvard, (as I remember it from the days when Harry James showed it to me) quite clearly provides mandate for restriction. I am wondering whether further limitation for access for a couple of years might not simplify matters for both of us.[53]

The imperative of monopoly has a selfish logic of its own, and it clearly operated with full force in Leon Edel's imagination.

Besieged by other scholars, whose habits of industry reproached his own dilatory progress, Edel answered back by trying to thwart competing projects. As we have seen, the librarian's desk at numerous repositories was his first line of defense; but Edel also used his growing influence in the realms of publishing and academia to disparage others' work and delay, or prevent, its way into print. "Let some other publisher lose money on it" was one editor's reaction to the manuscript of *Edith Wharton and Henry James*, after Edel had deprecated Millicent Bell's scholarship as "pedestrian and prosaic."[54] A former editor of *Nineteenth-Century Fiction* also has testified that when Edel was sent submissions to that journal for evaluation, he was "very selective in what he was willing to entertain, and was especially hostile to anything that might be seen going against the grain of his own writings on James."[55] Challenges to Edel's editorial work—especially his egregious handling of James's letters—were also suppressed.[56] So great was his power that in 1966 Edel could even turn up his nose at a chaired professorship at Harvard. Instead, he used the invitation as leverage to nudge NYU into naming him "Henry James Professor of English and American Letters"—and releasing him from almost all teaching responsibilities whatsoever (a precondition to which Harvard never would have acceded).[57]

Another batch of letters in which Edel showed interest were those James wrote to Violet Hunt, a mistress of Ford Madox Hueffer (with whom she helped found *The English Review* in 1908), whose adulterous conduct eventually cost her her friendship with the Master. James's letters to her and Hueffer had come into the possession of Harford Montgomery Hyde, an Anglo-Irish barrister, man of letters, and distant cousin of Henry James himself (a pedigree he was very fond of touting). Hyde was also a literary biographer (although Edel would have disavowed any kinship on those grounds); and it might be said that he had a dilettante's fond predilection for collecting source material. At any rate, Hyde responded generously when Edel made inquiries of him, graciously providing typescript copies of all the James letters he owned. The cordial reciprocity between the two men rapidly deteriorated, however, after Hyde became the official tenant of Lamb House and Henry James became the object of his own biographical interest. "H. Montgomery Hyde may turn out to be a bit of a nuisance," Edel warily reported to his publisher-friend Rupert Hart-Davis: "his tenancy of Lamb House has started him searching, and he will doubtless burst into print in the near future."[58] Edel also alerted Clifton Waller Barrett to the possibility that Hyde would want to see James material in his remarkable collection. On that score, he was reassured. "The way things stand at present," Barrett answered, "we have placed a reserve on all of the Henry James letters and they are not shown anybody without clearance from you."[59] Nevertheless, like Michael Swan before him, Hyde would soon become another biographical bête noire, the type Edel contemptuously dismissed as a publishing scoundrel, a sensationalist snooper whose interest in James was merely "journalistic."

To regard Hyde that way was certainly unfair—he had already published many more books (in many more disciplines) than Edel and had become recognized as one of the leading advocates in Britain for the decriminalization of homosexuality; but his suspicious rival began a kind of smear campaign when he was afraid that Hyde was closing in on sources that Edel considered exclusive to himself. Not long after he was tenanted in Lamb House, Hyde proposed to write a brief history of that noble dwelling for the National Trust, the British preservation organization that had been gifted the property by Harry James's widow in 1949. Such a work obviously would require research into the late career of its most famous occupant, and, with typical industry, Hyde quickly began to assemble source material for the project. Learning that Theodora Bosanquet's executrix had sold the secretary's papers and diaries to the Houghton Library in 1963, Hyde visited Harvard the following year, hoping to gain access to them. Fortuitously for Hyde, his visit coincided with the death of William A. Jackson, the curator who had long stood watch—*in loco Leonis*—against Jamesian interlopers. In his absence, Hyde was allowed to see Bosanquet's papers, including her copy of James's Napoleonic last dictations. When Edel learned of this, he knew he was in for a fight. "I am a little disconcerted at Montgomery Hyde's seeing the Bosanquet material," Edel modestly complained, "—especially since he has no scholarly intention and is quite likely to make superficial journalistic use of what he picks up."[60] Jackson's successor, eager to please, removed the dictation from the rest of Bosanquet's papers and locked it away in the Houghton vault.

That confiscatory gesture came too late. Hyde already had seen at least one copy of the document in Britain; and, for that matter, Bosanquet herself had read portions of it during the BBC radio program that Michael Swan ingeniously had organized back in the 1950s. After that series of interviews first aired, Edel had enjoined his British factotum, Rupert Hart-Davis, to get him a transcript: "the one they did in June," he specified, "with the unspeakable Michael Swan as narrator. I understand Theodora B. after enjoining us to silence proceeded to read HJ's final dictation or parts of it into the microphone—I wish she hadn't."[61] During that broadcast, before handing the mouthpiece over to Bosanquet, Swan had given the audience a kind of tantalizing anticipatory gloss of what they were about to hear. "It is not possible to give the whole of this strangely moving and absolutely characteristic final dictation of the Master," he acknowledged. "One may call it a vision—a vision in which he sees his own utterly dedicated life as in some way paralleled by the career of Napoleon."[62] Edel, we know, had spirited away his own copy of the dictation after he first uncovered it in the 1930s in the basement of Widener Library. Always wary of any evidence of mental instability within the family, Harry later confiscated the documents, removed them from the archive, and presumably destroyed them before giving the James papers, irrevocably, to Harvard.[63] As we have seen, Pelham Edgar first disclosed the existence of these weird snapshots of the Jamesian subconscious in his 1927 monograph (having learned of the dictation from Bosanquet), but no one had ever published so much as a word from the manuscript source. Its value to Edel, then, was capital: all along he had been planning to use the dictation to frame the majestic tableau of James's death— the natural culmination of his five-volume biography. Now his worst fears were being realized: he was going to be scooped, and every journalistic instinct in his wiry frame resented that possibility.

To ward off this prospect, Edel began a tortured correspondence with Hyde, sending him thinly veiled threats beneath a veneer of civility. After laying out the long history of his established "priorities," Edel then reminded Hyde of the need for respecting them. "I needn't tell you," he warned, "I would be most unhappy if there were some misunderstanding on this point and you anticipated some of the matters destined for my final volume."[64] Only one or two further exchanges were needed for the temperature to rise. Hyde kept reiterating the innocence of his motives and intentions; Edel kept accusing him of unwarranted trespass. To Hyde, as they had to so many others, Edel's monopolistic claims seemed preposterous. "I was not then aware," he confessed, "that you had reached an understanding with Dr. Bond's predecessor by which you had, so to speak, pre-empted the whole of the James and Bosanquet collections to the exclusion of all other students, including those who might wish to make a limited but reasonable use of them in their own published works. Indeed I am still in ignorance of the details of this extraordinary arrangement." Given the fact that Hyde had extended many courtesies to Edel—inviting him (twice) to stay at Lamb House, freely giving him copies of privately held source material ("without any thought of retaining it for prior publication by myself")—this stubborn obstructionist stance seemed unfathomable. "[W]hen I, as a kinsman of Henry James and the tenant of his old home, wish to quote a few paragraphs from original material over which you claim to exercise control, in a booklet I am writing for the use of visitors to the house and garden on the days when they are open to the public, you complain that I am poaching on your preserves and make all kinds of difficulties for me with Harvard where the material is located."[65] And this was just the beginning.

Later that year, Edel was tipped off that *Horizon* (a highbrow British literary periodical) was going to publish an article on "Henry James and Theodora Bosanquet," in which Hyde would quote from the secretary's manuscript diaries. Swinging into action, Edel protested to James Parton, the publisher of *Horizon*; and he got the Houghton librarian to chime in, too. "I have no recourse," William H. Bond insisted, "but to ask that the article be withdrawn," further claiming that Hyde's use of Bosanquet's diary was "a clear infringement of Mr. Edel's prior rights."[66] In the face of these legal arguments, the magazine caved and refused to publish Hyde's piece. But its rejection only galvanized the author's resolve to continue his archival research into the Master's domestic life history, which he now expanded to include not just James's years at Lamb House but the whole of his long residence in England. When the fruit of his extended labors, *Henry James at Home*, was ready for the press, another legal firestorm erupted. Rupert Hart-Davis (always on the lookout for Edel) learned that Methuen was planning to publish Hyde's book in Britain and that the American edition would be handled by Farrar, Straus and Giroux. Obligingly (and without Hyde's consent), Robert Giroux sent Edel a set of uncorrected proof sheets; after reading them, the biographer mounted an all-out assault to suppress publication. "I have a strong feeling," Edel confided to Hart-Davis, "that Hyde has worked at this not only to build himself up as a kinsman of the Jameses (he is descended from a sister in Ireland of the first W. J.) but also perhaps as a way to revenge himself on you, as my publisher, for having stopped him once before." Sensing that Hyde's volume would be a commercial success seems to have irked Edel the most. "He has created a gossipy book that will probably attract the very public I have created," Edel complained—oblivious to the irony of his own confession.[67]

In the proof sheets he had obtained, Edel could see that Hyde was going to finish his story with an account of James's last days and hours, including portions of the Napoleonic dictations he had seen. Rather than be scooped by the pestiferous Mr. Hyde, Dr. Edel chose instead to publish the texts of each "Last Dictation" in the pages of the *Times Literary Supplement*, the appearance of which also initiated an ugly exchange of letters in that same venue between the two antagonists. Edel threw down the gauntlet with typical hauteur. "It had been my intention," he revealed,

> to use this material in its relevant place in the *Life of Henry James* which I am now completing. But I have learnt that a certain writer in England, who gained access to Miss Bosanquet's papers, found copies of some of this dictation and is planning to make use of it in a forthcoming book along with other materials long ago made available to me by Miss Bosanquet, and reserved for my use. I have decided accordingly, in the interest of the record, and of accuracy, to make this document public, there being no objection now from the James descendants. If I am to be anticipated, it seems to me, I may as well be anticipated by myself.[68]

Not surprisingly, Hyde rose to the bait and, for the next six weeks, the "Letters" column of the *Times Literary Supplement* gleefully made room for their vicious war of words. Among other things, Hyde wanted to know how Edel had gained such intimate knowledge of his forthcoming book: certainly neither he nor his publisher had circulated proof sheets to him. (Even this minor literary brouhaha had its element of intrigue.) But the crux of their acrimonious correspondence brought into focus the issue (or absence) of scholarly courtesy.

Both writers described the friendliness of their first meeting, but Hyde was quick to counter that impression in rather lurid detail. "Mr. Edel makes much of the manner in which he received me in New York five years ago," he began.

> Since he told me then [in 1963] that he was working on the final volume of his Henry James biography, covering the years 1895 to 1916, which has yet to appear, I should add that I returned his courtesy by sending him typed copies of over fifty interesting unpublished letters of this period from Henry James to Violet Hunt and Ford Madox Ford, the originals of which were in my collection, and which I knew that he had never seen. I also offered him the originals at the price I paid for them. He declined this offer on the ground that he could not afford such an "exorbitant price," although he was glad to keep the copies I had given him.
>
> He has now repaid my friendly gesture by preventing me from using the Bosanquet diaries at Harvard, even for the purpose of my ignoble "pamphlet" [*The Story of Lamb House*], in spite of the fact that I have the permission of the controller of the copyright. For sheer selfishness, this seems to me hard to beat.[69]

As preliminary fanfare to the appearance of Hyde's book, this exchange sounded ominous indeed.

Determined to suppress *Henry James at Home*, Edel sought the assistance of his British publisher, Rupert Hart-Davis, whose legal advisers would act to defend their common interest in the James material. The rancorous crossfire that ensued certainly had its comic moments. Not only had Hyde made use of unpublished manuscripts to which Edel claimed first right but the poacher also had infringed upon the already-published volumes of his life of Henry James. "Even where Hyde has used common sources," Edel maintained,

> he has followed my sequence and often the very same quotation. He has on other occasion interlarded fuller quotation. Nevertheless if one follows through what he has done the effect is that of a paste-and-scissors job with a certain amount of word alteration, but nothing that can be tantamount to the creation of a work different from mine. The materials for a life of James, and for these specific years are so abundant (several thousand letters) that it would be the greatest of coincidence that two writers—if they did use the materials independently—would come up with similar sequences. He has lifted my frame and

my structure, and padded it out, and shuffled, but what he has lifted far exceeds what on this side of the water is regarded as "fair use."[70]

What clinched the argument, as far as Edel was concerned, was the fact that, when Hyde quoted from manuscript sources that thus far had appeared only in his own life of James, the interloper had replicated the same stupid errors of transcription for which Edel already was notorious. "He duplicates all my little errors in my quotations—whenever they occur," Edel almost boasted. "I omitted several words in one instance. He does so as well. He thus gives himself easily away."[71] It might have seemed a strange defense—to advance behind the shield of one's own incompetence—but that is where Edel planted his flag.

In further defense of his territory, the biographer also claimed that his own use of manuscript material had vested its statutory copyright exclusively in him—that he, in effect, was protecting the estate until such time as his long-delayed edition of James's letters was published and copyright in those volumes could be registered formally in the family's name. Exasperated by Hyde's remote genealogical filiation, Edel also asserted (somewhat remarkably) that living members of the James family (his staunch ally, Billy, had died in 1961) could not give permission to others to quote from unpublished letters, because such authority had been ceded to the literary agency of Paul Revere Reynolds in New York and that Reynolds had long accepted—and enforced—Edel's "priorities." Equipped with these arguments, the British barristers intended to seek an injunction against Methuen to bar that firm from publishing *Henry James at Home.*[72]

Methuen's legal team asked simply for the most basic piece of evidence: they wanted Edel to produce a document that would establish, indisputably, the legitimacy of his claims of privilege with respect to the James papers. *That*, of course, was the one piece of paper Edel could not produce, because all along his "priorities" had been based upon a kind of gentleman's agreement, periodically renewed through his cozy relations with various members of the James family and those who had physical possession of the manuscripts. With his long career in the law, Hyde himself likely was the author of Methuen's response to the threatened injunction, and this formidable document is worth quoting at length:

> If Professor Edel had never published a single line about Henry James, our author would still have followed substantially the same pattern in his narrative.

Such apparent similarities as exist, in the treatment of James's life from 1875 to 1895 in Hyde's book and your client's three works, are simply due to the two writers having used common sources, which is perfectly reasonable in the circumstances. As regards our author's few short quotations from James letters which your client was the first to publish, we are of the opinion that these would be covered by the fair dealing clause in the Copyright Act for the purpose of research or criticism, even if our author did not have the permission of the James trustees, which he has. . . . Whatever your client's understanding may be of the role of Paul Reynolds & Son in the matter, our author doubts whether this firm of literary agents were ever "the sole persons authorized to enter into contracts on behalf of the estate," except possibly in respect of contracts for the reprint of James's published works during the fifty years after his death, when these works were still in copyright and Reynolds acted as agents for the collection of the fees due to the estate. Mr Hyde informs us that he first obtained a copyright permission direct from his cousin the late William James as long ago as 1948 or 1949 for material used in a BBC broadcast, and nothing whatever was said at that time about having to go through Reynolds. Nor did William's son John, the present senior trustee, mention Reynolds when he gave Mr Hyde the permission he required for the present book. This is corroborated by the authors of six works containing extensive quotations from James letters which have appeared since the publication of the first volume of Edel's biography in 1953. In each instance the acknowledgment is either specifically to Mr John James or (if before 1962) to his father William James, or else generally to "the trustees of the James estate." None of these acknowledgments makes any mention of Reynolds. . . . Finally, our author would like us to draw your attention to the fact that his book is dedicated by permission to the present principal trustee of the James estate, Mr John James, and his wife.[73]

Since Edel could not provide conclusive evidence of his privileged status, his attorneys had no real answer to Hyde's counterarguments. "We should either start proceedings immediately," they advised, "and apply for an interlocutory injunction, which would be a gamble, or do no more about it other than perhaps continue the correspondence until either they decide not to publish the book or, more likely, until they call our bluff."[74] Call it they did, and Methuen brought out *Henry James at Home* in 1969. Coincidentally, perhaps, Hyde's next project was a massive biography of another tyrannical personality: Josef Stalin. When it was featured in the *New York Times Book Review*, Edel clipped the notice for his files, scribbling (gratefully) in the margin, "At least he's been driven from the James field."

## Chairman of the Board

How tenaciously Edel maintained his priorities (not infrequently at the expense of other scholars' careers) has already become a matter of public record. Less well appreciated is the fact that he often used the family's deep-seated phobias to reinforce his claims, even while he himself intended to exploit certain kinds of material for ends not unlike those of the "publishing scoundrels" he so actively discouraged. From a very early stage in his research about James, Edel certainly knew that he would have to tackle the issue of the writer's (homo)sexuality; but he also knew how timidly the writer's nearest relatives approached that subject and how determined they were to shield Uncle Henry from what they considered unwarranted speculation.[75] When he was wrestling with this problem, Edel had occasion to discuss his dilemma with Harold Nicolson, whose unzipped diary provides a curious glimpse of the biographer. "I lunch with Edel at the Century Club," Nicolson recorded,

> and he shows me the portrait of the young James [by John La Farge]. He is distressed how, in this third volume, he will deal with James' homosexuality. He was a late-flowering bugger and the Boston puritanism retarded him until it was too late to get full satisfaction from it. Edel is . . . perplexed how to handle this problem. I advise him to treat it as a matter of course, making no apologies or evasions.[76]

Despite Nicolson's frank advice, it was most unlikely that Edel ever would refer to the Master as a "late-flowering bugger." As he later admitted, Edel "was very careful not to offend the Jameses," always cautious not to "give them too much mental anguish."[77] How best, then, to quiet the family's fears and circumvent their anticipated objections? For one thing, time was on his side. Harry James was dead before the first volume of the biography was completed; Billy was gone before the second appeared. At the slow pace with which he proceeded, Edel would not get to the more sensitive material until the penultimate (fourth) volume, not published until 1969, and by then even the next James executor was dead. One might almost say (after *The Wings of the Dove*): He waited, Leon Edel. At any rate, he took his time.

He also took precautions. When (at an MLA convention, of all places!) another researcher queried Edel about letters "of the Hendrik Andersen type," he immediately sounded the alarm to both family and librarians. "I seem to sense a possible journalistic enterprise behind it," he warned.[78] Ever vigilant, the Houghton librarian reassured Edel that the suspected poacher had been "working in our Reading Room long enough for us all to become aware of the fact that she is a little eccentric." Not to worry, he insisted; "she is certainly not going to see anything she's not supposed to see."[79] At all the major repositories, Edel's jealous priorities were in safe hands.    And to each of the literary executors in turn, Edel periodically waved the red flag of journalistic revelation to remind them that publishing scoundrels were lurking: all the more reason to extend his monopoly. Not long after John Sumner Runnells James (1914–69) succeeded his father, Billy, as guardian of the literary estate, Edel passed on a "curious rumor" that had reached him from London that some letters from James to Edmund Gosse had turned up—letters "of an unusually 'frank' nature in which he discusses his sexual problems freely." Edel doubted the authenticity of this, but passed it along as a safeguard to thwart any "attempt at sensationalism" that might follow.[80] Privately, however, Edel almost hoped that the rumor was true. If some other author "outed" the Master, Edel shrewdly calculated that "this may actually be helpful for Vol. IV. It would relieve me of the onus of 'breaking' the story and thereby inviting the accusation (among a few) of invasion of privacy: for I would then be in the position of setting the record straight, as I did with the castration story in Vol. I."[81] Ironically, the "outing" story never got written, because the source material for it—transcripts of the Andersen letters that Michael Swan had deposited in the British Library—had been withdrawn from the collection at Edel's insistence.[82]

Of all the family literary executors, John James gave Edel the most trouble. Irascible and often unpredictable, John was much less complacent than his predecessors and far more difficult to manage. As we have seen, he was only too encouraging (as Edel would have felt) to a meddler like Hyde: a cozy cousin indeed, when he gave Hyde his consent to use James manuscripts, Edel's rival could trump all the long-standing restrictions that had kept those sources off limits. Since most requests to publish from the archive routinely were forwarded to Paul Reynolds in New York, all along Edel had pressured the agent either to deny them outright or at least to consult him first before granting permission. As interlopers began to evade his control with greater success, Edel ratcheted up his demands—so much so that by 1968 (provoked by the Hyde debacle) Reynolds wanted to wash his hands of the whole business. At the biographer's private instigation, Reynolds wrote to the surviving James heirs, described the situation as "chaotic," and recommended that they cede all rights in the unpublished letters to Edel and give him "the power to deal with all publication matters."[83] John James bristled at this suggestion and repudiated Reynolds's claim that managing the rights in the unpublished letters had become "chaotic." "The majority of Henry James and William James letters are in the hands of college libraries," he responded, taking a very pragmatic view of the whole question. "I receive each year on the average of forty requests from authors and students for permission to quote in part or in full from the letters and publications. I rarely refuse them. There is no financial gain to me nor will there ever be one." Obviously unaware that Reynolds's proposal originated with the biographer, John James added, "I have known, liked and admired Leon Edel for over thirty years. I would be surprised, if he, any more than I, would consider such a plan for the letters."[84] Well, surprise, surprise.

When John James died unexpectedly the following year, Edel and Reynolds pressured his successor, Alexander James (1918–95), to accede to the same plan that John sternly had rejected. Much to their surprise, Alex, too, repudiated the proposal. Seeing that he would have to ingratiate himself with the newest executor, Edel proposed a luncheon at the Century Club during which he could explain the long history of his "priorities" and the need for maintaining them. Like most of his predecessors, Alex seemed willing to defer to Edel's informed judgment, and their relationship soon followed the familiar pattern: when a permissions request came to him, Alex referred the supplicant to Edel, whose refusal was almost guaranteed. To ensure such continuity, Edel also resumed his usual strategy, insisting that with him alone the family secrets were safe. Having been told by Alex that a biographer had approached him about doing a book on Alice James, Edel immediately raised his suspicions and his hackles. "It would be easy for someone to do a nasty book about Alice," he warned, "because of her mental troubles, and her attachment to Katharine Loring—the attachment of a sick woman of brilliant mind in the old companion sense. But these people who write the new stuff often latch on to this and I can see a sensational Women's Lib, Lesbian, book written dramatizing Alice's neurosis—instead of the delicate, fine book that could be done."[85] That project (whatever its possible tenor) died quietly. Those people, writing the new stuff, had to be kept at bay.

All along, however, Edel himself was nursing ideas about how best to exploit the material he had discovered in his long years of research. James's late letters to younger men seemed especially suitable for such a purpose, and, when the time seemed right, Edel was ready to strike. Years before even one of his four-volume set of James letters was in print, the editor envisioned making a separate book of "the so-called 'homosexual' letters"—those written to Andersen, Jocelyn Persse, and Hugh Walpole.[86] "The entire gay world is waiting for these," he gloated.[87] Rather coyly entitled *Letters to Three Friends*, this volume, as Edel acknowledged to the director of Harvard's imprint, would not have the character of a university press book: its subject matter was far more topical and even, frankly, sensational. But when Harvard (never deaf to commercial prospects) expressed some interest in it, Edel grossly miscalculated by trying to start a bidding war between that press and his trade publisher, Lippincott. "I will simply have to be mercenary," he confessed; "my agent will be instructed to sell it to the publisher offering the best contract."[88] Seldom having to confront such tactics, Harvard sternly reminded Edel that he was still under contract (and had been, since 1958) to produce a multivolume edition of James letters for their imprint, an obligation that should take precedence over anything else. Like all the others he had frustrated, *this* publishing scoundrel now had to retreat.

Fully to examine the "mercenary" relation that Edel established with James's literary property would almost require another book, but it is certainly fair to say that, from the very start, he was hardly blind to the pecuniary value of the materials over which he ultimately would exert almost total control. (Not for nothing did his 1971 *New Yorker* profile carry the title "Chairman of the Board.")[89] As far back as the 1940s, when he was assembling and editing his collection of James's plays, Edel already anticipated that their publication might attract not just an audience of scholars but possibly the attention of stage actors or even Hollywood producers. "I should expect substantial royalty on the sales of the book," he frankly told the family, "and also, if, as a result of publication, some of the plays should reach the stage or screen, a reasonable percentage of royalties therefrom."[90] Edel's unexpected avarice touched a nerve in Harry James, whose early and steadfast enthusiasm for his scholarship was unprepared for it. After some delicate negotiation, Edel settled for a more modest share of possible returns (though it is doubtful that he got much or any). With Harry's death in 1947, Edel had much greater latitude in arranging his publishing contracts with the estate, not least because Billy James was convinced that he had done "more for the dear Uncle than anyone else."[91] Perhaps he had done more because no one else had been—or would be—permitted to do much at all? The biographer's jealous prerogatives made sure of that.

When Edel returned to the United States at the end of the Second World War, Henry James was still a secondary occupation for him. To make a living, once again Edel had to ply his trade in the inky substratum of journalism, all the while nursing his professional ambition and growing more confident that his advantageous relation to the James descendants (and their archive) someday would win him fame and its pecuniary equivalent. Very much like the Master, he, too, could stand a good deal of gold.[92] As we have seen, before he shipped out to France, Edel had initiated commercial contact with James Laughlin at New Directions for an anthology of James short stories. Matthiessen had landed that deal; but not long after he was back in New York, Edel resumed his correspondence with New Directions, hoping to interest the firm not merely in his edition of the Master's plays (then still in progress) but also in the biography of James that he had begun as a kind of companion piece. Laughlin had heard about these projects from Matthiessen and Harry Levin (his former professors at Harvard), and, wanting to know more about them, he set up a meeting between Edel and one of his scouts. That man's report to Laughlin offers some telling insights. "Mr. Leon Edel—the James dramatic mss man—has just been in," the memo began:

There are twelve plays and a scenario—all edited and ready BUT he is also writing a Biography entitled the Dramatic Years—which he feels should be published before the plays. He claims to have had several nibbles from commercial houses for the Biography and thinks that the plays should be published by the same people. He obviously believes that he is on to a good thing and is after BIG SALES, but is certainly prepared to talk business with you.[93]

Eventually, of course, Edel sold both the *Complete Plays* and his life of James to J. B. Lippincott; but these anonymous off-the-cuff remarks speak volumes about Edel's emerging conception of himself as a mercenary man of letters.

Not long after, his star in the ascendant, Edel frankly told Rupert Hart-Davis that "in my new status as 'homme de lettres' I say Yes to everything that can be sold in the literary marketplace."[94] When Frederick W. Dupee managed to secure permission to publish all three of the Master's autobiographical volumes between one pair of covers—Edel, in a rare instance, stepping aside—the biographer also insisted that it would be the last time anyone would get a foot in the door ahead of him. "In future I will not abdicate as readily," he impudently remarked, "but will take *all* HJ as my province and tell all comers that I am doing Everything!"[95] Ten years later, with an ever-tighter grip on the vastly expanding market for James reprints, Edel was able to negotiate extremely high fees for the various prefaces and introductions he supplied for them—"on the theory," he blandly said, "that my name on a James book has acquired a certain *cachet.*" R. P. Blackmur, who had worked with Dell Publishers to produce an inexpensive series of James paperbacks, was Edel's only significant competitor in this arena; and when Blackmur died in 1965, Edel had the field essentially to himself. With so many of the Master's works lapsing from copyright, the James estate received nothing from the sales of such books, but Edel always got his ample cut: after all, as he said, "my name represents a kind of 'trade-mark' on a James book."[96]

It is hardly surprising that Edel should have come to assert a kind of imperial equivalence between himself and the Master whom he had monopolized so effectively. Over the years, he surrounded himself with many Jamesian artifacts—often freely given to him by the Master's heirs. Most famous, probably, was the glittering topaz ring worn by James when he sat for the imposing Sargent portrait that now hangs in Britain's National Portrait Gallery. Bruce Porter (Peggy's husband) sent the ring to Edel in 1953 as a kind of trophy after the publication of the first volume of the biography. "The ring fits my finger— the same one HJ wore it on—as if it were made for it," the biographer rather complacently observed.[97]

Other association items Edel acquired at a fraction of their value—notably books from the Master's personal library and inscription copies James had given to friends and other members of the family. Harry James's second wife,

Dorothea Draper, had little interest in her husband's family history or its material accoutrements; soon after his death, she deeded the property in Rye to the National Trust and dispersed the contents of the Lamb House library for two hundred pounds ("a ridiculously trifling sum").[98] Edel quickly snatched up many of these from the bookseller who had purchased the inventory, and he also persuaded Dorothea to let him have many of the more desirable volumes that Harry personally had taken back to America because of their value (inscription copies, for example, that had been presented to James by Robert Louis Stevenson and Rudyard Kipling). Likewise, when John Sumner Runnells James inherited the Cambridge residence at 95 Irving Street, Edel implored him not

Leon Edel with a copy of John Singer Sargent's 1913 portrait of Henry James (1963). Edel is wearing the same topaz ring that glistens in Sargent's painting of the Master. By permission of the Rare Books and Special Collections Division, McClellan Library, McGill University.

to empty the house simply by handing over to Harvard the books and manuscripts he would find there. When John later decided to sell a large portion of the family library, Edel jumped at the chance to acquire the choicer parts of it wholesale. The deal he made with John James was simple and direct:

> [O]nce Goodspeed or whatever bookseller has named his price, allow me to acquire from you—at their price—the HJ volumes you may wish to sell. I would add them to the collection I have formed of volumes from Lamb House which have a particular biographical importance. I began this when Dorothea dispersed the books in Lamb House; but she sold to the booksellers and I usually had to pay their mark-up for volumes I wanted, which is just about 100 per cent.

Obligingly, John James offered the biographer "first crack at the books," and Edel's gathering of Jamesiana grew apace.[99] It should be noted that, before moving to Honolulu in the early 1970s, Edel sold his James collection to Clifton Waller Barrett for twenty-nine thousand dollars.[100]

Edel may have wanted—and needed—to think of himself as the Master's surrogate, but in all of his dealings, he betrayed a much closer affinity with James's nephew Harry: the indefatigable litigator, hardheaded businessman, and jealous guardian of family privilege. He certainly shared Harry's virtual contempt for younger scholars to whom a valuable archive was little more than an academic rumpus room. Having established his own monopoly of the James papers, Edel did not hesitate to proclaim himself an expert on the subject of archival ethics. In a 1970 symposium "On the Use of Private Papers," he warned that libraries had a duty to prevent such materials from falling into the hands of "future inexperienced and often unlettered graduate students for whom these archives are accumulated."[101] Three years earlier, Edel even had bemoaned the proliferation of the Xerox machine, which to him was a dreaded weapon of invasion. "Indiscriminate Xeroxing of collections is tantamount to publishing them," he insisted. And the most frequent benefactors of the new technology were those he most dreaded. "The great increase in Ph.D. candidates seeking an exercise to fulfill degree requirements has created an unjustifiable clamour for access to unpublished papers," he warned. While a small minority might know how to handle such sources, "some control of access is necessary. . . . [I]t should be recognized that some barrier needs to be erected by literary executors and libraries against a growing race of privacy-invaders, sensation-mongers, Xerox collectors and voyeurs, as well as curious amateurs who never intend to write a serious work."[102] These were exactly the same fears (and exactly the same arguments) that Harry expressed when he erected the formidable defensive perimeter around the James archive. From what we have seen of his behavior (and heard from his lips), it seems unlikely that Edel ever would have remarked—as the Master famously did—that in human life only three things were important: "The first is to be kind. The second is to be kind. And the third is to be kind."[103]

A higher priority for him was to be controlling. Edel's most faithful apologists (notably Lyall Powers) have excused this obvious tendency as a result of his Jewish ancestry, the burden of which made him a perpetual outsider and, at least initially, hampered his chances for securing a permanent academic appointment. Always working from the margins (so the argument goes) made Edel particularly wary about losing or compromising his hard-won status as the most privileged Jamesian, presumably justifying his aggressive—even ruthless—attitude toward others whom he could only regard as competitors. "He rode fence diligently around his Jamesian domain," as Powers acknowledged, "alert to the threat of encroachment by other scholars."[104] After the last volume of the biography was completed, when asked if he had ever felt "possessive" of James, Edel shot back his answer: "Certainly not. I never did." But, almost as quickly, he then went on to say, "I wasn't going to tolerate trespassers."[105]

In light of all that has happened since, it is almost amusing to wonder what Harry James's reaction would have been had he known that the meticulous young scholar who first approached him with queries about his uncle's obscure dramatic works eventually would seek to publish, and profit from, the most intimate letters in the epistolarium. Had such motives become apparent then, surely Edel would have been ostracized from the family's confidence as completely as the "publishing scoundrel" in "The Aspern Papers." But discretion had its day, and so did the careful Canadian. In those early years of research, Edel also had occasion (lucky man!) to interview Edith Wharton about her memories of James and other celebrated American expatriates. "Mrs. Wharton believed I was a gossip-mongering journalist," Edel admitted, but she nevertheless invited the interviewer to her suburban villa on the outskirts of Paris and gave herself up to his questions.[106] Again, discreet habits and a cosmopolitan demeanor were his best allies, and he was invited back several times: whatever suspicions Wharton harbored must have been put to rest. "Mrs. Wharton apparently was satisfied," he wrote, "that I wasn't some eager young newspaperman trying to write a sensational article about her secret 'love-life.'"[107] Perhaps her satisfaction was premature? Not many years later, when freelancing was still his profession, Edel tried to sell an article that he pitched this way:

> Whenever I think of Edith Wharton, I think of the talks I had with her the year before she died and of her fears that her papers would fall into inexperienced hands; when she died her private correspondence and manuscripts were locked up until 1965—until all those who lived in her time would be dead. And yet already the story of her love affair with—let's call him X—is leaking out. He is represented as the dark figure who wilted all passion from her writing; he read the manuscript of *Ethan Frome* page by page. He lived in the same apartment house as she did, in Paris. He was a robust, famous, American, of fine family, an international figure. He was a friend of Proust and of Henry James.[108]

What publishing scoundrel could have phrased it better? *Mr. X!* A secret lover—"of fine family," of course: why else should his true identity be of interest? It seems as if Mrs. Wharton's first instinct was the right one: this projected exposé of her private life would have been nothing if not titillating, appealing to all that is vulgar and prurient. He waited, Leon Edel. And we have to admit that, ultimately, he won.

All students and friends of Henry James should mark 4 May on their calendars. No, it's not the writer's birthday (one can celebrate that after filing one's taxes on 15 April) or even—for those who prefer morbid rites—his day of death (that is 28 February). Instead, it was the day in 1973 when prospects for Henry James scholarship were forever changed, liberated from the decades-old restrictions that had kept the novelist's manuscript letters and almost the entire archive of family papers at Harvard's Houghton Library beyond the inquiring reach of generations of scholars. On that day in 1973, Alexander James, great-nephew of the novelist and literary executor of the James estate, wrote to William H. Bond, head librarian at the Houghton, instructing him to rescind the encumbering regulations that for so long had prevented scores of researchers from accessing these desirable primary sources.[1] Leon Edel's monopoly at last was broken.

Even after the formal restrictions were lifted, however, more years passed before the library's long-standing presumption of refusal would fade from institutional memory. I can still recall a rather timid conversation, the first time that I ventured into Houghton to begin exploring possibilities for a doctoral dissertation on James, blindly unaware that—from the beginning—graduate students had been forbidden to consult the family archive. Long since superseded by its virtual successor, the card catalogue then was still just that: rows of varnished white maple cabinets, stacked in the bridge that used to link Houghton to the main Widener Library. There one would find the trove of three-by-five index cards that held the typewritten record of the library's vast acquisitions of printed books and manuscripts. Patrons were free to examine the drawers pertaining to the Jameses; and the hundreds of entries therein obviously had been well thumbed by hopeful (and, more likely than not, soon-to-be-disappointed) researchers. For across the top of many cards had been typed—with an ominously red ribbon—a discouraging warning: "James Restrictions Apply. Not to be consulted without Head Librarian's consent." Uncertain but not daunted, I filled out a few call slips for some of James's manuscript letters and took them to the main desk. "I don't want anyone to get in trouble," I said somewhat shyly, "in case I'm not supposed to see these." The librarian looked down at the slips, took note of the collection, and, for an instant, hung fire. "Well," she slowly answered, "Leon's done with his book, isn't he?" Immediately catching the drift of her query, I responded by saying that, yes, the last volume of Edel's biography had appeared some years earlier. "Oh, in that case," she brightened up, "I guess you can see anything you want!" It is even possible that mine was the first request to go unchallenged, so long had the custom of nay-saying been observed.

When in 1987 I first conceived the idea of publishing all of James's correspondence with his close friend William Dean Howells, my first concern had to be obtaining permission to proceed from both writers' families. From each I received gracious consent but also—remarkably—an unsolicited warning. "I was going to bring up Leon Edel's abortive plan to do such a volume . . . in the early sixties," Bill Howells (the novelist's grandson) told me, a project that Mildred Howells (his overly protective aunt) strenuously had quashed. After Mildred's death in 1966, Bill conceded that he "would have liked to have the plan go ahead, and I think Bill Jackson suggested this to Edel, who by that time had lost interest. But his loss turns out to be your gain. . . . I see he is about eighty and lives in Honolulu and is doubtless inactive."[2] With his greater familiarity, Alexander James was also less sanguine: "If there is overlap with Leon Edel," he dejectedly wrote, "I can not help it. 'Billy said I could' is his credential."[3] But by then, though not forced out, the Chairman of the Board no longer had all the crucial players in his pocket. A new era for James studies at last had come. We waited, Leon Edel.

# Reference Matter

# Sources and Abbreviations

To simplify citations—and distinguish among the easily confused members of the James family—the following abbreviations are employed in the endnotes to this volume:

AHGJ    Alice Howe Gibbens James (1849–1922), wife of William James

AJ      Alice James (1850–92), the novelist's younger sister

EW      Edith Wharton (1862–1937), fellow novelist and close friend of HJ

FOM     Francis Otto Matthiessen (1902–50), professor of history and literature at Harvard, author and editor of major works that inaugurated the James Revival of the 1940s

GL      Gaillard Lapsley (1871–1949), friend of HJ and confidant of Edith Wharton and Percy Lubbock

HJ      Henry James (1843–1916)

HJ3     Henry ("Harry") James (1879–1947), first son of WJ and AHGJ

HJSr    Henry James Senior (1811–82), the novelist's father

HMH     H[arford] Montgomery Hyde (1907–89), distant cousin of HJ, literary biographer, occupant of Lamb House (1963–67), and author of *Henry James at Home* (1969)

HS      Howard Sturgis (1855–1920), Anglo-American novelist and friend of HJ and Edith Wharton; proprietor of Queen's Acre (Qu'acre) on the lower fringe of Windsor Great Park, where he frequently entertained the Master and his other acolytes

JBP     James Brand Pinker (1863–1922), the novelist's literary agent

LE      Leon Edel (1907–97), the novelist's authorized biographer and editor of his letters

MJP     Margaret ("Peggy") James Porter (1887–1950), daughter of WJ and AHGJ

PL      Percy Lubbock (1879–1965), devoted acolyte of HJ and first editor of his letters

RPB     Richard Palmer Blackmur (1904–65), influential critic of modern poetry and compiler of *The Art of the Novel* (1934), the collected Prefaces from the New York Edition

TB      Theodora Bosanquet (1880–1961), the novelist's amanuensis

WAJ     William A. Jackson (1905–64), first librarian of the Houghton Library at Harvard, responsible for controlling access to the James Family Papers

WJ      William James (1842–1910), the novelist's elder brother

WJ2     William ("Billy") James (1882–1961), second son of WJ and AHGJ

Published volumes of primary sources to which frequent allusion is made can be identi-fied by these abbreviations:

*Works by Henry James*

A       *Henry James: Autobiography.* Ed. Frederick W. Dupee. New York: Criterion Books, 1956. A one-volume compilation of *A Small Boy and Others* (1913), *Notes of a Son and Brother* (1914), and *The Middle Years* (1917).

CN      *The Complete Notebooks of Henry James.* Ed. Leon Edel and Lyall H. Powers. New York: Oxford University Press, 1987.

CS      *Complete Stories.* 5 vols. New York: Library of America, 1996–99.

HJL     *Henry James Letters.* Ed. Leon Edel. 4 vols. Cambridge, MA: Belknap Press of Harvard University Press, 1974–84.

LC1     *Literary Criticism: Essays on Literature; American Writers; English Writers.* Ed. Leon Edel and Mark Wilson. New York: Library of America, 1984.

LC2     *Literary Criticism: French Writers; Other Writers; The Prefaces to the New York Edi-tion.* Ed. Leon Edel and Mark Wilson. New York: Library of America, 1984.

LHJ     *The Letters of Henry James.* Ed. Percy Lubbock. 2 vols. New York: Charles Scrib-ner's Sons, 1920.

LiL     *Henry James: A Life in Letters.* Ed. Philip Horne. New York: Penguin, 1999.

*Works by Others*

CWJ     *The Correspondence of William James.* Ed. Ignas K. Skrupskelis and Elizabeth M. Berkeley. 12 vols. Charlottesville: University of Virginia Press, 1992–2004.

LWJ     *The Letters of William James.* Ed. Henry James [III]. 2 vols. Boston: Atlantic Monthly Press, 1920.

*Manuscript Archives*

ARB     Anna Robeson Burr Papers, Manuscripts Division, Department of Rare Books and Special Collections, Princeton University Library, Princeton.

CSA     Archives of Charles Scribner's Sons, Manuscripts Division, Department of Rare Books and Special Collections, Princeton University Library, Princeton.

EWP     Edith Wharton Papers, Yale Collection of American Literature, Beinecke Rare Book and Manuscript Library, New Haven. Included in the Wharton collection is the correspondence of Percy Lubbock and Gaillard Lapsley.

HJC     Henry James Collection, Yale Collection of American Literature, Beinecke Rare Book and Manuscript Library, New Haven. Henry James correspondence from James B. Pinker Literary Agency.

LEP     Leon Edel Papers, Rare Book and Manuscripts Division, McGill University Library, Montreal.

MH    Houghton Library, Harvard University, Cambridge. In addition to the James Family Archive, also at Houghton are Theodora Bosanquet's diaries and correspondence, a portion of the James B. Pinker Archive, and the Archives of New Directions Publishers.

RPB   Richard Palmer Blackmur Papers, Manuscripts Division, Department of Rare Books and Special Collections, Princeton University Library, Princeton.

# *Notes*

*Preface*

1. The concept is central to much of Bourdieu's work, especially *Distinction: A Social Critique of the Judgement of Taste*, ed. Richard Nice (Cambridge, MA: Harvard University Press, 1984).

2. Northrop Frye, *Anatomy of Criticism* (Princeton, NJ: Princeton University Press, 1957), 18.

3. "Henry James and the Life of Art," *New Criterion* 11.8 (Apr. 1993): 5.

4. Michael Millgate, *Testamentary Acts: Browning, Tennyson, James, Hardy* (Oxford: Clarendon Press, 1992), 73–109; Pierre A. Walker, "Leon Edel and the 'Policing' of the Henry James Letters," *Henry James Review* 21 (2000): 279–89; and Brian Crane, "From Family Papers to Archive: The James Letters," *Henry James Review* 29 (2008): 144–62. Edel's own version of events, redacted in the introduction to the first volume of his *Henry James Letters* (Cambridge, MA: Belknap Press of Harvard University Press, 1974), obviously works to justify his privileged relation to the documents at hand.

5. Millgate, *Testamentary Acts*, 108.

6. Lionel Trilling, "Dreiser and the Liberal Mind," *Nation* 162 (20 Apr. 1946): 466.

*Chapter 1*

1. Preface to *The Tragic Muse, LC2*, 1103.

2. Ever breezy but influential, Clifton Fadiman asserted that "most of James's tales of writers are diluted by a certain infusion of self-pity," even though he felt obliged to include one ("The Middle Years") in *The Short Stories of Henry James* (New York: Modern Library, 1945), a popular anthology that appeared in the first wave of modern reprints that collectively became known as the "James Revival" (316). Even so discerning a critic as F. O. Matthiessen, whose 1944 edition of *Stories of Writers and Artists by Henry James* had also marked another step in the rehabilitation of the author's reputation, deliberately omitted from that collection certain works (such as "The Great Good Place") that betrayed "the vulgarity into which James could fall through the very dread of being vulgar." The writer George Dane's obvious delight in "every form of softness in the great good place"—the sanctuary for which he yearns after a career of ceaseless labor—convulsed Matthiessen with "a sickening sensation of everything that is least virile" in James's imagination. See *Henry James: The Major Phase* (New York: Oxford University Press, 1944), 144.

3. HJ to HJ3, 7 Apr. 1914, *HJL*, 4:806.

4. HJ, will dated 19 Dec. 1910; amended 25 Aug. 1915; proved 9 May 1916; London Probate Department, Family Division of the High Court of Justice, London.

5. HJ to Mrs. F. W. H. Myers, 8 Apr. 1904, *LiL*, 399.

6. HJ to Mrs. James T. Fields, 2 Jan. 1910, *HJL*, 4:541.

7. HJ to Edmund Gosse, 13 June 1910, *HJL*, 4:556.

8. AHGJ to HJ3, 5 June 1910 (bMS Am 2538 [15], MH).

9. HJ3 to Ralph Barton Perry, 31 Mar. 1933 (bMS Am 1938 [246], MH).

10. HJ to Robert Louis Stevenson, 31 July [1888], *HJL*, 3:240. Edel mistranscribes "abject" as "object."

11. HJ to Thomas Sergeant Perry, 26 Sept. [1884], in Virginia Harlow, *Thomas Sergeant Perry: A Biography* (Durham, NC: Duke University Press, 1950), 317.

12. HJ, "Criticism" [1891; 1893], *LC1*, 98.

13. Harriet Waters Preston, "The Latest Novels of Howells and James," *Atlantic Monthly* 91 (Jan. 1903): 82.

14. HJ to Bliss Perry, 23 Jan. 1903 (bMS Am 1343 [274], MH).

15. HJ to William Dean Howells, 17 Aug. 1908, in Michael Anesko, *Letters, Fictions, Lives: Henry James and William Dean Howells* (New York: Oxford University Press, 1997), 426.

16. JBP to Edward L. Burlingame, 3 Aug. 1904 (CSA, Author Files I, Box 81, Folder 2).

17. HJ to Charles Scribner's Sons [30 July 1905], *HJL*, 4:367.

18. Preface to *Roderick Hudson*, *LC2*, 1039.

19. Preface to *The Golden Bowl*, *LC2*, 1338–39.

20. Paul Armstrong, "Reading James's Prefaces and Reading James," in *Henry James's New York Edition: The Construction of Authorship*, ed. David McWhirter (Stanford: Stanford University Press, 1995), 127.

21. HJ to William Dean Howells, 17 Aug. 1908, in Anesko, *Letters, Fictions, Lives*, 426.

22. PL, "The Novels of Mr. Henry James," *Times Literary Supplement* (9 July 1909): 249.

23. [William] Morton Fullerton, "The Art of Henry James," *Quarterly Review* 212 (Apr. 1910): 393. This essay, with a detailed headnote explaining the complex history of its composition, is reprinted in Edith Wharton, *The Uncollected Critical Writings*, ed. Frederick Wegener (Princeton, NJ: Princeton University Press, 1996), 299–318.

24. William Crary Brownell to HJ, 28 Aug. 1906 (CSA, Author Files I, Box 81, Folder 3).

25. For a bibliographical compilation of contemporary reviews (and brief summaries of them), see Linda J. Taylor, *Henry James, 1866–1916: A Reference Guide* (Boston: G. K. Hall, 1982), 397–421.

26. HJ to Charles Scribner's Sons [30 July 1905], *HJL*, 4:366.

27. HJ to Witter Bynner, 20 [Sept.] 1908 (Bynner Papers [bMS Am 1891.19 (24)], MH).

28. Until 1909, the year in which the last volume of the Edition appeared, copyright in the United States was limited to an initial term of twenty-eight years, renewable for another fourteen. The Copyright Act of 1909 liberally extended the renewal term by another fourteen years. For a concise summary of copyright issues, see Alice D. Schreyer, "Copyright and Books in Nineteenth-Century America," in *Getting the Books Out*, Papers of the Chicago Conference on the Book in 19th-Century America (Washington, DC: Library of Congress, 1987), 121–36.

29. HJ to JBP, 3 May 1910 (HJC).

30. "The idea of the poor man, the artist, the man of letters, who all his life is trying—if only to get a living—to do something *vulgar*, to take the measure of the huge, flat foot of the public": such was James's donnée for "The Next Time," traceable to his first disappoint-

ment twenty years earlier when he quit his job as a correspondent for the *New York Tribune* after the editor of that paper demanded that he make his columns less literary—more breezy and chatty, more accommodating to a lower standard of taste. "Twenty years ago, and so it has been ever," James bitterly wrote, after the disastrous premiere of *Guy Domville*—yet another example of his inability to cater to marketplace demands (*CN*, 109–10).

31. For HJ's incomparably witty reaction to this event, see his letter to Howells, 25 Jan. 1902, in Anesko, *Letters, Fictions, Lives*, 368–69.

32. Edward L. Burlingame to HJ, 10 Apr. 1896, Burlingame Letterbooks 18:322–23 (CSA).

33. Millgate, *Testamentary Acts*, 1, 2.

34. Scribner's Library of Modern Authors included subscription editions of the works of James M. Barrie, Thomas Carlyle, Charles Dickens, Eugene Field, Rudyard Kipling, James Whitcomb Riley, F. Hopkinson Smith, Robert Louis Stevenson, Frank Stockton, William Makepeace Thackeray, Leo Tolstoi, and Ivan Turgenev. Houghton Mifflin's list of "Standard Works in Deluxe Bindings" included collected editions of Thomas Bailey Aldrich, Elizabeth Barrett Browning, Thomas Burroughs, Charles Dickens, Ralph Waldo Emerson, John Fiske, Bret Harte, Nathaniel Hawthorne, Oliver Wendell Holmes, James Russell Lowell, William Shakespeare, and Henry David Thoreau. Scribner's advertised their subscription editions in their house organ, *The Lamp*, aimed at potential book buyers (see, for example, vols. 26–27 [1903]: endpapers); Houghton Mifflin's subscription editions are catalogued in the firm's "Special Editions Book" (MS Am 2030 [85], Houghton Mifflin Archive, MH). Ellen Ballou discusses "Subscription Books and Limited Editions" in her magisterial house history, *The Building of the House: Houghton Mifflin's Formative Years* (Boston: Houghton Mifflin, 1970), 303–27.

35. Not to be outdone by the collusional tactics of other major industries—John D. Rockefeller's Standard Oil Company was just the most notorious example—the American Publishers Association also tried to regulate the haphazard (and seemingly suicidal) practice of trade discounting, especially with respect to the fiction titles its members sold. In 1914, the federal courts awarded retail giant W. H. Macy & Company large damages against the association for price fixing and practices in restraint of trade, an action that eventually led to the association's dissolution. For this and other aspects of modernization within the publishing industry, see Donald Sheehan, *This Was Publishing: A Chronicle of the Book Trade in the Gilded Age* (Bloomington: Indiana University Press, 1952), 225–34; and John Tebbel, *A History of Book Publishing in the United States*, vol. 2, *The Expansion of an Industry 1865–1919* (New York: R. R. Bowker, 1975), passim.

36. Edward L. Burlingame to Charles Scribner, 6 Apr. 1900 (CSA, Author Files I, Box 133, Folder 8).

37. William Crary Brownell's reaction to the manuscript of James's novel was partly tempered by his knowledge that the firm was in negotiations with the author about a collected edition. Here, too, the distinction between James's cultural and commercial values registers audibly. "It certainly makes a thoroughly disappointing impression on me," Brownell told Charles Scribner,

and this fact is in itself disappointing, because I gathered (& gather) from Burlingame that we half asked to see it, & there is the subscr[iption]-edition possibility, & anyhow I think a new book by James would become our list. I certainly expected, too, to be able to say that, if the terms proposed . . . were not prohibitory or if some modification of them were possible, the book itself seemed to me all right. Unfortunately it doesn't. It is surely the n+*th* power of Jamesiness—his peculiar manner carried to an excessive degree. I have had the greatest difficulty in following it—indeed I *couldn't* follow some of it. At times the suspense into wh[ich] he forces the mind (& keeps it there) is exceedingly irritating. It gets decidedly on one's nerves. It is like trying to make out page after page of illegible writing. The sense of effort becomes acutely exasperating. Your spine curls up, your hair-roots prickle & you want to get up and walk around the block.

Despite these profound reservations, Brownell conceded, "I should say we had better take it if we could get it for an advance of $1000 on a 15% royalty." Since James was in need of ready money, he preferred to lease the American copyright to Scribner's for five years in exchange for an up-front payment of £400 (approximately $2,000); the firm had the option of continuing the contract at the end of that term, paying James a royalty of 20 percent of the retail price ($1.50) on each copy sold. On the basis of a 20 percent royalty, the lease sum would have been the equivalent of an advance on the sale of sixty-seven hundred copies. The firm never recouped its money on *The Sacred Fount*. Brownell to Scribner, 7 Aug. 190 (CSA, Author Files I, Box 133, Folder 3); and Brownell to JBP, 14 Aug. 1900 (CSA, Brownell Letterbooks, 7:48).

38. Edward L. Burlingame to Charles Scribner, 12 Aug. 1904 (CSA, Author Files I, Box 133, Folder 9).

39. Most of these collected editions were graced with advertising metonyms that then became integral design elements of the books included in them: for example, the "Thistle" (Stevenson), the "Outward Bound" (Kipling), the "Homestead" (James Whitcomb Riley), the "Edinburgh" (Carlyle), the "Wayside" (Hawthorne). In like fashion, the title pages of the New York Edition carried a stylized emblem of the city's harbor: a steamship passing under the towering pylons of the Brooklyn Bridge.

40. Comparing James's Prefaces to those supplied by Joseph Conrad for Dent's "Collected Edition," Vivienne Rundle observes that Conrad's "grant the reader a place and a role, allowing the prefaces to function as living texts, while James's prefaces are transfixed and petrified because of the exclusion of any real readerly contribution from their narrative system" ("Defining Frames: The Prefaces of Henry James and Joseph Conrad," *Henry James Review* 16 [1995]: 69).

41. The text of Scribner's prospectus, "The Novels and Tales of Henry James," was reprinted verbatim in *The Book Buyer* 32 (Dec. 1907): 212–13.

42. Cf. "First Collected Edition of The Novels and Tales of Henry James: *Édition de Luxe*," (London: Macmillan, 1908), Macmillan Archive (Box 82), New York Public Library.

43. HJ to JBP, 6 June 1905, *LiL*, 412.

44. "The Novels and Tales of Henry James," 212.

45. HJ to William Dean Howells, 17 Aug. 1908, in Anesko, *Letters, Fictions, Lives*, 426.

46. As he told Robert Herrick, "[B]y the mere fact of leaving out certain things (I have tried to read over *Washington Square* and I *can't*, and I fear it must go!) I exercise a control, a discrimination, I treat certain portions of my work as unhappy accidents. (Many portions of many—of all—men's work are)." HJ to Robert Herrick, 7 Aug. 1907,

in *The Selected Letters of Henry James*, ed. Leon Edel (New York: Farrar, Straus & Cudahy, 1955), 159.

47. Namely, *Watch and Ward* (1878), *The Europeans* (1878), *Confidence* (1880), *Washington Square* (1880), *The Bostonians* (1886), *The Other House* (1896), and *The Sacred Fount* (1901).

48. Martha Banta, "The Excluded Seven: Practice of Omission, Aesthetics of Refusal," in *Henry James's New York Edition*, 240–60.

49. Michael Anesko, *"Friction with the Market": Henry James and the Profession of Authorship* (New York: Oxford University Press, 1986), 155–60.

50. When Edel first delivered his misleading paper on "The Architecture of Henry James's 'New York Edition'" at the 1950 convention of the Modern Language Association, he created such a sensation that New York University promptly rewarded him with his first standing appointment as a full-time faculty member. Coinciding with the untimely death of F. O. Matthiessen, Edel's triumph crowned him as the reigning monarch of the James Revival, just then gaining its full momentum. The *New England Quarterly* published Edel's essay the next year (vol. 24 [1951]: 169–78). See also Daniel Mark Fogel, "Leon Edel and James Studies: A Survey and Evaluation," *Henry James Review* 4.1 (Fall 1982): 8.

51. HJ to Charles Scribner's Sons, 12 June 1906, *HJL*, 4:408–9. HJ's emendation is not noted by Edel.

52. For graphic evidence of James's impossibly complex interlineations, see *The American: The Version of 1877 Revised in Autograph and Typescript for the New York Edition of 1907; Reproduced in Facsimile from the Original in Houghton Library, Harvard University* (Ilkley, UK: Scolar Press, 1976). At the behest of Scribner's, who feared a mutiny in the pressroom if such confusing copy continued to arrive, James eventually had to engage his private secretary to prepare cleaner typescripts for the more heavily revised portions of later works. One partial set of typescripts—for *The Portrait of a Lady*—survives at Harvard's Houghton Library (MS Am 1237.17).

53. "The Novels and Tales of Henry James," 212. Evidence of the publishers' concern about the revisions is implied in Pinker's response to the firm of 15 June 1906:

When your Mr. Charles Scribner was here, he told me that the very elaborate revision which he noted in "Roderick Hudson" had made you a little anxious lest Mr. James should so transform his early books that those who had known and delighted in them for years should feel disappointed with the new edition, owing to loss of freshness. I hinted at this to Mr. James, and he told me at once frankly that he rather anticipated the suggestion. He says we may rest perfectly happy on that score, that he has greatly improved the books, not only for himself but for the public. (CSA, Author Files I, Box 81, Folder 3)

54. "On Revised Versions," *New York Times Saturday Review of Books* (18 Jan. 1908): 30. Not surprisingly, Henry's brother William, who found the late style bothersome, expressed his doubts about the virtue of rewriting. When he had tackled the revised *Roderick Hudson*, he confessed to his brother, "My brain could hardly understand anything, much less *enjoy*. . . . I am not sure either, that in *that* case at all events, it was not labor lost, or that the simpler and more naïve phrasing of the original edition does n't keep a better harmony." WJ to HJ, 4 Feb. 1908, *CWJ*, 3:357.

55. HJ to JBP, 20 Oct. 1908, *LiL*, 468.

56. HJ to JBP, 1 Apr. 1909, *LiL*, 477. The amount in sterling was £7.14.2.

57. HJ to Frederick Macmillan, 17 Mar. 1909, in *The Correspondence of Henry James and the House of Macmillan: "All the Links in the Chain,"* ed. Rayburn S. Moore (Baton Rouge: Louisiana State University Press, 1993), 217.

58. WJ to HJ, 7 Jan. 1910, *CWJ*, 3:406.

59. According to the most up-to-date inflation calculator (http://www.westegg.com /inflation/), the cost of the least expensive version of the Edition in 2008 dollars would be $1,095.

60. Edward Clark Marsh, "Henry James: Auto-Critic," *Bookman* 30 (Oct. 1909): 138.

61. The fullest account of the British publishing history of the New York Edition is Michael Anesko, "Ambiguous Allegiances: Conflicts of Culture and Ideology in the Making of the New York Edition," in *Henry James's New York Edition*, 77–89.

62. For a vivid account of the complicated James-Roosevelt relationship, see Philip Horne, "Henry James and 'the Forces of Violence': On the Track of 'Big Game' in 'The Jolly Corner,'" *Henry James Review* 27 (2006): 237–47; quotation, 240.

63. WJ to AJ, 29 July [1889], *CWJ*, 6:516–17.

64. HJ, *A*, 30, 35, 278.

65. WJ would employ the same autobiographical diversion in *The Varieties of Religious Experience* (1902), in which the melodramatic account of his own nervous collapse (like that of his father's "vastation") is camouflaged by false attribution. See WJ, *Writings 1902–1910*, ed. Bruce Kuklick (New York: Library of America, 1987), 149–50.

66. Thomas Sergeant Perry provided Percy Lubbock with this account, which was included in *LHJ*, 1:9.

67. WJ to HJ, 9 Jan. 1883, *CWJ*, 1:344.

68. WJ, "Introduction," in *The Literary Remains of the Late Henry James* (Boston: James R. Osgood, 1884), 16.

69. R. W. B. Lewis, *The Jameses: A Family Narrative* (New York: Farrar, Straus & Giroux, 1991), 354.

70. HJ to WJ, 2 Jan. 1885, *HJL*, 3:62.

71. Habegger discloses that Henry Senior's "body had hardly grown cold when his sister-in-law, Catharine Walsh, began going through his papers and selectively burning them, and this process continued in his son William's posthumous edition of his papers, in Henry Jr.'s marvelous but not always trustworthy memoirs of life at home, and in the selective preservation of letters and other documents . . . by his grandson Henry III." See *The Father: A Life of Henry James, Sr.* (New York: Farrar, Straus & Giroux, 1994), 6. It should also be noted that, after her parents' deaths, Alice James apparently destroyed all the letters she had written to them, a gesture that brother Henry forgivingly regarded as "natural enough" (*LHJ*, 2:207).

72. Millgate, for example, asserts that James's "unhesitating and often radical adjustments of the texts of his brother's, his father's, and Minny Temple's letters remain fully reflective of the characteristic imperiousness of his irresistibly expansive imagination," his "usurping consciousness" (*Testamentary Acts*, 96). Even more aggressively, Holly claims that "assumptions about the family's need for and the right to justification"

allowed James to reconstruct the "psychological fabric" of the documents he tampered with, the result being "a massive display of evasion, manipulation and justification" (*Intensely Family: The Inheritance of Family Shame and the Autobiographies of Henry James* [Madison: University of Wisconsin Press, 1995], 190). Alfred Habegger first called attention to "Henry James's Rewriting of Minny Temple's Letters" in *American Literature* 58.2 (May 1986): 159–80.

73. Qtd. in Habegger, *The Father*, 4.

74. WJ to HJ, 24 Mar. [18]94; HJ to WJ, 25 and 28 May, 29 June 1894, *CWJ*, 2:302, 307, 310, 311, 309, 315. Somewhat more charitably—and honestly—HJ conceded, "Now that my sister is gone no one will fully know the long years of inestimable and disinterested devotion that [Katharine Loring] gave up to her. We owe her a debt we can never repay." HJ to William W. Baldwin, 21 Mar. [1892] (bMS Am 1094.1 [6], MH).

75. HJ to WJ, 28 May 1894, *CWJ*, 2:310.

76. Katharine P. Loring to Margaret James Porter, 6 June 1934 (bMS Am 1094.5 [53], MH).

77. For details of Robertson James's alcoholism, see Lewis, *The Jameses*, passim; and Jane Maher, *Biography of Broken Fortunes: Wilkie and Bob, Brothers of William, Henry, and Alice James* (Hamden, CT: Archon Books, 1986).

78. In 1920, Percy Lubbock had printed HJ's letter to his brother of 28 May 1894 (expressing his appreciation of the diary's merits); but, at the family's insistence, Lubbock omitted large portions of the text in which HJ vented his alarm that the work would fall into the hands of their brother Robertson. Lubbock's brief headnote to the letter also conveyed the misleading impression that the diary, if it had survived at all, was still in manuscript. See *LHJ*, 1:214–17.

79. Burr chastises Pelham Edgar, whose recent *Henry James, Man and Author* (Boston: Houghton Mifflin, 1927) had made this claim. See *Alice James: Her Brothers—Her Journal* (New York: Dodd, Mead, 1934), 64.

80. Burr, *Alice James: Her Brothers—Her Journal*, 61, 65.

81. Ibid., 65–66.

82. Ibid., [i].

83. Katharine P. Loring to Anna Robeson Burr, 11 May [1934] (MS C0618, Box 1, Folder 15, ARB).

84. Edward Holton James to Anna Robeson Burr, 15 May 1934 (MS C0618, Box 1, Folder 11, ARB).

85. John Chamberlain, Rev. of *Alice James: Her Brothers—Her Journal*, *New York Times* (17 May 1934): 21; see also C. Hartley Grattan's review in the *Sunday Times Book Review* (20 May 1934): 3+.

86. HJ3 to MJP, 11 May 1934 (bMS Am 1094.5 [53], MH).

87. MJP to Mary Vaux [May 1934] (bMS Am 1094.5 [53], MH).

88. MJP to Katharine Loring, 11 June 1934 (bMS Am 1094.5 [53], MH).

89. HJ3 to Ralph Barton Perry, 10 May 1934 (bMS Am 1094.5 [53], MH). Burr's Jamesian credentials were not as slight as Harry presumed. One of her earliest works of scholarship was a pioneering study of the genre of autobiography, a book in which she dealt intelligently with both Henry James Senior and Harry's own father. In fact, when

William James received a copy of the book, he congratulated the author in no uncertain terms. "Hurrah! hurrah! hurrah!" he scribbled. "What could have induced you," he asked Burr, "first to write just the book I have longed to see in existence, and second, to send it to poor unknown me? I'm grateful anyhow!" WJ to Anna Robeson Burr, 16 Oct. 1909 (MS C0618, Box 1, Folder 12, ARB). See also Anna Robeson Burr, *The Autobiography: A Critical and Comparative Study* (Boston: Houghton Mifflin, 1909).

90. HJ3 to MJP, 9 Jan. 1935 (Bruce Porter Papers, additions [BANC/MSS 72/35c], Box 1, Bancroft Library, University of California, Berkeley).

91. [Percy Lubbock], Rev. of *Alice James: Her Brothers—Her Journal*, *Times Literary Supplement* (11 Oct. 1934): 690. Lubbock could not have known that "Miss" Burr was, in fact, the widow of Charles Burr.

92. HJ to AHGJ, 29 Mar. 1914, *HJL*, 4:706–7.

93. As Susan Gunter reports, "According to Harry, Alice start[ed] examining and organizing William's letters in 1911, eventually destroying some. He claims that her children told her she must decide which ones to keep. It is impossible to know how she made her decisions, but she may have felt that ordinary, daily letters did not present William at his best. And as they often quarreled by mail during his frequent absences, she also may have preferred to keep their marital differences private. Harry believed that she destroyed many of the early letters, written before their marriage, and he himself destroyed others later, letters that 'would be liable to misinterpretation if not accompanied by explanations that I couldn't find the time to compile.'" See *Alice in Jamesland: The Story of Alice Howe Gibbens James* (Lincoln: University of Nebraska Press, 2009), 317–18; and HJ3, "Memorandum Concerning Letters Between my Father and Mother" (bMS Am 1096.2 [66b], MH).

94. HJ to HJ3, 26 Nov. 1911, *LiL*, 505.

95. HJ to JBP, 7 Aug. [1912] (HJC).

96. Darrell Figgis [J. M. Dent & Sons] to JBP, 7 Mar. 1912 (Berg Collection, New York Public Library).

97. Macmillan offered to pay a royalty of 25 percent of the retail price, an unprecedented figure for HJ, together with an advance payable on the first thousand copies. See JBP to Frederick Macmillan, 2 Sept. 1912 (Macmillan Archive, Add. MS 54905, British Library).

98. HJ to JBP, 30 Aug. 1912 (HJC). Constable's advance was £300.

99. In the same letter, James outlined his anticipated plans for publication. "The 'Family Book,' *as a vehicle for William's Early Letters*, has had wholly to break down," he wrote,

—after drawing me along into the delusion that I might make the whole thing *one*. It was becoming far too copious & complicated to *be* one, at all; absolutely it will have to be two—but with the Early Letters, as a publication by themselves, the 1st now to be thought of. It has been an immense relief to see the case thus beautifully simplified—for I shall accompany the Letters with as much "Family," all along, as *immediately* concerns them, & with thereby the light so much more completely focussed on William himself. I am in very auspicious treaty with the Scribners for the volume—"Early Letters of William James, with Notes by Henry James," & with the Notes (the simplest &

best name for *my* part) I can do *everything* I want. Charles Scribner, who is in England, is keenly interested & eager, & it's pretty clear that I shall be able to make highly advantageous terms. (HJ to AHGJ, 26 Aug. 1912, in *Dear Munificent Friends: Henry James's Letters to Four Women*, ed. Susan E. Gunter [Ann Arbor: University of Michigan Press, 1999], 94)

100. When HJ later was obliged to abandon an edition of WJ's letters, the generous royalty advance from Scribner's was paid against future royalties of *A Small Boy and Others* and *Notes of a Son and Brother*. Charles Scribner to JBP, 13 Jan. 1913 (HJC).

101. *Scribner's Magazine* 52 (Nov. 1912): endpaper.

102. AHGJ to HJ3, 14 Nov. 1912 (bMS Am 2538 [16], MH).

103. HJ3 to JBP, 15 Nov. 1912 (bMS Am 1237.14 [25], MH).

104. In the "Prefatory Note" he composed for this volume, Harry laid down his commitment to textual accuracy as an article of faith. All of the pieces he included had been previously published by WJ in various magazines, but the author had left marked-up drafts and proof sheets among his papers at the time of his death. "Comparison with the original texts will disclose slight variations in a few passages," Harry explained, and "in these passages the present text follows emendations of the original which have survived in the author's own handwriting" (*Memories and Studies* [New York: Longmans, Green, 1911], i).

105. HJ to HJ3, 11 June 1912 (bMS Am 1094 [1389], MH).

106. "Literary Gossip," *Athenaeum* 4416 (15 June 1912): 681.

107. Percy Lubbock first published a much-abbreviated version of HJ's last answer to Harry, dated 15–18 Nov. 1913, in *LHJ*, 2:345–48. In an appendix ("The Autobiographies") added to the fourth volume of *Henry James Letters* published in 1984 (*HJL*, 4:793–804), Leon Edel reprinted excerpts from two other letters (dated 23–24 Sept. 1912 and 25 Nov. 1912) that further address the compositional history of *A Small Boy and Others* and *Notes of a Son and Brother* and the techniques of selection that James defensively employed while writing them. Quotations from HJ's letters to HJ3 in the next several paragraphs in the text are drawn from *HJL* 4, unless otherwise noted. Where necessary, Edel's incorrect transcriptions have been emended.

108. HJ3 to HJ, 6 Oct. 1912 (bMS Am 1094 [1393], MH). In the margin of that portion of HJ's 23–24 Sept. letter in which he urges the economic necessity of settling with Scribner's, Harry penciled, "Financial delusion!"

109. HJ to HJ3, 19 Jan. 1913, *LHJ*, 2:290.

110. HJ to HJ3, 24 Apr. 1913, *LiL*, 521.

111. HJ to AHGJ, 5 Aug. 1913, in *Dear Munificent Friends*, 105; HJ to Theodora Bosanquet, 11 Sept. 1913 (bMS Eng 1213 [55], MH).

112. HJ to HJ3, 30 Sept. 1913 (bMS Am 1094 [1402], MH).

113. Charles Scribner to JBP, 27 Oct. 1913 (HJC).

114. HJ to Charles Scribner, 4 Nov. 1913 (CSA, Author Files I, Box 81, Folder 5).

115. Tamara Follini, "Pandora's Box: The Family Correspondence in *Notes of a Son and Brother*," *Cambridge Quarterly* 26 (1996): 33. Even those critics who have most thoroughly analyzed this astonishing document have overlooked the fact that its most famous passage (in which James justifies his emendation of a reference to Abraham Lincoln) concerns a letter of William's that is *not* printed in *Notes of a Son and Brother*. In

a letter to his father of 12 Sept. 1865, WJ sorrowfully recalled Lincoln's assassination: "Poor old Abe! What is it that moves you so about his simple, unprejudiced, unpretending, honest career? I can't tell why, but 'albeit unused to the melting mood,' I can hardly ever think of Abraham Lincoln without feeling on the point of blubbering" (*CWJ*, 4:123). Recasting this text, Henry James substituted the slain president's full Christian name and defended the preference to his nephew:

> I may mention however that your exception that particularly caught my eye—to "poor old Abraham" for "poor old Abe"—was a case for change that I remember feeling wholly irresistible. Never, *never*, under our Father's roof did we talk of Abe, either *tout court* or as "Abe Lincoln"—it wasn't *conceivable*: Abraham Lincoln he was for us, when he wasn't either Lincoln or Mr. Lincoln.

With a better ear, perhaps, than his uncle, Harry scribbled in the margin, "Its the adjective *old* that makes *Abe* right—'Old Abraham' sounds like Genesis" (bMS Am 1094 [1406], MH).

116. HJ to HJ3, 15–18 Nov. 1913 (bMS Am 1094 [1406], MH). After *Notes of a Son and Brother* was published, HJ offered his sister-in-law a different piece of advice about the disposition of WJ's letters:

> I think more yearningly than I can say of the time Harry hopes to be able to give to his Father's letters. You said something in one of yours to Peg about the peculiarly characteristic beauty of William's to his children—& that has made me wish, or wonder, in respect to the issue of those to begin with, in a vol. by itself (if a volume could, or can, come of them:) *W.J.'s Letters to his Children* would be *such* a compelling title & announcement. But perhaps it's one of those things that are just too good [to] be feasible? (HJ to AHGJ, 24 July 1914 [bMS Am 1094 (1747), MH])

HJ seems not to have imagined that *those* letters—so intimate and familial—would have been the *least* likely that WJ's heirs would have wanted to see in print.

117. Charles Scribner to HJ, 3 Dec. 1913; HJ to Charles Scribner, 19 Dec. 1913 (CSA, Author Files I, Box 81, Folder 5).

118. *LC*2, 1332.

119. As might be expected, HJ amended the texts of *all* the documents he "quoted" in *Notes of a Son and Brother*, including thirty-four letters from his father, fifteen from brother Wilky, and nineteen from Minny Temple, the cousin whose early death profoundly affected his creative imagination.

120. *A*, 309.

121. WJ to the James Family [10 Nov. 1861]; comparison of *CWJ*, 4:50–51, and *A*, 327. The strike-throughs indicate HJ's deletions, and the bracketed carets enclose HJ's insertions.

122. *LWJ*, 1:viii–ix.

123. *HJL*, 4:800.

124. How successfully Harry managed these tasks can be read in the overwhelmingly positive reviews his work received. "In what other collection of Letters shall we find a writer so swift, so vivid, so varied and so spontaneous?" If Harry's collection could spark that kind of enthusiasm from the normally staid *North American Review*, for what more could he hope? The *Boston Evening Transcript* added laurel to the crown. "Let-

ters rarely disclose so much of a man in his entirety as do these," that paper applauded. "They are not merely 'The Letters of William James'; they are the record of an epoch in the history of philosophy and the chronicle of a notable family." Revs. of *The Letters of William James, North American Review* 213 (May 1921): 693; *Boston Evening Transcript* (8 Dec. 1920): 10.

125. HJ, Rev. of *Correspondence of William Ellery Channing, D.D., and Lucy Aikin, from 1826 to 1842*, ed. Anna Letitia Le Breton [1875], *LC1*, 212.

126. Cf. *LWJ*, 1:289–90, and *The Diary of Alice James*, ed. Leon Edel (1964; rpt., New York: Penguin Books, 1982), 57–58. On the corresponding page in WJ's copy of the Loring privately printed *Diary*, HJ3 noted, "P. 72 of *A Small Boy* etc. seems to be inspired by this reminder. Compare A.J. & H.J.'s ways of recalling." See *The Diary of Alice James* (Cambridge, MA: John Wilson & Son, 1894), 44 [*AC85 J2312 894d, MH].

127. HJ3 to the President and Fellows of Harvard University, 23 Apr. 1923 (bMS Am 1095.2 [44], MH).

128. HJ to Frederick Macmillan, 19 Apr. 1883, *HJL*, 2:412.

129. HJ to WJ2, 13 May 1913, *HJL*, 4:673.

130. HJ3, entry for 13 July [1898], Pocket Diary, p. 23 (bMS Am 1094.5 [23], MH).

131. HJ, "The Turning Point of My Life," *CN*, 438, 437 (erroneously dated 1901).

132. HJ, *A*, 438.

133. HJ, "The Jolly Corner" [1908], *CS*, 5:706, 707. Subsequent references to this edition will be cited parenthetically in the text.

134. To fulfill his responsibility as legal executor of Henry Senior's estate, HJ did once travel to Syracuse in January 1883 to inspect the family's holdings firsthand. "The 'property' is very good," he reported to WJ, "much better than I supposed—in the very best position in town, in good order, & occupied by prosperous 1st class tenants." Rents from these commercial buildings would yield a net income of more than five thousand dollars per year, to be divided among the heirs. With obvious pride, the author also noted that he had been escorted down James Street—"the 5th Avenue of Syracuse, one of the handsomest American strts. I have ever seen" (HJ to WJ, 23 Jan. [1883], *CWJ*, 1:358). HJ would also use quotation marks to set off the word *property* in "The Jolly Corner" (cf. *CS*, 5:698).

135. Lewis, *The Jameses*, 594–96.

136. HJ to HJ3, 21 Aug. 1906 (bMS Am 1094 [1364], MH).

137. For two representative examples of these approaches, see Daniel Mark Fogel, "A New Reading of Henry James's 'The Jolly Corner,'" in *Critical Essays on Henry James: The Late Novels*, ed. James W. Garagano (Boston: G. K. Hall, 1987), 190–203; and Eric Savoy, "The Queer Subject of 'The Jolly Corner,'" *Henry James Review* 20 (1999): 1–21.

138. See, for example, Deborah Esch, "A Jamesian About-Face: Notes on 'The Jolly Corner,'" *ELH* 50.3 (Autumn 1983): 591–92; and Lee Clark Mitchell, "'Ghostlier Demarcations, Keener Sounds': Scare Quotes in 'The Jolly Corner,'" *Henry James Review* 28 (2007): 223–31.

139. *HJL*, 4:802–3.

140. HJ to HJ3, 16 July 1912 (bMS Am 1094 [1391], MH).

141. *HJL*, 4:804.

142. HJ to HJ3, 15–18 Nov. 1913 (bMS Am 1094 [1406], MH).

*Chapter 2*

1. HJ to HJ3, 15–18 Nov. 1913 (bMS Am 1094 [1406], MH).

2. HJ, "The Death of the Lion" [1895], *CS*, 4:391. The missing WJ letters eventually were found and sent back to Harry, who did, indeed, include some of them—including the one in which his father refers to "Poor old Abe!"—in *LWJ*, 1:53–70.

3. On 4 March 1910, HJ confided to his close friend Howard Sturgis, "I've been having again, my 50th relapse—though at times it all seems one large & continuous lapse without any 're,' in which I hopelessly welter. My only present better news is that my blest elder nephew, Harry, has most mercifully come out to [me] & that I cling to him almost in the frenzy of despair" (bMS Am 1094 [1272], MH). Edith Wharton, on the other hand, felt that Harry's understanding of his uncle's nervous breakdown was rather callous. "Seeing more of the nephew," she wrote to Fullerton, "I have decided that, all his family having been the victims of the neurotic, unreliable Wm James, he has had to harden himself against 'nerves,' & does not see that the sudden break-down of a solid équilibré character like Henry's is very different, (& must be differently dealt with) from the chronic flares & twitches of the older brother—William o' the wisp James. And for this reason, while he is of great practical help, I don't think he understands how serious the situation is." EW to W. Morton Fullerton, 24 Mar. 1910, in *The Letters of Edith Wharton*, ed. R. W. B. Lewis and Nancy Lewis (New York: Charles Scribner's Sons, 1988), 205.

4. HJ3 to WJ2, 6 Jan. [1915] (bMS Am 2538 [54], MH).

5. HS to TB, 7 Feb. 1916 (MS Eng 1213.3 [191], MH).

6. AHGJ to HJ3, 14 Dec. 1915 (bMS Am 2538 [18], MH).

7. TB, entries for 8 and 31 Jan. 1916, in *Henry James at Work* (1924; rpt., Ann Arbor: University of Michigan Press, 2006), 87, 89. This modern reprint of Bosanquet's commemorative essay, which was first issued by Leonard and Virginia Woolf's Hogarth Press, includes significant portions of her invaluable manuscript diaries.

8. HJ, "Greville Fane" [1892], *CS*, 4:233.

9. AHGJ to HJ3, 28 Dec. 1915 (bMS Am 2538 [18], MH).

10. TB, entry for 29 Dec. 1915: "We talked too of his disposition of his unfinished works—I told what he told me the morning after his stroke, and she quite understood the force of it all" (*Henry James at Work*, 86).

11. AHGJ to JBP, 5 Mar. 1916 (HJC).

12. AHGJ to HJ3, 6 Mar. 1916 (bMS Am 2538 [19], MH).

13. Charles Scribner to HJ, 27 Sept. 1912; for this and other documents relating to the secret diversion of Wharton's royalties, see *HJL*, 4:789–92. Half the amount was paid when HJ agreed to the offer; the remainder due upon delivery of the manuscript. Since James never completed the work, he received only the first installment, modestly whittled down to a still-hefty thirty-six hundred dollars after Pinker's 10 percent commission was subtracted.

14. As HJ told Pinker in a letter of 8 October 1912, "[A]t the very most immediate blush of the thing, I felt quite dazzled and elated," though he was also concerned that Scribner's proposal would entail the surrender of his copyright in the yet-to-be-written novel. "That affects me as awkward and depressing and unadvisable—though the proposal has otherwise a certain superficial 'liberality' which slightly hypnotises and

makes the temptation (the temptation *to* make the surrender) rather cruel in its vividness" (*HJL*, 4:626–27).

15. EW to Mary Cadwalader Jones, 23 Sept. 1911, in *The Letters of Edith Wharton*, 259.

16. WJ2 to [William Sturgis] Bigelow, 3 Apr. 1913 (HJ2d, James Family Papers, Creighton University). This contretemps almost cost Wharton James's friendship. Shortly after the uproar, Percy Lubbock asked James if he and Wharton were "straight again"? And James replied, "Not *yet*—but we shall be." Lubbock sensed that James was "in the mood to forgive everybody & forget everything now," but he also had to wonder, "will that satisfy *her*?" PL to GL, 16 Apr. 1913 (EWP, Box 58, Folder 1688).

17. In her diary entry for 16 December 1915, TB noted that, even though her continued presence at Carlyle Mansions was becoming superfluous, she was glad to have been there that day because she "wouldn't willingly have missed hearing Mrs. James's indignant repudiation of Mrs. Wharton and all her works (due to her shocked feelings when she read 'The Reef')" (*Henry James at Work*, 86).

18. HJ3 to [Henry L.] Higginson, 27 Mar. [1913] (HJ2i, James Family Papers, Creighton University). Edith Wharton, we should note, responded in kind:

Dr. Bigelow has sent me a letter from young Henry James wh. has made me simply speechless with indignation. He says they (the family) had considered it their duty to notify H. J. of the Birthday gift, as I had already twice "tried to relieve" their uncle, & had "been stopped"—by them, I suppose!

I shall not tell Henry of this, but shall write to the young man, & ask him to put an immediate stop to the circulation of this outrageous lie. I shd like to ask, in addition, why they permitted their uncle to accept an equivalent amount from strangers, if they wd not consent to their compatriots' gift?—Certainly, once he had refused ours, he put himself doubly in the wrong by accepting the English present. (EW to William Morton Fullerton, 3 May 1913, in *The Letters of Edith Wharton*, 301)

See also R. W. B. Lewis, *Edith Wharton: A Biography* (New York: Harper & Row, 1975), 339–41.

19. EW to TB, 17 Jan. 1916, in *Henry James and Edith Wharton: Letters, 1900–1915*, ed. Lyall H. Powers (New York: Charles Scribner's Sons, 1990), 390.

20. TB, entry for 14 Dec. 1915, in *Henry James at Work*, 85.

21. EW to HJ3, 22 Feb. and 1 Mar. 1916 (Autograph File W; bMS Am 1095.2 [34], MH).

22. AHGJ to MJP, 17 Dec. 1915 (bMS Am 2538 [23], MH).

23. [Percy Lubbock], "Henry James, O. M.," *London Times* (29 Feb. 1916): 9.

24. AHGJ to WJ2, 14 Mar. 1916 (bMS Am 2538 [40], MH). In the same letter, Alice confessed her surprise that, in his will, James had not bequeathed Lubbock some kind of honorary legacy (as he had for Walpole, Jocelyn Persse—a stranger to her—and Lucy Clifford, who each were to receive one hundred pounds): surely he was as deserving as they—and probably more so. "Perhaps he does not need the money?" she wondered.

25. PL, "Henry James," *Quarterly Review* 203 (July 1916): 73.

26. TB, entry for 29 Dec. 1915, in *Henry James at Work*, 86.

27. HJ3 to JBP, 7 Apr. 1916 (HJC).

28. TB, entry for 3 May 1916, in *Henry James at Work*, 92, 93. The entry for this date records some events that had taken place several weeks earlier.

29. TB to JBP, 1 May 1916 (HJC).

30. TB, entry for 3 May 1916, in *Henry James at Work*, 93.

31. PL to GL, 12 June 1916 (EWP, Box 58, Folder 1694).

32. MJP to EW, qtd. in EW to EG, 6 June 1916, in *Letters of Edith Wharton*, 376.

33. EG to EW, 8 June 1916 (EWP, Box 25, Folder 783).

34. For a concise overview of this group (which also included Wharton's lover, Morton Fullerton; her more chaste companion, Walter Berry; and, eventually, Bernard Berenson, among others), see Susan Goodman, *Edith Wharton's Inner Circle* (Austin: University of Texas Press, 1994), passim. The literary and historical significance of this cluster of figures was first suggested by Edmund Wilson in his discerning 1947 review of Lubbock's *Portrait of Edith Wharton*; see "Edith Wharton: A Memoir by an English Friend," in *Classics and Commercials: A Literary Chronicle of the 1940s* (1950; rpt., New York: Noonday Press, 1967), 412–18.

35. GL to EW, 2 June 1916 (EWP, Box 29, Folder 868). Goodman argues that Wharton's "campaign to control the publication of James's letters"—those written, at least, to members of her inner circle—originated in a desire "to keep their own privacy intact" (Goodman, *Edith Wharton's Inner Circle*, 32). Such an emphasis obscures their deeper concern that the provincial prejudices of the family would shortchange and distort the complexity of HJ's epistolary relationships.

36. HS to EW, 11 June 1916 (EWP, Box 30, Folder 927).

37. EW to MJP, June 1916, in *Letters of Edith Wharton*, 378.

38. EW to HS, 17 June 1916, in ibid., 380–81.

39. MJP to EW, 18 June [1916] (EWP, Box 27, Folder 833).

40. PL to GL, 26 July 1916 (EWP, Box 58, Folder 1694).

41. EW to Edmund Gosse, 6 Aug. 1916 (Edmund Gosse Papers, Brotherton Collection, University of Leeds).

42. PL to GL, 20 Aug. 1916 (EWP, Box 58, Folder 1694).

43. Copy of contract for *The Letters of Henry James*, 16 Nov. 1916 (bMS Am 1435 [13], MH).

44. PL to GL, 17 Nov. 1918 (EWP, Box 58, Folder 1696).

45. The phrase was attributed to HJ by Preston Lockwood in "Henry James's First Interview," *New York Times Magazine* (21 Mar. 1915): 4. Despite the byline, this "interview" was in fact dictated by HJ himself; cf. TB, entry for 1 Mar. 1915, in *Henry James at Work*, 80–81.

46. PL to EW, 6 Aug. 1916 (EWP, Box 29, Folder 873).

47. PL to JBP, 15 Aug. 1916 (HJC).

48. HJ3 to JBP, 6 Sept. 1916 (HJC).

49. HJ3 to JBP, 1 Nov. 1916 (HJC). Entries in Bosanquet's diaries suggest that she continued her work at least through the middle of October 1916; see *Henry James at Work*, 95.

50. PL to GL, 20 Aug. 1916 (EWP, Box 58, Folder 1694).

51. TB, entry for 23 Aug. [1916], in *Henry James at Work*, 95. Lubbock's more restrained anticipation of their meeting is worth comparing. Just three days earlier, he had written rather dispassionately that "the question of a copyist has to wait. As to that, Mrs James has very explicitly pronounced her wish . . . that it shall *not* be little Bosanquet—Peggy has more or less emphatically dissented from this view—& Edith has said it will kill

little B. if she is not chosen—so there we are. I face the question by inviting little B. to dine with me next week, when I shall merely just talk to her about it all—after all we are both hard English folk, with no appreciation of fine shades of feeling." PL to GL, 20 Aug. 1916 (EWP, Box 58, Folder 1694).

52. PL to EW, 6 Aug. 1916 (EWP, Box 29, Folder 873). The year before, Bosanquet had begun collaborating with her friend Clara Smith on an epistolary novel, *Spectators*, published by Constable & Co. in 1916. She also published a number of literary parodies (including several of James) in the *Westminster Gazette*. See the introduction to *Henry James at Work*, 5–9.

53. TB, entry for 8 Nov. 1916 (MS Eng 1213.2 [1], MH).

54. EW to TB, 1 Mar. [1916], in *Henry James and Edith Wharton: Letters*, 391.

55. TB, entry for 1 Aug. 1916, in *Henry James at Work*, 106.

56. TB, entry for 17 July 1916, in ibid., 20.

57. HS to TB, 10 Nov. 1916 (MS Eng 1213.3 [196], MH).

58. TB to JBP, 11 Mar. 1917 (bMS Am 2540 [15], MH).

59. TB, "Henry James," *Fortnightly Review* 101 (June 1917): 1004, 1008.

60. EW to GL, 15 July 1917 (EWP, Box 59, Folder 1711).

61. TB, "The Revised Version," *Little Review* 5.4 (Aug. 1918): 59, 57.

62. TB to JBP, 1 May 1916 (HJC); TB, entry for 4 May 1916, in *Henry James at Work*, 94. Harry's reaction came after seeing *The Middle Years* serialized in *Scribner's Magazine*; HJ3 to JBP, 29 Sept. 1917 (HJC).

63. JBP to Charles Scribner, 15 June 1916 (CSA, Author Files I, Box 81, Folder 6).

64. AHGJ to JBP, 31 Mar. 1917 (bMS Am 1237.14 [23], MH).

65. TB, *Henry James at Work*, 57; cf. TB, "The Record of Henry James," *Yale Review* 10.1 (Oct. 1920): 156.

66. PL, Rev. of *Henry James at Work*, *Nation & Athenaeum* 36 (13 Dec. 1924): 416, 415.

67. PL to TB, 18 Nov. [1924] (MS Eng 1213.3 [157], MH).

68. On 13 December 1915, PL reported to GL that, according to TB, "yesterday [HJ] dictated quite a long passage, & all coherent, she says, about Napoleon" (EWP, Box 58, Folder 1693).

69. TB to EW, 12 Dec. 1915, in *Henry James and Edith Wharton: Letters*, 377.

70. Ferris Greenslet to HJ3, 15 and 30 Apr. 1925; HJ3 to Ferris Greenslet, 28 Apr. 1925 (bMS Am 1435 [9], MH). At that time, Harry may have overlooked the document's existence. Leon Edel would later claim that he found the complete texts of HJ's last dictations (including material unknown to Bosanquet, transcribed in her absence by niece Peggy) among the James Family Papers when he first was given access to them in 1937. Sometime after Edel made an unauthorized copy of them, Harry James destroyed the originals, unknowingly leaving Edel in sole possession of their complete contents. Edel first published the texts of HJ's last dictations in the *Times Literary Supplement* (2 May 1968): 459–60; he reprinted them in *HJL*, 4:808–12.

71. HJ3 to Eric Pinker, 16 July 1925 (LEP, Box 17, Folder 21).

72. Pelham Edgar, *Henry James, Man and Author* (Boston: Houghton Mifflin, 1927), 99.

73. "Recollections of Henry James in His Later Years," BBC Third Programme, 14 June 1956 (MS Eng 1213.4 [20], MH).

74. TB to LE, 25 Sept. 1932 (LEP, Box 17, Folder 21).

75. Rupert Hart-Davis to TB, 27 May 1948 (MS Eng 1213.3 [105], MH).

76. Needing some information for a reprint edition of *The Other House* that he hoped to publish, Hart-Davis turned in a pinch to Bosanquet. "I realise that your Mr. Edel—I might almost say *our* Mr. Edel—is just the chap to answer this question, but he is so far away, and even Air Mail letters take a time. Incidentally I am more than grateful for your having given me his name. We have corresponded in a very friendly way, and I am hoping to publish the fruits of his various Jamesian labours in due course." Aside from serving as the British publisher for almost all of the American's future books, Hart-Davis would become one of Edel's most valuable confidantes and research minions in the years ahead. Rupert Hart-Davis to TB, 18 Sept. 1946 (MS Eng 1213.3 [94], MH).

77. "Notes on a Sitting with Mrs. Hester Dowden," 15 Feb. 1933, qtd. in Pamela Thurschwell, *Literature, Technology and Magical Thinking, 1880–1920* (Cambridge: Cambridge University Press, 2001), 102.

78. TB, automatic writing, "Monday March 20th, 1933," in ibid., 109.

79. HJ, "The Real Right Thing," *CS*, 5:122, 121, 127, 131–32.

80. TB, automatic writing, "Monday March 20th, 1933," in Thurschwell, *Literature, Technology and Magical Thinking*, 109.

81. TB to LE, 21 Nov. 1935 (LEP, Box 17, Folder 21).

82. For other details of Bosanquet's relationship with Edel, see Lyall Powers's running commentary in *Henry James at Work*, esp. 130, 139–42.

83. TB, "The Son and Brother," rev. of *Henry James: The Untried Years, 1843–1870*, by Leon Edel, *Time and Tide* (4 July 1953): 888.

84. PL, *The Craft of Fiction* (1921; rpt., London: Jonathan Cape, 1954), viii, x.

85. In his keenly discriminating essay about the New York Edition in the *Times Literary Supplement* (8 July 1909: 249–50), Lubbock was probably the first person to recognize in print the distinctive value of James's Prefaces—important for the volumes to which they were individually attached but also important because, collectively, "their appearance" marked "an event, indeed the first event, in the history of an art almost as confusedly apprehended as it is enormously practised": the genuine articulation of a theory of the novel. James commended Lubbock's notice to his brother William as "much the most intelligent series of remarks ever dedicated, I think, to H. J." No less effusively, the author told Howard Sturgis that "Percy's admirable & exquisite article" was altogether "a very superior & a charmingly distinguished thing," in response to which he could but "intensely & gratefully & almost tearfully appreciate it." HJ to WJ, 17 Aug. 1909, *CWJ*, 3:398; and HJ to HS, 11 July 1909, in *Dearly Beloved Friends: Henry James's Letters to Younger Men*, ed. Susan E. Gunter and Steven H. Jobe (Ann Arbor: University of Michigan Press, 2001), 152. Lubbock had already published two well-regarded biographical works: *Elizabeth Barrett Browning in Her Letters* (London: Smith, Elder, 1906), and *Samuel Pepys* (London: Hodder & Stoughton, 1909). Others would follow his work on James. It seems rather anomalous that no book-length study of Lubbock's life or work has ever been published: his central position in the literary field of his time would seem to have warranted one. In its absence, the best briefer assessments of Lubbock's various talents are Robert Liddell, "Percy Lubbock," *Kenyon Review* 29 (1968): 493–511; and D. W. Jefferson, "Percy

Lubbock," in *Late Nineteenth- and Early Twentieth-Century British Literary Biographers*, Dictionary of Literary Biography, vol. 149, ed. Steven Serafin (Detroit: Gale Research Press, 1995), 138–47. See also Charles W. Mayer, "Percy Lubbock: Disciple of Henry James," PhD diss., University of Michigan, 1968.

86. Lubbock's appeal appeared in the *Times Literary Supplement* (11 Jan. 1917): 21.

87. PL to JBP, 8 July [1917] (HJC).

88. PL to EW, 6 Aug. 1916 (EWP, Box 29, Folder 873).

89. Sturgis's reaction when he first read James's notes for *The Ivory Tower* (appreciated in Lubbock's edition for the way that they illuminated the Master's technique) also speaks to their different scale of values. "It is exactly like hearing him talk," Sturgis gleefully wrote Wharton. "A ghost is nothing to it. I feel like the dog in the advertisement of the gramophone, 'His Master's Voice.'" HS to EW, 16 Sept. 1917 (EWP, Box 30, Folder 927).

90. The Jameses were much put out when Elsie Hueffer, the estranged wife of Ford Madox Ford, threatened to sue Macmillan and the estate for damages, because Violet Hunt, Hueffer's mistress, had been identified in the *Letters'* index as "Mrs. F. M. Hueffer." Pinker was obliged to deduct one hundred pounds from the estate's royalty account to settle her claim. JBP to AHGJ, 14 Dec. 1920 (bMS Am 1435 [13], MH).

91. PL to Lucy Clifford, 9 May 1917, qtd. in *"Bravest of women and finest of friends": Henry James's Letters to Lucy Clifford*, ed. Marysa Demoor and Monty Chisholm (Victoria, BC: English Literary Studies, 1999), 20.

92. On 23 March 1918, Lubbock wrote to Wharton, "Your packet of letters reached me safely yesterday. They are very opulent letters—some of the best he ever wrote I think. They will be copied with the due omissions, as before, & *your* copies destroyed" (EWP, Box 29, Folder 873).

93. HJ3 to PL, 20 May 1919 (LEP, Box 19, Folder 12).

94. LE, "Introduction," in *HJL*, 1:xxiii.

95. HJ3 to Edmund Gosse, 21 May 1919 (Edmund Gosse Papers, Brotherton Collection, University of Leeds). Lubbock reported to Gosse that Harry had been repelled by his uncle's endearing forms of address to men such as Hugh Walpole ("Beloved little Hugh," excised *LHJ*, 2:236; "Dearest little Hugh," excised *LHJ*, 2:244; "Belovedest Hugh," excised *LHJ*, 2:322; "Darlingest & deligthtfullest old Hugh!" excised *LHJ*, 2:352). "H.J. jr suggests certain omissions in this connexion," Lubbock explained, "which I very nearly made myself, and which can be made with advantage, I don't doubt. Ah, Hugh Walpole needn't be alarmed! I most carefully cut out very nearly all the extravagances he has in mind, and only left in one or two that struck me as pleasant and easy. (But they shall go too if he doesn't like them). You may be quite sure I shall watch this point attentively, and indeed I had it in mind throughout. But don't you find that such things don't *now* strike outsiders as they wd have a generation or so ago?—that kind of effusive expression is so much commoner among people of all sorts than it used to be" (PL to Gosse, 1 June 1919 [Edmund Gosse Papers, Brotherton Collection, University of Leeds]).

96. At the time of his death, Howells was at work on a review of *The Letters of Henry James*, a censored draft of which was included as an appendix by his daughter Mildred in her own *Life in Letters of William Dean Howells* (1928). A plain-text version of Howells's

surviving manuscript (exposing his alarm at his sense of James's "oddity") appears in the next chapter.

97. HJ3 to JBP, 3 Apr. 1919 (bMS Am 2538 [56], MH).

98. HJ3 to JBP, 17 Apr. 1919 (bMS Am 1453 [13], MH).

99. HJ3 to AHGJ, 18 Apr. 1919 (bMS Am 2538 [53], MH).

100. Lewis, *The Jameses*, 596; "Miss Cutting One of Brides of a Day," *New York Times* (12 June 1917): 13.

101. Caroline Moorehead, *Iris Origo: Marchesa of Val d'Orcia* (Boston: David R. Godine, 2002), 88. With grounds landscaped by Frederick Law Olmsted, Westbrook is now the Bayard Cutting Arboretum, a state park created through the joint bequest of Olivia and her mother, both of whom died in 1949.

102. Lewis, *The Jameses*, 602.

103. Qtd. in Moorehead, *Iris Origo*, 17.

104. "W. B. Cutting, Jr.'s Will," *New York Times* (18 May 1910): 10. The Cuttings' daughter, a precocious young girl, would later be known to the world by her married name, Iris Origo, and recognized as an accomplished writer and memoirist.

105. Moorehead, *Iris Origo*, 60; Lady Sybil Lubbock, *The Child in the Crystal* (London: Jonathan Cape, 1939), 244.

106. Mary Berenson to Geoffrey Scott, 12 Jan. 1918, qtd. in Richard M. Dunn, *Geoffrey Scott and the Berenson Circle: Literary and Aesthetic Life in the Early 20th Century* (Lewiston, NY: Edwin Mellen Press, 1998), 179.

107. EW to Mary Berenson, 3 Mar. 1918, in ibid., 185.

108. Geoffrey Scott to Mary Berenson, 2 Jan. 1918, in ibid., 176.

109. Sybil Cutting to Bernard Berenson, 18 Dec. 1917 (Berenson Archive, Villa I Tatti, Fiesole). Perhaps not surprisingly, Berenson penciled a note in the margin of this letter: "Keep carefully."

110. "Divorce Division: Lady Sybil Scott's Petition," *London Daily Telegraph* (21 Apr. 1926): 6. Scott, who in reality had been having an adulterous affair with Vita Sackville-West, wanted to keep her name out of the case and so provided himself with an escort whom (in Vita's words) "he didn't like at all, and whom he thought a wicked waste of money." Vita advised Scott to send a bill for the woman's services to Sybil, "but he said no, that wasn't done" (qtd. in Victoria Glendinning, *Vita: The Life of V. Sackville-West* [London: Weidenfeld & Nicolson, 1983], 148).

111. No doubt from Sturgis, Percy Lubbock also learned how to knit and purl. In her recent biography of Edith Wharton, Shari Benstock offers a tableau of Lubbock, kept by the fireside at 53 Rue de Varenne like a kind of Red Cross boy-bitch, knitting caps and scarves for Belgian refugees through the first winter of the Great War. See *No Gifts from Chance: A Biography of Edith Wharton* (New York: Charles Scribner's Sons, 1994), 311.

112. HJ3 to MJP, 30 Jan. 1917 (Bruce Porter Papers: additions [BANC/MSS 72/35c], Box 1, Bancroft Library, University of California, Berkeley).

113. See Lewis, *The Jameses*, 614–19; and Linda Leavell, "Marianne Moore, the James Family, and the Politics of Celibacy," *Twentieth Century Literature* 49.2 (Summer 2003): 219–45.

114. Lubbock and Scott were both early recipients of the prestigious James Tait Black

Memorial Prize for biography; the jury selected Lubbock's 1922 memoir, *Earlham*, and Scott's 1925 *Portrait of Zelide* for the distinction.

115. PL, *Shades of Eton* (New York: Charles Scribner's Sons, 1929), 207.

116. In his biographical study *Mary Cholmondeley: A Sketch from Memory* (London: Jonathan Cape, 1928), Lubbock modestly recalled his invitation to become part of Sturgis's charmed circle of friends:

> A silent but appreciative youth was introduced into it, many years ago; he can't have added much to the gaiety of that ready-witted circle, but they were good to him, and he used his eyes and ears and mind, which weren't dull, with a dazzled and bewitched attention. It was wonderful to begin to feel at home there. The banquet of grace and glee was perpetually renewed; it became a legend among the partakers, and those who are left to cherish it will never be tired of reminding each other of that which they will never forget. (59–60)

117. HJ to HS, 4 Feb. 1904 (bMS Am 1094 [1220], MH).

118. PL to GL [18 Mar. 1911] (EWP, Box 57, Folder 1685).

119. Entry for 25 Feb. 1906, in *The Diary of Arthur Christopher Benson*, ed. Percy Lubbock (New York: Longmans, Green, 1926), 139. For many decades, Lubbock's scrupulously circumspect edition of this diary provided the only access to it; the bulk of Benson's unpublished work remained sealed in a special cabinet in the Magdalene College Library, Cambridge.

120. Such an inference might be justified from a letter of 20 April 1908 in which Lubbock disclosed the contents of a dream to Lapsley: "I dreamt of you so clearly & circumstantially last night, visiting you in the strangest little tiny room at Cambridge, with a window in a sloping wall, that it seems a leading to write to you, which indeed I have been meaning to do" (EWP, Box 57, Folder 1684).

121. David Newsome, *On the Edge of Paradise: A. C. Benson: The Diarist* (Chicago: University of Chicago Press, 1980), 292. This book was the first to print additional excerpts from Benson's diary; most of them (dealing with same-sex attraction) would have been deemed unfit for publication by Lubbock.

122. PL to GL, 23 Feb. 1926 (EWP, Box 58, Folder 1699).

123. PL to GL, 10 June 1911 (EWP, Box 57, Folder 1685).

124. HJ to PL, 9 Mar. 1902, *LHJ*, 1:391.

125. PL to GL, 27 Mar. [1912] (EWP, Box 58, Folder 1686).

126. PL to GL, 1 Jan. 1914 (EWP, Box 58, Folder 1690). Any doubt about the context of these remarks would be erased by another confidence in the same letter. "Do you know, by the way, that a flashing-eyed black-haired young pupil of yours, *Law*, is now the most junior of the juniors in the Embassy here? He lives with Loch of the Times, so I see a good deal of him, & take to him not a little." Lubbock was referring to James Law, eldest son of Andrew Bonar Law, British statesman who would later serve briefly as prime minister. James Law was shot down over France in 1917; his body was never recovered. See R. J. Q. Adams, *Bonar Law* (Stanford: Stanford University Press, 1999), 260–61.

127. The insights of queer theory have encouraged provocative reexaminations of many of James's titles, especially those of his later years. See, for example, Eve Kosovsky Sedgwick, "The Beast in the Closet: James and the Writing of Homosexual Panic," in *Sex,*

*Politics, and Science in the Nineteenth-Century Novel*, ed. Ruth Bernard Yeazell (Baltimore: Johns Hopkins University Press, 1986), 147–86; Hugh Stevens, *Henry James and Sexuality* (New York: Cambridge University Press, 1998); Wendy Graham, *Henry James's Thwarted Love* (Stanford: Stanford University Press, 1999); and Michael Anesko, "What We *Don't* Talk About When We Talk About Love: Henry James's Last Words," in *A Companion to Henry James*, ed. Greg W. Zacharias (Chichester, UK: Wiley-Blackwell, 2008), esp. 237–39.

128. PL to GL, 1 Jan. 1914 (EWP, Box 58, Folder 1690). Much later in life, Lubbock observed that James, often bored by his generational peers, preferred "the company & conversation of young people who treated him with more freedom and addressed him with less decorum!" (PL to LE, 1 June 1950 [LEP, Box 19, Folder 10]).

129. PL to HJ, 19 Dec. 1913 (bMS Am 1094 [340], MH).

130. HJ to EW, 16 Feb. 1914, in *Henry James and Edith Wharton: Letters*, 276. Walter Van Rensselaer Berry (1859–1927), Edith Wharton's adviser and companion for thirty years, was a distinguished American lawyer and Francophile.

131. PL to GL, 13 Apr. 1914 (EWP, Box 58, Folder 1690).

132. EW to Bernard Berenson, 16 Apr. [1914], in *Letters of Edith Wharton*, 318.

133. PL to GL, 10 Mar. 1909 (EWP, Box 57, Folder 1684).

134. PL to GL, 23 Aug. 1909 (EWP, Box 57, Folder 1684).

135. PL to EW, 22 Jan. 1914 (EWP, Box 29, Folder 873).

136. Qtd. in *Henry James and H. G. Wells: A Record of Their Friendship, Their Debate on the Art of Fiction, and Their Quarrel*, ed. Leon Edel and Gordon N. Ray (Urbana: University of Illinois Press, 1958), 39.

137. TB, entry for 1 Aug. 1916, *Henry James at Work*, 106.

138. Virginia Woolf, entry for 9 Mar. 1918, in *The Diary of Virginia Woolf*, 5 vols., ed. Anne Olivier Bell (New York: Harcourt Brace Jovanovich, 1977–84), 1:125–26.

139. Edel and Ray, *Henry James and H. G. Wells*, 248, 261, 267.

140. PL to JBP, 12 Feb. 1919 (EWP, Box 59, Folder 1711). See also *LHJ*, 2:485–90.

141. PL to GL, 24 Feb. 1919 (EWP, Box 58, Folder 1697).

142. PL to JBP, 26 Apr. 1919 (HJC).

143. HJ3 to PL, 20 May 1919 (LEP, Box 19, Folder 12).

144. HJ, "The Figure in the Carpet" [1896], *CS*, 4:579.

145. PL, "Introduction," in *LHJ*, 1:xv. Subsequent references to this edition in the next few pages will be cited parenthetically in the text.

146. Lubbock would repeat this assertion in his review of Bosanquet's *Henry James at Work*, in which he claimed "it was a matter of scrupulous pride" with James "to sweep away the litter of his workshop, to leave no signs of labour, notes or sketches or fragments of any kind, strewn about his finished work" (*Nation & Athenaeum* 36 [13 Dec. 1924]: 415).

147. Louis Auchincloss, "'My Dear Blest Percy,'" *New Criterion* 3.9 (May 1985): 85. Auchincloss was thinking of Lubbock's 1921 book on George Calderon (*A Sketch from Memory*); his 1923 novel (*Roman Pictures*); his 1928 biography of Mary Cholmondeley (*A Sketch from Memory*); his 1929 academic memoir (*Shades of Eton*); and his 1947 *Portrait of Edith Wharton*.

148. HJ3 to MJP, 6 Sept. 1919 (Bruce Porter Papers: additions [BANC/MSS 72/35c], Box 1, Bancroft Library, University of California, Berkeley).

149. As the proofs passed from one member of the family to another, so too did the composite list of their objections, inviting subsequent recipients to record additional comments (and reservations). This document and other related notes and memoranda are among the Leon Edel Papers (Box 19, Folder 12).

150. PL to AHGJ, 12 Sept. 1919, LEP (Box 19, Folder 12).

151. PL to JBP, 29 Oct. 1919 (HJC).

152. Rev. of *The Letters of Henry James*, *Bookman* 51 (May 1920): 364.

153. Lawrence Gilman, Rev. of *The Letters of Henry James*, *North American Review* 211 (May 1920): 682.

154. Rev. of *The Letters of Henry James*, *Times Literary Supplement* (8 Apr. 1920): 1.

155. "A Disappointed Reader," *Times Literary Supplement* (27 Feb. 1919): 113.

156. HJ3 to JBP, 6 Aug. 1917 (HJC).

157. Frederick Macmillan to PL, 23 Sept. 1919 (Macmillan Letterbooks, Add. MS 55556, p. 977, Macmillan Archive, British Library).

158. This meant that seventeen short stories (almost all first published in magazines prior to 1875) were deliberately omitted from the 1921–23 Macmillan edition.

159. PL to JBP, 4 May 1919 (HJC).

160. HJ3 to JBP, 5 July 1919, qtd. in Horne, *Henry James and Revision: The New York Edition* (Oxford: Clarendon Press, 1990), 320; the passage from the Macmillan advertisement is also quoted here.

161. David J. Supino, *Henry James: A Bibliographical Catalogue of a Collection of Editions to 1921* (Liverpool: Liverpool University Press, 2006), 479–80.

162. "The Novels of Henry James," *Times Literary Supplement* (12 May 1921): 297.

163. PL to Frederick Macmillan, 10 Dec. 1920 (Add. MS 55033, f. 188, Macmillan Archive, British Library).

164. Frederick Macmillan to PL, 30 Jan. 1922 (Macmillan Letterbooks, Add. MS 55576, p. 528, Macmillan Archive, British Library).

165. EW to GL, 13 May 1922, *Letters of Edith Wharton*, 452.

166. PL, *Roman Pictures* (London: Jonathan Cape, 1923), 10. Subsequent references to this edition will be cited parenthetically in the text.

167. PL to GL, 23 Aug. 1909 (EWP, Box 57, Folder 1684). One might also note a touch of grim prophecy (or self-caricature) in Lubbock's remarks, since he was destined to become a fixture of Anglo-Florentine society himself.

168. Marjory Gane Harkness, "Introduction," in *Percy Lubbock Reader* (Freeport, ME: Bond Wheelwright, 1957), 14.

169. [Arthur Sydney McDowell], Rev. of *Roman Pictures*, by Percy Lubbock, *Times Literary Supplement* (7 June 1923): 385.

170. L. P. Hartley, Rev. of *The Region Cloud*, by Percy Lubbock, *Saturday Review* 140 (21 Nov. 1925): 600.

171. PL, *The Region Cloud* (London: Jonathan Cape, 1925), 7. Subsequent references to this edition will be cited parenthetically in the text. It is worth noting that, years later, Lubbock described his own relation to James in very similar terms. "As for *my* part in H.J.'s later years," he told Leon Edel, "important as it was to me, you must not suppose that it was of great importance to him. You see I was always the admiring and upward-

gazing disciple; and kind as he ever was to me, and I dare say pleased with my homage (which he recognized as being not unintelligent), that was not the sort of thing that really interested and entertained him" (PL to LE, 1 June 1950 [LEP, Box 19, Folder 10]).

172. Lorinne Pruette, Rev. of *The Region Cloud*, by Percy Lubbock, *New York Evening Post Literary Review* (9 Jan. 1926): 4.

173. The artist's full name was Adrian Keith Graham Hill; he was an early theorist and practitioner of what we would now call "art therapy." See Susan Hogan, *Healing Arts: The History of Art Therapy* (Philadelphia: Jessica Kingley, 2001), 133ff.

174. Newsome, *On the Edge of Paradise*, 367. Just as summarily, Benson dismissed the draft he had seen of *The Region Cloud*, telling Gosse that, even though the chapters he had read "were full of clever things," they didn't seem to "to have any reality or vitality & to be dreadfully reminiscent in style of H.J. in his most high-piled mood" (Arthur Christopher Benson to Edmund Gosse, 3 Aug. 1924 [Edmund Gosse Papers, Brotherton Collection, University of Leeds]).

175. EW to GL, 27 Mar. 1924 (EWP, Box 59, Folder 1713).

176. PL to GL, 17 May 1924 (EWP, Box 58, Folder 1698).

177. W. Somerset Maugham, "The Most Selfish Woman I Ever Knew," *Hearst's International/Cosmopolitan* 79 (Sept. 1925): 90–91. The quoted text (somewhat revised from the serial) is from Maugham's *Complete Short Stories*, 2 vols. (Garden City, NY: Doubleday, 1952), 2:533. For book publication, Maugham also changed the story's title to "Louise."

178. EW to GL [26 Oct. 1925] (EWP, Box 59, Folder 1715).

179. EW to GL, 30 Oct. 1925, in *Letters of Edith Wharton*, 487. Many years earlier (another queer twist) Lubbock and his then-sometimes-companion Oliffe Richmond claimed to have been in love with the same young woman, a London debutante named Celia Newbolt (daughter of the poet Sir Henry John Newbolt). The announcement of her engagement to a different man (Lt. Col. Sir Ralph Dolignon Furse) in 1913 prompted Lubbock to take the *Times* assignment in Vienna, a departure that he announced with all the histrionic melodrama of a third-rate romance. "You will have heard perhaps of an announcement of marriage, which puts an end to life as I have lived it for the last four years," he wrote Lapsley on 10 October 1913. "This means that without a minute's unnecessary delay I must now arrange a different sort of life—& it must be one that for some time to come will take me out of this country." For all the rhetorical gnashing of teeth, Lubbock immediately added that he had no idea "that I was so soon to see for myself the strange face of the more or less foreseen possibility," a queer contradiction that rather evacuates his professed feeling of romantic abandonment, since he seems to have been anticipating the "news" for some time (EWP, Box 58, Folder 1689).

180. Arthur Christopher Benson to GL, 30 Mar. 1925 (EWP, Box 57, Folder 1679).

181. PL to GL, 1 Dec. 1926 (EWP, Box 58, Folder 1699).

182. EW to Margaret Terry Chanler, 11 Aug. 1926, in *Letters of Edith Wharton*, 492. The Lewises mistakenly transcribe "lubric" as "lubie," erasing its salacious connotation as a shortened form of *lubricious*.

183. EW to GL, 16 Mar. 1916 (EWP, Box 59, Folder 1710).

184. PL to GL, 19 Mar. 1933 (EWP, Box 58, Folder 1700). As she first told Lapsley (in a letter of 2 March 1933), Wharton seemed to recall that James had said, "So it's you at

last, august stranger!" but she was uncertain about the accuracy of her memory (*Letters of Edith Wharton*, 557; see also EW, *A Backward Glance* [New York: D. Appleton-Century, 1934], 367).

185. PL to GL, 17 Aug. 1937 (EWP, Box 59, Folder 1701).

186. PL to GL, 14 Nov. 1937 (EWP, Box 59, Folder 1701).

187. PL, *Portrait of Edith Wharton* (New York: Appleton-Century-Crofts, 1947), 5, 8.

188. Deborah Hecht offers a concise overview of this subject in "The Poisoned Well: Percy Lubbock and Edith Wharton," *American Scholar* 62.2 (Spring 1993): 255–59.

*Chapter 3*

1. William Dean Howells to Frederick A. Duneka, 7 Mar. 1916, in *Selected Letters of William Dean Howells*, 6 vols., ed. George Arms, Don L. Cook, et al. (Boston: Twayne, 1979–83), 6:92–93.

2. HJ to Herbert H. Asquith, 28 June 1915, in *HJL*, 4:764. Certain pragmatic considerations also entered into James's decision, because, legally, his "alien" status restricted his freedom of movement between London and Rye during wartime.

3. William Dean Howells to Thomas Sergeant Perry, 24 July 1915, in *Selected Letters*, 6:83.

4. William Dean Howells to Frederick A. Duneka, 23 Mar. [1916], in ibid., 6:94. In a very curious slip of the pen, Howells dated this letter *1915*, almost as if to suggest that his sentiments were still akin to those he had expressed to Perry the year before.

5. Arthur C. Benson, "Henry James," *Cornhill*, n.s., 40.512 (Apr. 1916): 511–19; the essay is reprinted in Benson's *Memories and Friends* (London: John Murray, 1924), 192–204.

6. See TB, "The Record of Henry James," *Yale Review* 10.1 (Oct. 1920): 143–56; Edmund Gosse, "Henry James," *London Mercury* 1 (Apr. 1920): 673–84; 2 (May 1920): 29–41; and EW, "Henry James in His Letters," *Quarterly Review* 234 (July 1920): 188–202.

7. T. S. Eliot, "In Memory of Henry James," *Egoist* 5 (Jan. 1918): 1–2. This essay—its title shortened to "In Memory"—was later reprinted together with an important supplement ("The Hawthorne Aspect") in the "Henry James" number of the *Little Review* 5.4 (Aug. 1918): 44–53. For ease of reference, all quotations from Eliot's remarks on James (which, in this instance, can be found on page 46) will be based upon the *Little Review* text.

8. T. S. Eliot to Charlotte Eliot, 29 Mar. 1919, in *The Letters of T. S. Eliot*, vol. 1, ed. Valerie Eliot (New York: Harcourt Brace Jovanovich, 1988), 280.

9. Eliot, "In Memory," 46.

10. Ford Madox Ford, *Henry James: A Critical Study* (1913; rpt., New York: Albert & Charles Boni, 1915), 68.

11. T. S. Eliot, "Tradition and the Individual Talent" [1919], in *Selected Essays: New Edition* (New York: Harcourt, Brace & World, 1964), 11.

12. Eliot, "In Memory" and "The Hawthorne Aspect," 44, 50, 51.

13. HJ, *Hawthorne*, in *LC1*, 352, 351.

14. T. S. Eliot, *Notes Towards the Definition of Culture* (New York: Harcourt, Brace & World, 1949), 30. John Carlos Rowe has also found other variations on this Jamesian theme. See "What the Thunder Said: James's *Hawthorne* and the American Anxiety of Influence: A Centennial Essay," *Henry James Review* 4.2 (Winter 1983): 81–119.

15. Ezra Pound, "In Explanation; Brief Note; A Shake Down," *Little Review* 5.4 (Aug. 1918): 5, 9, 7, 22, 31, 29, 35.

16. Pound, "Brief Note," 7–8.

17. "The Henry James Number," *Little Review* 5.7 (Nov. 1918): 50.

18. Pound, "A Shake Down," 9.

19. See Martha Banta, "From 'Harry Jim' to 'St. James' in *Life Magazine* (1883–1916): Twitting the Author; Prompting the Public," *Henry James Review* 14 (1993): 237–56; also useful is E. R. Hagemann, "*Life* Buffets (and Comforts) Henry James, 1883–1916: An Introduction and an Annotated Checklist," *Papers of the Bibliographical Society of America* 62 (1968): 207–25.

20. Edel and Ray, *Henry James and H. G. Wells*, 248–49; as first published, see *Boon, The Mind of the Race, The Wild Asses of the Devil, and The Last Trump: Being a First Selection from the Literary Remains of George Boon, Appropriate to the Times* (New York: George H. Doran, 1915).

21. Rebecca West, *Henry James* (London: Nisbet, 1916), 26, 27–28, 107.

22. E. M. Forster, *Aspects of the Novel* (New York: Harcourt, Brace & World, 1927), 159–61; Forster's lengthy (and approving) quotation from *Boon* appears on pages 162–63.

23. E. M. Forster, *The Longest Journey* (1922; rpt., New York: Vintage Books, 1962), 79.

24. Lubbock himself anticipated this problem. As he explained to Pinker, "The difficulty, as I have always foreseen, will be that the last 15 years or so of his life will be very much more fully represented than the years 1870–1900. This can't be helped—his later letters are so much the best that it would be absurd to use the space with earlier & inferior ones (sacrificing later & better) simply for symmetry's sake" (PL to JBP, 6 Jan. 1919 [HJC]).

25. *LHJ*,1:xxii–xxiii, xxiv, xxv, xxvi.

26. Van Wyck Brooks, *The Ordeal of Mark Twain* (New York: E. P. Dutton, 1920).

27. Van Wyck Brooks, *The Pilgrimage of Henry James* (New York: E. P. Dutton, 1925), 51–52, 138.

28. Joseph Warren Beach, *The Method of Henry James* (New Haven, CT: Yale University Press, 1918), 109, 110. Significantly, Beach also recognized the distinctive value of James's Prefaces, suggesting (well in anticipation of R. P. Blackmur's 1934 edition of *The Art of the Novel*) that "few but professional students would have the hardihood and pertinacity to make their way through these explanatory reviews distributed over twenty-four volumes. It remains for the student to collect and set in order these scattered considerations, to view them in connection with the stories themselves, and, from the whole, to put together some connected account of the aims and method of our author" (2).

29. Edgar, *Henry James, Man and Author*, 70.

30. Cornelia Pulsifer Kelley, *The Early Development of Henry James* (Urbana: University of Illinois Press, 1930). Somewhat unfairly, a reviewer for the *New England Quarterly* dismissed Kelley's labors as adding "nothing to one's essential knowledge or appreciation of the novelist or of his works" (vol. 4.3 [July 1932]: 577). Because Kelley's work began as a dissertation, she had been obliged to cover "neglected" ground: the relatively arid first decade of James's professional career, when almost everything he wrote the author later repudiated.

31. Brooks, *The Pilgrimage of Henry James*, v.

32. Ernest Sutherland Bates, Rev. of *Henry James, Man and Author*, by Pelham Edgar, *Saturday Review of Literature* 4 (3 Sept. 1927): 89.

33. A. Hutchison, "Henry James, a Victim of the Jamesians," *New York Times Book Review* (13 Feb. 1927): 2.

34. Vernon Louis Parrington, *Main Currents in American Thought*, vol. 3, *The Beginnings of Critical Realism in America, 1860–1920* (New York: Harcourt, Brace, 1930), 239–40.

35. Morris R. Cohen, Rev. of *Main Currents in American Thought*, by Vernon Louis Parrington, *New Republic* 65 (28 Jan. 1931): 303.

36. Wyndham Lewis, *Men Without Art* (1934; rpt., New York: Russell & Russell, 1964), 153. Characteristically, the chapter devoted to the Master is entitled "Henry James (The Arch-Enemy of 'Low Company')."

37. André Gide, "Henry James" [from an unsent letter to Charles Du Bos], *Yale Review* 19 (1930): 643.

38. C. Hartley Grattan, *The Three Jameses, a Family of Minds: Henry James, Sr., William James, Henry James* (New York: Longmans, Green, 1932), 272, 339, 340.

39. T. S. Eliot, "Cousin Nancy" [1915]: "Upon the glazen shelves kept watch / Matthew and Waldo, guardians of the faith, / The army of unalterable law" (*The Complete Poems and Plays, 1909–1950* [New York: Harcourt, Brace & World, 1971], 18).

40. Eliot, "In Memory," 44 (emphasis added).

41. Mitzi Berger Hamovitch, ed., *The Hound and Horn Letters* (Athens: University of Georgia Press, 1982), 22, 67, 193–94. See also David Garrett Izzo, "The Henry James Revival of the 1930s," in *Henry James Against the Aesthetic Movement: Essays on the Middle and Late Fiction*, ed. David Garrett Izzo and Daniel T. O'Hara (Jefferson, NC: McFarland, 2006), 13–34.

42. Marianne Moore, "Henry James as a Characteristic American," *Hound & Horn* 7 (Apr.–May–June 1934): 372, 365.

43. Edna Kenton, "Henry James in the World," ibid., 513, 507.

44. In *Hound & Horn*'s prefatory "Homage to Henry James 1843–1916," the editors announced that they had hoped to have contributions from T. S. Eliot, Gertrude Stein, and Ezra Pound but that none of them could provide new material for the special number (361).

45. Morton Fullerton's and Lubbock's appreciative notices have been cited previously. When Ford Madox Ford turned to the question of James's artistic method, he confessed that the best any critic could do would be to paraphrase the Master's own Prefaces. "There is nothing left," he conceded, "but the merest of quotations" (*Henry James: A Critical Study*, 152).

46. HJ to William Dean Howells, 17 Aug. 1908, in Anesko, *Letters, Fictions, Lives*, 426.

47. RPB, "The Critical Prefaces," *Hound & Horn* 7 (Apr.–May–June 1934): 473. Apparently unknown to Blackmur at this time was the parallel work recently completed by Leon Edel, whose *The Prefaces of Henry James* (Paris: Jouve, 1931) also analyzed those compositions through the classification and division of narrative themes and techniques.

48. Quentin Anderson, "Why R. P. Blackmur Found James's *Golden Bowl* Inhumane," *ELH* 68.3 (Fall 2001): 725.

49. RPB, "Introduction," in *The Wings of the Dove* (New York: Dell, 1959); rpt. in *Stud-*

*ies in Henry James,* ed. Veronica A. Makowsky (New York: New Directions, 1983), 161. Rather uncannily, many years later Leon Edel would testify to an almost identical *initiation première* to the Master's oeuvre; see his confessional essay, "How I Came to Henry James," *Henry James Review* 3.3 (Spring 1982): 163.

50. Denis Donoghue, "Blackmur on Henry James," in *The Legacy of R. P. Blackmur: Essays, Memoirs, Texts,* ed. Edward T. Cone, Joseph Frank, and Edmund Keeley (New York: Ecco Press, 1987), 23.

51. Russell Fraser, *A Mingled Yarn: The Life of R. P. Blackmur* (New York: Harcourt Brace Jovanovich, 1981), 166. Less comprehensive but still useful is Gerald J. Pannick, *Richard Palmer Blackmur* (Boston: Twayne, 1981).

52. Edward W. Said, "The Horizon of R. P. Blackmur," in *The Legacy of R. P. Blackmur,* 101.

53. RPB to John Hall Wheelock, 30 Jan. 1934 (CSA, Author Files I, Box 81, Folder 7). Blackmur would make a similar claim in the opening paragraph of his *Hound & Horn* essay.

54. RPB to John Hall Wheelock, 5 Feb. 1934 (CSA, Author Files I, Box 81, Folder 7).

55. John Hall Wheelock to RPB, 7 Mar. 1934 (RPB, Correspondence, Box 8, Folder 6).

56. RPB to John Hall Wheelock, 8 Mar. 1934 (CSA, Author Files I, Box 81, Folder 7).

57. John Hall Wheelock to RPB, 15 Mar. and 1 May 1934 (CSA, Author Files I, Box 81, Folder 7).

58. Alpheus Smith to Charles Scribner's Sons, 1 Feb. 1934 (CSA, Author Files I, Box 81, Folder 7).

59. Charles Scribner Jr. to RPB, 23 Nov. 1959 (RPB, Correspondence, Box 8, Folder 6).

60. RPB to Charles Scribner Jr., 3 Dec. 1959 (RPB, Correspondence, Box 8, Folder 6).

61. Contrary to the publisher's expectations, initial sales of *The Art of the Novel* totaled more than eight hundred copies within six months of publication. One editor wrote to James's literary executor, "We think that this is a very fair showing for the book under present conditions and for so limited a time." From their payment of $126.15 to HJ3, one can infer a total sale of 841 copies at a retail price of $3.00 and a royalty rate of 5 percent. [W. D. Howe] to HJ3, 3 Sept. 1935 (CSA, Author Files I, Box 81, Folder 8).

62. C. Hartley Grattan, Rev. of *The Art of the Novel,* by Henry James, *New York Times Book Review* (18 Nov. 1934): 2.

63. The author of many broken promises, Blackmur once averred that "the game of literature is mostly shit; the shit of deliberate misunderstanding, the shit of ill-will, the shit of patronage, and the worst shit of intellectual snobbery" (qtd. in Fraser, *A Mingled Yarn,* 176). Blackmur also reneged on a contract to edit the *Henry James Reader* for Scribner's, although to them he returned his $750 advance. That project then fell into the hands of Leon Edel. RPB to Wayne Andrews, 1 June 1963 (CSA, Author Files IV, Box 37, Folder 4).

64. HJ to William Dean Howells, 17 Aug. 1908, in Anesko, *Letters, Fictions, Lives,* 426; Blackmur, "The Critical Prefaces," 445, 446.

### Chapter 4

1. FOM to WAJ, 21 Apr. 1943, Harvard University Archives (UAIII.8.11.3 [Box 54—"James Papers"]).

2. Well meaning but certainly mistaken, Warren acknowledged his debt to Perry, whom he identified as "literary executor of the James manuscripts." Harry James had never surrendered that legal authority to him. Cf. Austin Warren, *The Elder Henry James* (New York: Macmillan, 1934), ix.

3. In a note of warning to Ralph Barton Perry, Harry dismissed one of them with obviously patronizing condescension:

A little aspirant for a Ph.D. degree, Miss Cornelia Pulsifer Kelley, has just called on me to ask to get at my uncle's papers in the library. She apparently knows they're there and knows that you are working on that group of papers. She's going to be working in the library this summer, and remarked cheerfully that she hoped to see you and talk with you. This is merely to warn you and to say that I told her that the papers are not in such condition that I could give her permission to consult them. I have decided to make it a rule not to consider applications from students who are trying to write theses—even Ph.D. theses. (HJ3 to Ralph Barton Perry, 18 June 1930 [bMS Am 1095.2 (66), MH])

4. HJ3, *Richard Olney and His Public Service: With Documents, Including Unpublished Diplomatic Correspondence* (Boston: Houghton Mifflin, 1923), 109.

5. It is surely worth noting that one of Harry's sisters-in-law, Alice Runnells James (Billy's wife), was the daughter of the general counsel of the Pullman Palace Car Company. For years John Sumner Runnells brought his family from Chicago to spend their summers at Chocorua, New Hampshire, where they were nearby neighbors of the Jameses.

6. HJ3, *Richard Olney*, 12.

7. A later historian of education, Hugh Hawkins, generously refers to James's work as "one of the finest examples of the life-and-letters form of biography" and credits his use of archival sources as "careful and thorough." See *Between Harvard and America: The Educational Leadership of Charles W. Eliot* (New York: Oxford University Press, 1972), 304. For more on HJ3's close connection with Harvard, see Lewis, *The Jameses*, 598–603.

8. H. L. Mencken, Rev. of *Charles W. Eliot*, by Henry James, *Nation* 131 (3 Dec. 1930): 617.

9. Henry James, *Charles W. Eliot: President of Harvard University, 1869–1909*, 2 vols. (Boston: Houghton Mifflin, 1930), 1:x.

10. Ralph Barton Perry, *The Thought and Character of William James: As Revealed in Unpublished Correspondence and Notes, Together with His Published Writings*, 2 vols. (Boston: Little, Brown, 1935), 1:vii.

11. David Leslie Murray, Rev. of *The Thought and Character of William James*, by Ralph Barton Perry, *Times Literary Supplement* (17 Oct. 1936): 821.

12. John Dewey, Rev. of *The Thought and Character of William James*, by Ralph Barton Perry, *New Republic* 85 (12 Feb. 1936): 24.

13. HJ3 to Ralph Barton Perry, 17 Feb. 1931 (bMS Am 1938 [246], MH).

14. HJ3 to Lucy Clifford, Aug. 1927, qtd. in *"Bravest of women and finest of friends,"* 20.

15. Jacques Derrida, *Archive Fever: A Freudian Impression*, trans. Eric Prenowitz (Chicago: University of Chicago Press, 1996), 12. The relevance of this theoretical framework to tales such as "The Aspern Papers" (and HJ's personal bonfires) is fairly clear, as Eric Savoy has pointed out ("Aspern's Archive," *Henry James Review* 31 [2010]: 61–67).

16. HJ3, entry for 22 Aug. [1898], Pocket Diary, p. 29 (bMS Am 1094.5 [23], MH).

17. Another student of the family, curious to learn more about Alice James's particular medical and psychological symptoms, was disappointed to find that portions of certain letters in the archive had been mutilated. As Leon Edel explained:

There are one or two letters portions of which have been cut away and Harry scribbled on the margin something about his feeling that posterity had no business with Alice's minute symptoms on which HJ reported to the medical William. It must have been very much like those letters in which Henry tells William about his constipation. I would suspect that he probably wrote about Alice's urine, or other excreta etc etc HJ being very exact in such matters. (LE to Saul Rosenzweig, 24 Jan. 1979 [LEP, Box 13, Folder 22])

18. William James, "The Ph.D. Octopus," *Harvard Monthly* 36 (Mar. 1903): 1–9.

19. HJ3 to Alfred C. Potter, 18 June 1930, Librarian's Files: James Collection—Early Correspondence (MH). Two years earlier, when he presented the Harvard library with the remarkable copy-text of *The American* that his uncle had so heavily revised for the New York Edition, Harry added a stern restriction to the bequest. "During my lifetime," he insisted, "none of the pages of this volume of the manuscript are to be reproduced. I make an exception to this stipulation in favor of any one holding a Harvard Faculty appointment with the rank of not less than Assistant Professor." Feeling a need to explain himself further, Harry added a postscript: "The last paragraph is a measure of precaution against random and foolish hunters after 'copy.'" HJ3 to Harvard College Library, 27 Dec. 1928 (bMS Am 1237.14 [25], MH).

20. Arthur T. Hamlin, "Personal Papers in the Harvard Library," *Harvard Alumni Bulletin* (21 Jan. 1938): 442, 445.

21. HJ3 to Keyes D. Metcalf, 31 Jan. 1938, Harvard University Archives (UA III.8.11.3 [Box 55—"Henry James"]).

22. I am grateful to Susan Halpert, reference librarian at Houghton, for sharing with me her unpublished paper "The Real Thing" (first delivered at the 2002 Paris Conference "Henry James Today"), in which she assembled a concise history of the restrictions surrounding the James Family Papers. The "Application for the Examination of Manuscripts" specifically prohibits publication of any material to which the petitioner has been given access, without another separate written application to the appropriate curator at Harvard.

23. HJ3 to Harvard University, 16 Dec. 1941, Harvard University Archives (UA III.8.11.3 [Box 54—"James Papers"]). These restrictions were formally announced by Ralph Barton Perry shortly after Harry gifted the collection; see "The James Collection," *Harvard Library Notes* 4.2 (Mar. 1942): 79. Harry's first letter of intent was sent to Metcalf on 13 Apr. 1939, Harvard University Archives (UA III.8.11.3 [Box 55—"Henry James"]).

24. WAJ to HJ3, 26 Aug. 1942, Librarian's Files: James Collection—Henry James (1942–47) (MH).

25. "James' Works in Houghton" (8 Mar. 1943), www.thecrimson.com/article.aspx?ref=191178.

26. Labels from "Henry James Exhibition," Feb.–Apr. 1943 (Harvard Deposit Library, Harvard University).

27. "It was from James' example," Matthiessen observes, "that Eliot and Pound, living among Georgians, learned 'that poetry ought to be as well written as prose'; and by

extending and tightening up such a note as this of James', Eliot could have arrived at his formulation of the 'objective correlative,' which now stands as one of the classic definitions of wholeness of composition" (*American Renaissance: Art and Expression in the Age of Emerson and Whitman* [New York: Oxford University Press, 1941], 305).

28. Ibid., ix.

29. William Cain has sketched its outlines in "Criticism and Politics: F.O. Matthiessen and the Making of Henry James," *New England Quarterly* 60.2 (June 1987): 163–86.

30. Matthiessen's letters to Cheney, quoted in chronological sequence, are dated 15 Jan., 10 Feb., 1 Mar., and 21 Mar. 1943 (F. O. Matthiessen Papers, Box 4, Folder 61, Yale Collection of American Literature, Beinecke Rare Book and Manuscript Library). Some of these and other relevant letters are included in *Rat & the Devil: Journal Letters of F. O. Matthiessen and Russell Cheney*, ed. Louis Hyde (Hamden, CT: Archon Books, 1978).

31. Even though many notable contributors (including Alfred Kazin, Lionel Trilling, and Allen Tate) backed out, "the James issue," according to one historian, "was outstanding and diversified." If not exactly pioneering, "the issue certainly was timely: it helped launch the James revival in the 1940s and stimulated critical concentration on James's final period." See Marian Janssen, *"The Kenyon Review" 1939–1970: A Critical History* (Baton Rouge: Louisiana State University Press, 1990), 101, 102.

32. FOM, "Henry James's Portrait of the Artist," *Partisan Review* 11.1 (Winter 1944): 71–87.

33. FOM, *Henry James: The Major Phase* (New York: Oxford University Press, 1944), ix, xiii, x.

34. FOM, comp., *The James Family* (New York: Knopf, 1947), v.

35. Maxwell Perkins to HJ3, 19 Mar. 1943; HJ3 to Perkins, 25 Mar. 1943 (CSA, Author Files I, Box 81, Folder 9). Edel, it should be noted, was born in the United States.

36. *Henry James: Representative Selections*, ed. Lyon Richardson (New York: American Book, 1941). This compact volume was the first commercial anthology of James's writing designed for classroom use.

37. HJ3 to JBP, 6 Sept. [1919] (HJC).

38. HJ3 to LE, 5 May 1932 (LEP, Box 23, Folder 8). Two years later, when R. P. Blackmur was preparing the one-volume compilation of the Prefaces (*The Art of the Novel*) for Scribner's, Harry expressed regret that Edel's work was not cited. Commenting to the Scribner editor in charge of the book, Harry thought that Blackmur "might well . . . have found room for a reference to Leon Edel's monograph on the Prefaces, for its worth the attention of anyone who wants to study them carefully and its little known." HJ3 to W. D. Howe, 29 Nov. 1934 (CSA, Author Files I, Box 81, Folder 7).

39. Importantly, Edel's volumes also were circulated among other branches of the family, bringing his name to their attention. When Billy James, Harry's younger brother, saw Edel's review of C. Hartley Grattan's *The Three Jameses* in the *Saturday Review of Literature*, he commended the author on his acuity and even invited him to visit the James homestead at 95 Irving Street in Cambridge or their country retreat at Chocorua, New Hampshire. "I think that you write of H. J. with a more sympathetic understanding and with more thorough knowledge than anyone else has done," Billy complimented. "And you write beautifully." WJ2 to LE, 14 Nov. 1932 and 23 Sept. 1933 (LEP, Box 24, Folder 4).

40. HJ3 to PL, 16 May 1932; PL to HJ3, 30 June 1932 (LEP, Box 18, Folder 29). Besides to Harry, Edel sent copies of his Sorbonne essays to Wharton, Lubbock, Lapsley, and a handful of others who had known the Master. All of them were favorably impressed by his diligent research and would become important allies in his quest to monopolize the James material. Lubbock commended Edel's work to Lapsley, saying, "I thought those two books of little Edel's quite honest & meritorious pieces of work—particularly the années dramatiques, a job well worth doing, usefully done: don't you agree?" (EWP, Box 58, Folder 1700). Wharton was so taken with his essay on the Prefaces that she hoped he would undertake to compile a selection "of all the passages of purely literary interest" from them (a project she had advocated for years): "I am sure you are the person to do it," she added. Of course, Blackmur's *The Art of the Novel*, published two years later, superseded that design. EW to LE, 16 June 1932 (LEP, Box 21, Folder 5).

41. LE, "An Amazing Family," rev. of *The Three Jameses: A Family of Minds*, by C. Hartley Grattan, and *Theatre and Friendship: Letters from Henry James to Elizabeth Robins*, by Elizabeth Robins, *Saturday Review of Literature* 9.1 (12 Nov. 1932): 236.

42. LE to HJ3, 20 Sept. 1937 (LEP, Box 23, Folder 8).

43. Discovery of the notebooks even prompted Edel—momentarily—to think of abandoning his edition of James's plays. "My first impulse," he later wrote, "was to telephone the nephew in New York and tell him I was ready to forget the plays—the notebooks cried for editing. But a second thought suggested caution: the novelist's executor might consider this capricious, and I went on with my work." LE, untitled draft of a memoir, n.d. (LEP, Box 60, Folder 10).

44. Edel himself provides the best account of his wartime years; see his posthumously published *The Visitable Past: A Wartime Memoir* (Honolulu: University of Hawai'i Press, 2000), 8, passim.

45. In the spring of 1945, Harry informed the Houghton librarian that Edel had found the aged Fullerton in Paris, very hard up for money, and eager to sell his James letters. "As you know," Harry wrote, "I have never gone into the market to buy my Uncle Henry's letters for a variety of reasons, and I don't want to do it now. But if Fullerton wants to sell his papers, including my uncle's, to the Library and you want to buy them, let me know what the figure would be and I will see how much of a contribution I could make." HJ3 to WAJ, 5 Mar. 1945, Librarian's Files: James Collection—Henry James (1942–47) (MH).

46. FOM to LE, 24 Apr. [1943] (LEP, Box 19, Folder 18).

47. Harry Levin to LE, 9 May 1943 (LEP, Box 8, Folder 26). The New Directions book was *Stories of Writers and Artists*, ed. F. O. Matthiessen (1944).

48. James Laughlin, the New Directions publisher (and one of Matthiessen's students at Harvard), had been in correspondence with his former professor for some time about the James project. When Edel got wind of this, he tried an end run by proposing such a volume himself, but New Directions gave *Stories of Writers and Artists* to Matthiessen instead. FOM to James Laughlin, 21 Mar. [1943]; LE to James Laughlin, 1 May 1943 (bMS Am 2077 [2472], MH).

49. Robert B. Heilman, Rev. of *Henry James: The Major Phase*, by F. O. Matthiessen, *New England Quarterly* 18 (June 1945): 268.

50. LE to FOM, 15 Mar. 1945 (F. O. Matthiessen Papers, Yale Collection of American Literature, Beinecke Rare Book and Manuscript Library).

51. FOM to LE, 24 Apr. [1943] (LEP, Box 19, Folder 18).

52. LE to HJ3, 19 July 1947 (LEP, Box 23, Folder 8).

53. HJ3 to LE, 11 Aug. 1947 (LEP, Box 23, Folder 8). When *Henry James: The Major Phase* appeared, Harry found occasion to voice a qualified dissent. "Matthiessen is not an interesting writer," he wrote,

> and his treatment of his subject is suited more to student readers, whether undergraduate or mature, than to general readers. But you will be impressed by his thoroughness and care; and he seems to be unusually sensitive and discriminating in his interpretations and on the whole in his judgments. He is a bit obsessed by his own social philosophy which is that of a lot of left-wing people. They tend to demand of an author something like their own interest in social reform; and some of them have gone off into absurdities in the way of finding fault with Uncle Henry because he didn't share their interest or their approach to social questions. It is childish to write about an author that way because when you are trying to interpret and appraise an author, the only sensible thing to do is to consider how he handled the sort of thing that he was interested in. It is idle to spend time wailing or finding fault because he wasn't interested in what happens to interest you. The structural elements of the social economic order in the 19th century just didn't interest Uncle Henry. He had no personal contact with practical affairs, was as innocent as a child about them, and knew that he didn't understand them. (HJ3 to John W. Lapsley, 23 Apr. 1945 [LEP, Box 23, Folder 7])

Whether Harry James was aware of Matthiessen's closeted homosexuality is a tempting, but probably unknowable, question.

54. When Matthiessen had finished the manuscript of *The Major Phase*, he took it down to New York to deliver it to Oxford University Press. Dining beforehand with a member of the Century Club, he was chagrined when his luncheon companion welcomed Harry James to their table. "That meant a lunch of walking on egg shells," Matthiessen confided, "since I didn't want to take any chance of offending his pinch-faced decorously mean little spirit." FOM to Russell Cheney, 5 Mar. [1944] (F. O. Matthiessen Papers, Box 4, Folder 22, Yale Collection of American Literature, Beinecke Rare Book and Manuscript Library).

55. LE to WAJ, 14 Aug. and 2 Sept. 1947; WAJ to LE, 18 Aug. 1947 (LEP, Box 7, Folder 13). In the last letter, Jackson informed Edel that the library "recently had a communication from Mr. James concerning the use of the material in which he specifically states that you, Matthiessen, and Murdock are to have priority over other applicants. With this we heartily concur, and I, for one, look forward to your publications in this field." Not surprisingly, Edel was relieved by this news and he thanked Jackson "for telling me about the priority matter, which is both flattering, and comforting."

56. LE, Rev. of *The James Family*, by F. O. Matthiessen, *PM* (19 Oct. 1947): m15.

57. FOM to LE, 10 Nov. [1947] (LEP, Box 19, Folder 18).

58. LE to FOM, 3 Dec. 1947 (LEP, Box 19, Folder 18). Matthiessen probably never came across another hostile notice that Edel had written in response to *The Major Phase*. In his review of that book, Edel called his rival to task for underestimating the full extent of the Master's late creativity and for failing to grasp the broader significance of

it. "Impression and intuition in such circumstances run the risk of being divorced from fact," Edel lamented, "and this makes one wonder whether, at bottom, Mr. Matthiessen, in his 'intuitive' appreciation of literature and ideas, does not minimize unduly the spadework of scholarship." LE, Rev. of *Henry James: The Major Phase*, by F. O. Matthiessen, *University of Toronto Quarterly* 16 (1947): 428.

59. WJ2 to LE, 5 Nov. 19[47] (LEP, Box 24, Folder 4).

60. WJ2 to LE, 12 June 1948 (LEP, Box 24, Folder 4).

61. LE, "Introduction," in *Henry James: A Collection of Critical Essays* (Englewood Cliffs, NJ: Prentice-Hall, 1963), 7.

62. Roger du Béarn [Jacques Barzun], "The Henry James Boom," *New Yorker* 21 (22 Dec. 1945): 30.

63. As Lehmann later recalled, "The revival in Henry James, one of our favourite authors, was reaching its height [in 1946]; Graham Greene at Eyre and Spottiswoode was planning, we heard, to republish the later novels of 'James the Old Pretender,' so we decided to start on the novels and stories of the early and middle periods which were, with very rare exceptions, totally unobtainable and likely to remain so. We began with *Roderick Hudson*, and by the end had ten volumes in print." John Lehmann, *The Ample Persuasion: Autobiography 3* (London: Eyre & Spottiswoode, 1966), 171.

64. In 1944 Macmillan offered to sell Laughlin a set of plates for the entire 1921–23 Pocket Edition of James's *Novels and Tales*, with delivery after the war. Leon Edel tried to persuade Laughlin to follow through with the plan but was unsuccessful. Macmillan & Co. to James Laughlin, 15 Feb. 1944; and LE to James Laughlin, 15 May 1946 (bMS Am 2077 [2472], [499], MH).

65. John Hall Wheelock to RPB, 21 Jan. 1946 (RPB, Correspondence, Box 8, Folder 6). Five years later, a different proposal to reissue James's autobiographical volumes met the same fate. Scribner's editor rebuffed the idea, remarking, "The James 'revival,' while it has shown definite vitality in the field of criticism, thus far has involved loss for the publishers who have participated in it." W[allace] M[eyer] to Sara Fine Rubenstein, 4 May 1951 (CSA, Author Files III, Box 45, Folder 12). Just five years later, Criterion Books reissued all of HJ's memoirs in one volume, *Autobiography* (1956).

66. In addition to reissues of works like *Roderick Hudson*, *The Bostonians*, and *The Princess Casamassima*, important new editions of works previously uncollected by James also appeared for the first time: *The Scenic Art: Notes on Acting & the Drama*, ed. Alan Wade (New Brunswick, NJ: Rutgers University Press, 1948); and *The Complete Plays of Henry James*, ed. Leon Edel (Philadelphia: J. B. Lippincott, 1949). Both of these titles were issued in England by Rupert Hart-Davis.

67. "Did you notice that the intervals in the B.B.C. Third Programme last week were filled in with readings from Henry James?" Hart-Davis happily queried Theodora Bosanquet. "I see also that someone has made a play out of 'The Turn of the Screw.' Have you read Matthiessen's book, which I believe the Oxford Press are bringing out this autumn? It appeared, I believe, two years ago in America. All these events, together with Eyre & Spottiswoode's forthcoming reprints of *The Wings of the Dove* and *The Ambassadors*, are surely forerunners of The Boom." Rupert Hart-Davis to TB, 7 Oct. 1946 (MS Eng 1213.3 [96], MH).

68. Philip Rahv, "Henry James's America" [rev. of *The American Novels and Tales of Henry James*, ed. F. O. Matthiessen], *New York Times Book Review* (2 Mar. 1947): 4. Rahv had voiced similar views in an earlier essay written in anticipation of the James centennial; see "Attitudes to Henry James," *New Republic* 108 (15 Feb. 1943): 22–24.

69. Alfred Kazin, "Critics at the Feast of Henry James" [rev. of *The Question of Henry James*, comp. F. W. Dupee], *New York Times Book Review* (2 Dec. 1945): 39.

70. Granville Hicks, *The Great Tradition: An Interpretation of American Literature Since the Civil War*, rev. ed. (New York: Macmillan, 1935), 108.

71. F. R. Leavis, *The Great Tradition: George Eliot, Henry James, Joseph Conrad* (London: Chatto & Windus, 1948), 16.

72. Philip Rahv, "A Biographical Introduction," *The Great Short Novels of Henry James* (New York: Dial Press, 1944), vii.

73. Clifton Fadiman, "The Revival of Interest in Henry James," *New York Herald Tribune Weekly Book Review* (14 Jan. 1945): 2. Fadiman reprinted this essay as the introduction to his Modern Library anthology, *The Short Stories of Henry James* (1945).

74. As one aficionado wrote to Billy James, "The Fadiman volume is disappointing. We had no great reason to expect much from the introduction or the notes but some to expect a larger collection and a subtler choice. Dr. Matthiessen's three volumes (to come) will overshadow the attempts of C.F. and Dupee to cash in on a good market." Donald Brien to WJ2, 24 Oct. [1945] (bMS Am 1938 [18], MH). A sales manager for a New England shoe manufacturer, Brien had a minor passion for Jamesians and Jamesiana. Besides collecting James first editions and manuscript letters, he became a kind of unpaid agent for Leon Edel, often doing research for the biographer when business trips took him to locations where he could access manuscripts that were still in private hands. After he retired from business in 1960, he described himself as Edel's "research associate."

75. Jonathan Freedman, *The Temple of Culture: Assimilation and Anti-Semitism in Literary Anglo-America* (New York: Oxford University Press, 2000), 186, 198.

76. Qtd. in Lewis, *The Jameses*, 608.

77. Paul Rosenfeld, "The Henry James Revival: The Expatriate Comes Home," *Commonweal* 43 (11 Jan. 1946): 329–32.

78. Hilton Kramer, "Henry James & the Life of Art," *New Criterion* 11.8 (Apr. 1993): 7.

*Chapter 5*

1. A[rthur] B[ingham] W[alkley], "Henry James's Letters," *London Times* (14 Apr. 1920): 12:1.

2. Robert Herrick, "A Visit to Henry James," in *The Manly Anniversary Studies in Language and Literature* (Chicago: University of Chicago Press, 1923), 232.

3. AHGJ to HJ3 [n.d., 1920?] (bMS Am 1092.10 [95], MH).

4. AHGJ to HJ3, 4 May 1921 (bMS Am 2538 [21], MH). At least part of Alice James's despair originated as a reflex against her earlier enthusiasm for Lubbock's candidacy. In numerous letters to her children, she had confirmed her approval of his choice to edit HJ's correspondence. To HJ3, for example, she commended Lubbock as "very interesting and satisfactory about the letters"; likewise, she told WJ2 that Lubbock was a man "whom one likes more the more one sees him," and she expressed some surprise when

234 Notes to Pages 159–163

she discovered that HJ had overlooked him in the list of modest bequests included in his last will and testament. See AHGJ to HJ3, 31 July 1916 (bMS Am 2538 [19], MH); AHGJ to WJ2, 16 Apr. 1916 and 14 Mar. 1916 (bMS Am 2538 [40], MH). To calm his mother, HJ3 defended Lubbock's handling of the *Letters* by saying that if his "editing was not fault-less . . . no one else's would have been faultless either. *Nothing*," Harry insisted, "would have been so wrong and so contrary to all Uncle Henry's beliefs and literary instincts as for you or me or any member of the family to have stood over Lubbock's elbow, or for any of us to set out now to patch and 'remedy it.'" The Jameses may not have stood over Lubbock's elbow, but they certainly went over his proof sheets with watchful eyes and, previously, had carefully edited the typescript copies of letters sent to him from America. HJ3 to AHGJ, 21 May 1921 (bMS Am 2538 [53], MH).

5. [Louis Umfreville Wilkinson], "The Better End: Conclusion of a Chapter from the Unpublished Novel, What Percy Knew, by H*nr* J*m*s" ([1912]; London: Privately printed, 1969), 3. See also Adeline Tintner, *Henry James's Legacy: The Afterlife of His Figure and Fiction* (Baton Rouge: Louisiana State University Press, 1998), 84–85.

6. See, for example, Max Beerbohm, "The Mote in the Middle Distance," in *A Christmas Garland* (London: Heinemann, 1912), 1–10; or, as pointedly, his caricature ("A Rage of Wonderment") of a wide-eyed Master, kneeling down and staring at two pairs of shoes—a man's boots and a woman's pumps—placed on the threshold of a closed hotel room door (reproduced in Fred Kaplan, *Henry James: The Imagination of Genius* [London: Hodder & Stoughton, 1992], following page 304).

7. *Letters to A. C. Benson and Auguste Monod*, ed. E. F. Benson (London: Elkin Matthews & Marrot, 1930), 14, 28. As Sheldon Novick has commented on the homoeroticism of these letters, "A minimum of discretion was observed, he wrote in double entendres, but he was reassuring Benson of his love and his language could hardly be misunderstood" (*Henry James: The Mature Master* [New York: Random House, 2007], 250).

8. Qtd. in *A Bibliography of Henry James*, 3rd ed., comp. Leon Edel and Dan H. Laurence (with the assistance of James Rambeau) (Oxford: Clarendon Press, 1982), 264.

9. HJ3 to PL, 23 Dec. 1932 (LEP, Box 19, Folder 12).

10. HJ3 to Mrs. Alice Dew-Smith, 23 Dec. 1932 (LEP, Box 19, Folder 12).

11. The best source of information about Andersen and his complicated relation with the Jameses is the supplemental editorial matter in *Beloved Boy: Letters to Hendrik C. Andersen, 1899–1915*, ed. Rosella Mamoli Zorzi, with an additional introduction by Millicent Bell and afterword by Elena di Majo (Charlottesville: University of Virginia Press, 2004), 123–24.

12. WJ to Hendrik C. Andersen, 18 Jan. 1901, *CWJ*, 9:411.

13. Lewis, *The Jameses*, 570.

14. Hendrik C. Andersen to WJ2, 18 July 1933 (Museo Andersen, Rome).

15. Hendrik C. Andersen to Alice Runnells James, 19 Dec. 1933 (Museo Andersen, Rome).

16. WJ2 to Hendrik C. Andersen, 13 Mar. 1934 (Museo Andersen, Rome).

17. Hendrik C. Andersen to WJ2, 14 Apr. 1934 (Museo Andersen, Rome).

18. HJ3 to Hendrik C. Andersen, 28 Dec. 1934 (Museo Andersen, Rome).

19. Hendrik C. Andersen to HJ3, 8 Jan. 1935 (Museo Andersen, Rome). Only a month

later, Andersen repeated his request, which naturally elicited from Harry an even blunter rejection. As Andersen then told Billy,

> I have had one or two letters from good Henry James regarding the letters I sent him—those I had received from big, lovable Henry James—that I wished to have published. As he did not approve of issuing them in a little volume which I had intended to illustrate with photographs of Rye and its surroundings, as well as many others which I felt would make a little gem of his letters "to an unknown artist," the matter has fallen through. It seemed to me that these letters showed a richness in his affections that is not to be found in the two volumes of letters already published, which I have read carefully. In any case, since Henry James's decision is final and his reasons well defined I must of course accept this decision and raise no objection. (Hendrik C. Andersen to WJ2, 16 Mar. 1935 [Museo Andersen, Rome])

20. HJ3 to Hendrik C. Andersen, 21 Jan. 1935 (Museo Andersen, Rome).

21. Hendrik C. Andersen, "Introduction to Letters with a Few Explanatory Notes" [1934?] (Museo Andersen, Rome).

22. HJ3 to WAJ, 16 Oct. 1942, Librarian's Files: James Collection—Henry James (1942–47) (MH).

23. Simon Nowell-Smith to WJ2, 30 Sept. 1946 (bMS Am 1938 [104], MH).

24. Adele Neville, the woman who had helped Andersen transcribe the correspondence, told Edel (exaggeratedly) that the sculptor had "hundreds of letters" from James and that he was planning to publish them. Because Harry had withheld consent to publish, Andersen extended that prohibition to others and refused Edel access. Adele Neville to LE, 5 Sept. 1939; Hendrik C. Andersen to LE, 23 Oct. 1939 (LEP, Box 17, Folder 5).

25. Frederick B. Adams Jr. to LE, 18 Mar. 1953 (LEP, Box 10, Folder 5).

26. Lehmann, *The Ample Persuasion*, 18, 33.

27. "It would be interesting to know," Swan speculated, "just what psychological complications in James's mind allowed him to write, when advanced in years, of the successful late fulfilment of love, after his youth and middle age had been spent in showing that love, like the full discovery of life, demands too much and may strain the finer sensibility to the point of destruction" (*Henry James* [London: Arthur Barker, 1952], 90–91). Edel would maintain that the principal catalyst for James's mature analysis of "the great relation" was the author's belated recognition (and acceptance) of his own same-sex desires, a thesis much dependent upon the letters to Andersen. In 1950, Swan also had contributed a brief pamphlet on James to the British Book News Series, Writers and Their Work (London: Longmans, Green), which was revised and reprinted in 1957 and 1969.

28. Michael Swan, "Henry James and H. G. Wells: A Study of Their Friendship Based on Their Unpublished Correspondence," *Cornhill Magazine* 997 (Autumn 1953): 43–65.

29. Edel and Ray, *Henry James and H. G. Wells*, 10. In 1949, Rupert Hart-Davis told Edel that he had received a book proposal for a book called *James and Wells: A Record of Their Controversy over the Form and Function of the Novel*; Edel discouraged him from accepting it, saying, "Very interesting your report of a volume on James and Wells—I can see an article in it but wonder how it can be stretched to a book." This is just one of many examples where Edel piggybacked or leapfrogged with others' ideas. Rupert Hart-Davis to LE, 15 Aug. 1949; LE to Rupert Hart-Davis, 7 Sept. 1949 (LEP, Box 5, Folder 47).

30. Michael Swan, *A Small Part of Time: Essays on Literature, Art and Travel* (London: Dufour Editions, 1961), 43, 44.

31. Michael Swan, comp., "Recollections of Henry James in His Later Years," transcriptions of initial interviews (MS Eng 1213.4 [20], MH).

32. Michael Swan, *A Small Part of Time*, 45.

33. The description of Barrett's largesse as a patron was offered by Leon Edel in *A Salute to Clifton Waller Barrett on His Eightieth from Friends & Admirers* (Charlottesville, VA: Privately printed, 1981), n.p.

34. Clifton Waller Barrett Library, "Re: acquisitions question," message to the author, 30 Nov. 2007.

35. WAJ to LE, 7 Feb. 1955, Librarian's Files: Leon Edel (MH).

36. LE to Clifton Waller Barrett, 27 Feb. 1961 (LEP, Box 1, Folder 36).

37. Clifton Waller Barrett to LE, 3 Mar. 1961 (LEP, Box 1, Folder 36).

38. Michael Swan, "Henry James and the Heroic Young Master," *London Magazine* 2 (May 1955): 78–86; and also in *Harper's Bazaar* 89 (Sept. 1955): quotation, 227. Swan did get permission from the literary agent who managed the James family's literary property in Great Britain, but it is evident that license to publish would have been refused had the executor himself been consulted. See also Walker, "Leon Edel and the 'Policing' of the Henry James Letters," 280.

39. WJ2 to Paul Revere Reynolds, 12 Oct. 1955 (Paul Revere Reynolds Papers, Box 100, Folder 4, Rare Book and Manuscript Division, Butler Library, Columbia University).

40. Paul Revere Reynolds to WJ2, 10 Nov. 1955 (Paul Revere Reynolds Papers, Box 100, Folder 4, Rare Book and Manuscript Division, Butler Library, Columbia University).

41. WJ2 to LE, 12 Nov. 1955 (LEP, Box 24, Folder 5).

42. LE to WJ2, 10 Nov. 1953 (LEP, Box 24, Folder 4). The articles in question were Carl J. Weber, "Henry James and His Tiger-Cat," *PMLA* 68.4 (Sept. 1953): 672–87; and Burdett Gardner, "An Apology for Henry James's 'Tiger-Cat,'" *PMLA* 68.4 (Sept. 1953): 688–95. Edel's rejoinder appeared later as "Henry James and Vernon Lee," *PMLA* 69.3 (June 1954): 677–78.

43. WJ2 to LE, 12 and 23 Nov. 1953 (LEP, Box 24, Folder 4).

44. Steven H. Jobe, "The Leon Edel Papers at McGill University," *Henry James Review* 21 (2000): 292.

45. LE, Letter, *Times Literary Supplement* (21 Oct. 1949): 681.

46. LE to WAJ, 17 May 1954 (LEP, Box 7, Folder 13).

47. Noel Perrin, "The Henry James Papers," *New Yorker* 36 (12 Nov. 1960): 198.

48. LE to Rupert Hart-Davis, 11 Mar. 1964 (LEP, Box 6, Folder 2).

49. Donald Gallup to LE, 1 Feb. 1962 (LEP, Box 18, Folder 14).

50. WAJ to LE, 16 Feb. 1951 (LEP, Box 7, Folder 13).

51. WAJ to Herman E. Spivey, 8 Sept. 1948, Librarian's Files: James Requests (MH).

52. The worst offenders, in Edel's view, had published James material in spite of his express veto. Among them were George Montiero ("Letters of Henry James to John Hay," *Texas Studies in Literature and Language* 4 [1963]: 639–95); Robert F. Sayre (*The Examined Self: Benjamin Franklin, Henry Adams, Henry James* [Princeton: Princeton University Press, 1964]); and Millicent Bell (*Edith Wharton and Henry James: The Story of Their Friend-*

*ship* [New York: Braziller, 1965]). When in 1963 he wrote to congratulate Edel for having been awarded the Pulitzer Prize for the second and third volumes of his biography, Monteiro included, as a courtesy, a copy of his James-Hay piece. The angry response he received could hardly have been anticipated. "Your offprint came to me as a surprise," Edel admonished. "I had assumed you had understood that when permission to publish is refused one respects such decisions. I am making vigorous protests, some of which will doubtless reach you. . . . I regret very much that a young scholar, starting on a career in publication, should have made so serious an error—or been counseled so unwisely in the matter" (LE to George Monteiro, 3 Oct. 1963 [LEP, Box 10, Folder 1]).

53. LE to William H. Bond, 8 Feb. 1965 (LEP, Box 2, Folder 8). Bond succeeded William A. Jackson as Houghton librarian after the latter's death in 1964.

54. LE to Richard Garnett (for Rupert Hart-Davis), 1 Feb. 1965; Richard Garnett to LE, 9 Feb. 1965 (LEP, Box 4, Folder 41).

55. Thomas Wortham, message to the author, 1 June 2009.

56. See, for example, Christoph K. Lohmann and George Arms, "Commentary," *Nineteenth-Century Fiction* 31.2 (Sept. 1976): 244–51.

57. LE to Rupert Hart-Davis, 10 Mar. 1966 (LEP, Box 6, Folder 2). Harvard had offered him the Powell M. Cabot Professorship in American Literature, the position previously held by Perry Miller, who died in 1963.

58. LE to Rupert Hart-Davis, 2 Dec. 1963 (LEP, Box 6, Folder 2).

59. Clifton Waller Barrett to LE, 28 Nov. 1964 (LEP, Box 1, Folder 36).

60. LE to William H. Bond, 9 Nov. 1964 (LEP, Box 2, Folder 8).

61. LE to Rupert Hart-Davis, 10 Aug. 1956 (LEP, Box 5, Folder 49).

62. "Recollections of Henry James in His Later Years" (MS Eng 1213.4 [20], MH).

63. *HJL*, 4:809. In the early 1940s, when Harry got wind that Dr. Saul Rosenzweig, a leading psychoanalytic researcher, was nosing into the significance of his uncle's "obscure hurt"—the unspecified disability (disclosed by HJ in *Notes of a Son and Brother*) that disqualified him from service in the Union Army—he immediately warned the Harvard librarians to fend him off. "Thank you for sending me word about Dr. Rosenzweig," Keyes Metcalf answered. "I'll watch out for him. I am warning the attendants in the Houghton Library, so that they will not give him access to the James papers without bringing up the matter with me." Despite these hurdles, in 1943 Rosenzweig published a very influential analytical study of James in the scientific journal *Character and Personality* (vol. 11–12 [Dec. 1943]: 79–100). The next year, the *Partisan Review* reprinted Rosenzweig's essay as "The Ghost of Henry James" (vol. 11 [1944]: 436–55). No manuscript sources are cited in his study. Keyes D. Metcalf to HJ3, 16 July 1942, Harvard University Archives (UA III.8.11.3 [Box 54—"James Papers"]).

64. LE to HMH, 20 May 1965 (LEP, Box 18, Folder 18).

65. HMH to LE, 6 June 1965 (LEP, Box 18, Folder 18).

66. William H. Bond to Marshall B. Davidson [*Horizon Magazine*], 8 Oct. 1965 (LEP, Box 18, Folder 18).

67. LE to Rupert Hart-Davis, 8 May 1968 (LEP, Box 5, Folder 46).

68. LE, "Henry James's 'Last Dictation,'" *Times Literary Supplement* (2 May 1968): 459.

69. HMH, Letter, *Times Literary Supplement* (30 May 1968): 553. The other letters in

their exchange appeared on 9 May (p. 481), 23 May (p. 529), 6 June (p. 597), and 13 June (p. 621).

70. LE to Rodney Blumer [Rupert Hart-Davis Ltd], 15 June 1968 (LEP, Box 18, Folder 18).

71. LE to Rupert Hart-Davis, 18 May 1968 (LEP, Box 5, Folder 46).

72. In his recent legal study, Brian Crane has accepted this logic to defend Edel against critics who have deplored his virtual monopoly of the family papers. What Crane conspicuously overlooks is that Edel took this position largely out of self-interest, not from any fiduciary concern for James's heirs. Cf. "From Family Papers to Archive: The James Letters," *Henry James Review* 29 (2008): 144–62.

73. Methuen & Co. Ltd to Goodman, Derrick & Co., 26 Aug. 1968 (LEP, Box 18, Folder 18).

74. Goodman, Derrick & Co. to Mr. Davis-Poynter [Rupert Hart-Davis Ltd], 20 Nov. 1968 (LEP, Box 18, Folder 18).

75. Shortly after completing his own concise account of James's life, Frederick W. Dupee asked Edel if he had ever interviewed a Dr. Joseph Collins on the subject of James. This physician had examined the novelist on one of his later trips to New York. Dupee himself had talked with Collins the previous winter and "found him very eager to talk about his former patient, especially about his possible homosexuality." Frederick W. Dupee to LE, 9 Aug. 1949 (LEP, Box 3, Folder 51).

76. Harold Nicolson, entry for 31 Jan. 1963, *Diaries and Letters, 1930–1964*, ed. Stanley Olson (New York: Atheneum, 1980), 407.

77. Jeanne McCulloch, "The Art of Biography I: Leon Edel," *Paris Review* 98 (Winter 1985): 184. Edel later denied to Alexander James that the word "bugger" was used in their colloquy. Somewhat defensively, he alleged that Nicolson, "being a 'bugger' himself, obviously enlarge[d] our conversation" (LE to Alexander R. James, n.d. [Apr. 1984] [LEP, Box 23, Folder 1]).

78. LE to John James, 29 Dec. 1964 (LEP, Box 24, Folder 1).

79. William H. Bond to LE, 31 Dec. 1964 (LEP, Box 2, Folder 8).

80. LE to John James, 9 Apr. 1963 (LEP, Box 24, Folder 1).

81. LE to Rupert Hart-Davis, 9 Apr. 1963 (LEP, Box 6, Folder 2).

82. Vincent Brome, Letter, *Times Literary Supplement* (13 June 1968): 621.

83. Paul Revere Reynolds Jr. to John James et al., 2 July 1968 (Paul Revere Reynolds Papers, Series II, Box 221, Folder 1, Rare Book and Manuscript Division, Butler Library, Columbia University).

84. John James to Paul Revere Reynolds, 29 July 1968 (Paul Revere Reynolds Papers, Series II, Box 221, Folder 1, Rare Book and Manuscript Division, Butler Library, Columbia University).

85. LE to Alexander R. James, 6 Mar. 1972 (LEP, Box 23, Folder 1).

86. LE to Mark Carroll [Harvard University Press], 10 Apr. 1972 (LEP, Box 6, Folder 7). Dudley Jocelyn Persse was an extremely debonair man-about-town whom HJ met in 1903. After that he was a frequent escort when HJ went to London theaters and the recipient of some of the Master's most erotically charged epistles. When the letters were offered to Harvard (for one hundred dollars), HJ3 paid half the cost "to keep them," he confided, "from being hawked around and getting into the hands of persons who would

make a silly use of them" (HJ3 to WAJ, 22 Mar. 1945, Librarian's Files: James Collection— Henry James [1942–47] [MH]).

87. LE to Maud Wilcox [Harvard University Press], 29 July 1980 (LEP, Box 6, Folder 7).

88. LE to Maud Wilcox [Harvard University Press], 10 July 1972 (LEP, Box 6, Folder 7).

89. Geoffrey T. Hellman, "Chairman of the Board," *New Yorker* 47 (13 Mar. 1971): 44–86.

90. LE to HJ3, 11 May 1942 (LEP, Box 23, Folder 8).

91. WJ2 to LE, 20 Oct. 1948 (LEP, Box 24, Folder 4).

92. Desmond MacCarthy reported that HJ made that remark to him as they were standing "in an exceptionally gilt and splendid drawing-room" (*The Legend of the Master*, 25).

93. Internal memo to James Laughlin [May 1946] (bMS Am 2077 [2472], MH).

94. LE to Rupert Hart-Davis, 12 Dec. 1952 (LEP, Box 5, Folder 48).

95. LE to Rupert Hart-Davis, 7 Mar. 1955 (LEP, Box 5, Folder 49).

96. LE to James Michie [The Bodley Head], 17 Nov. 1965 (LEP, Box 2, Folder 5).

97. LE to WJ2, 10 Sept. 1953 (LEP, Box 24, Folder 4).

98. LE to WAJ, 19 Apr. 1950 (LEP, Box 7, Folder 13). See also Edel's introduction to *The Library of Henry James*, comp. Leon Edel and Adeline R. Tintner (Ann Arbor, MI: UMI Research Press, 1987), esp. 6–9.

99. LE to John James, 6 Aug. 1962; John James to LE, 8 Aug. 1962 (LEP, Box 24, Folder 1).

100. Clifton Waller Barrett to LE, 14 May 1972 (LEP, Box 15, Folder 4). Barrett believed that he was acquiring "not only the James part of your archive but everything relevant to your writing so that the complete Leon Edel collection will be at the University of Virginia." In this Barrett was deceived: the vast bulk of Edel's papers were later sold to McGill University in Montreal; other than Edel's collection of books, almost nothing of value was shipped to Charlottesville.

101. LE [respondent], "On the Use of Private Papers," *Proceedings of the American Academy of Arts and the National Institution of Arts and Letters*, 2nd ser., 21 (1971): 46.

102. LE, Letter, *Times Literary Supplement* (23 Feb. 1967): 147.

103. WJ2 to LE, 20 Feb. 1941 (LEP, Box 24, Folder 4).

104. Lyall H. Powers, "Leon Edel: The Life of a Biographer," *American Scholar* 66 (1997): 598, 603.

105. McCulloch, "The Art of Biography I: Leon Edel," 199.

106. LE, "Walter Berry and the Novelists: Proust, James, and Edith Wharton," *Nineteenth-Century Fiction* 38.4 (Mar. 1984): 521.

107. LE, "Henry James, Edith Wharton, and Newport" (Newport, RI: Redwood Library & Athenaeum, 1966), 24.

108. LE to William Morris Agency [Mar. 1949] (LEP, Box 10, Folder 9).

*Afterword*

1. Alexander R. James to W. H. Bond, 4 May 1973, Librarian's Files: William H. Bond (1964–90), file J-1973 (MH).

2. William W. Howells to the author, 9 June 1987.

3. Alexander R. James to the author, 9 June 1987.

# Index